World Wisdom
The Library of Perennial Philosophy

The Library of Perennial Philosophy is dedicated to the exposition of the timeless Truth underlying the diverse religions. This Truth, often referred to as the *Sophia Perennis*—or Perennial Wisdom—finds its expression in the revealed Scriptures as well as the writings of the great sages and the artistic creations of the traditional worlds.

The Perennial Philosophy provides the intellectual principles capable of explaining both the formal contradictions and the transcendent unity of the great religions.

Ranging from the writings of the great sages of the past, to the perennialist authors of our time, each series of our Library has a different focus. As a whole, they express the inner unanimity, transforming radiance, and irreplaceable values of the great spiritual traditions.

Sufism: Love & Wisdom appears as one of our selections in the Perennial Philosophy series.

The Perennial Philosophy Series

In the beginning of the twentieth century, a school of thought arose which has focused on the enunciation and explanation of the Perennial Philosophy. Deeply rooted in the sense of the sacred, the writings of its leading exponents establish an indispensable foundation for understanding the timeless Truth and spiritual practices which live in the heart of all religions. Some of these titles are companion volumes to the Treasures of the World's Religions series, which allows a comparison of the writings of the great sages of the past with the perennialist authors of our time.

Cover: Arabic calligraphy on a painted wood panel from Morocco

Sufism: Love & Wisdom

Edited by

Jean-Louis Michon
&
Roger Gaetani

Foreword by

Seyyed Hossein Nasr

World Wisdom

Sufism: Love & Wisdom

For complete bibliographical information on the articles
in this anthology, please see pp. 286-287.

Library of Congress Cataloging-in-Publication Data

Sufism : love and wisdom / edited by Jean-Louis Michon & Roger Gaetani ; foreword by Seyyed Hossein Nasr.
p. cm. -- (Perennial philosophy series)
Includes bibliographical references and index.
ISBN-13: 978-0-941532-75-4 (pbk. : alk. paper)
ISBN-10: 0-941532-75-5 (pbk. : alk. paper) 1. Sufism. I. Michon, Jean-Louis. II. Gaetani, Roger, 1954- III. Series.
BP189.S783 2006
297.4--dc22

2006003803

Printed on acid-free paper in Canada.

For information address World Wisdom, Inc.
P.O. Box 2682, Bloomington, Indiana 47402-2682

www.worldwisdom.com

Contents

Table of Transliteration System

Consonants	
ء	ʾ
ب	b
ت	t
ث	th
ج	j
ح	ḥ
خ	kh
د	d
ذ	dh
ر	r
ز	z
س	s
ش	sh
ص	ṣ
ض	ḍ
ط	ṭ
ظ	ẓ
ع	ʿ

consonants (cont)	
غ	gh
ف	f
ق	q
ك	k
ل	l
م	m
ن	n
ه	h
و	w
ى	y
ة	a (*-at* in construct state)

Vowels	
ـَا	ā
ـِي	ī
ـُو	ū
ـَ	a
ـِ	i
ـُ	u

FOREWORD

The present work is one of the most valuable anthologies devoted to Sufism in a Western language and is in fact unique in its authenticity combined with diversity. In order to understand the value of this work, it is necessary to turn briefly to the history of the study of Sufism in the Occident. In contrast to the fields of theology, philosophy, and the sciences, there were no translations of Sufi texts into Latin during the Middle Ages. The knowledge received about Sufism in the West by such men as Dante and, somewhat later, St. John of the Cross came from vernacular languages, oral transmission, and personal contact. The first work to use the term "Sufism," as *taṣawwuf* has come to be known in the West, was in fact written in 1821 by a German scholar by the name of August Tholuck, who wrote a study of the subject entitled *Sufismus: sive Theosophia Persarum pantheistica.* The later eighteenth and the nineteenth centuries were also witness to the translations of Sufi texts from both Persian and Arabic into English, German, French, and some other European languages. The works of such translators as Sir William Jones, von Hammer Purgstall, and Rückert began to be read in literary and even philosophical circles and attracted major figures such as Goethe and Emerson. But the influence of Sufism during the Romantic Movement remained for the most part literary, and not philosophical and metaphysical, at least not as these terms are understood in a traditional context.

With the rise of Orientalism more and more translations of Sufi texts into European languages began to see the light of day, and detailed studies of the subject also began to appear. Nearly all these studies, however, lacked authenticity. Some were simply philological, without any attention being paid to the meaning of the texts involved. Others were merely historical, many seeking to prove in one way or another that Sufism had a pre-Islamic origin, whether that be early Christianity, Hinduism, or the earlier Iranian religions; others tried to demonstrate how one Sufi scholar influenced another Sufi writer. And yet other studies were sociological, often carried out on behalf of the colonial powers to enable them to keep an eye on Sufi orders.

The metaphysical and esoteric knowledge necessary to understand Sufism in depth had become eclipsed in the West. As for the domain of practice, Christian mysticism as it had existed in the Middle Ages has also more or less disappeared in Europe and the meaning of following an authentic spiritual path based on appropriate teachings and methods has mostly been forgotten. Consequently, Western scholars did not possess the intellectual and spiritual means necessary to study Sufism seriously. One need only remember here the principle that only the like can know the like. It remained for the twentieth century to provide serious works on Sufism in Western languages.

At the beginning of the last century the Swedish painter and esoterist Ivan Aguéli traveled to the Islamic world, was initiated into Sufism, and began to write seriously on the doctrines of Ibn ʿArabī and other Sufi masters. A small number of people who were seekers followed suit as far as initiation into Sufism is concerned; these people were especially from France and Italy. It is true that some have claimed that Richard Burton and H. Wilberforce-Clarke had been initiated into Sufi orders, but such claims remain unproven. In any case ʿAbdul Hādī, as Aguéli was known in the Islamic world and later in Europe, must be given his due as a pioneer in the serious introduction of Sufism to the West. It must also be recalled that by the early twentieth century René Guénon had already come into contact with this current and that after 1930, when he migrated to Cairo, he lived openly as a Shādhilī *faqīr*. The traditionalist or perennialist school that Guénon, known in the Islamic world as Shaykh ʿAbd al-Wāḥid Yaḥya, "inaugurated" was to be of the utmost importance to the West in the presentation of authentic Sufism, in both doctrine and practice, his theoretical works being complemented by the operative teachings and spiritual practices issuing from the Algerian Shaykh Aḥmad al-ʿAlawī. In the 1930s the appearance of the colossal figure of Frithjof Schuon (Shaykh ʿĪsā Nūr al-Dīn Aḥmad) brought about the serious presence of the Shādhilīyya Order in the West, accompanied by writings on Sufism which were unparalleled in their depth and authenticity. His works were complemented by those of several of his companions such as Titus Burckhardt (Sidi Ibrāhīm ʿIzz al-Dīn), and Martin Lings (Shaykh Abū Bakr Sirāj al-Dīn), and including also the co-editor of this work himself (i.e., Jean-Louis Michon) and many others.

Meanwhile, from the 1920s onward a number of Western academic scholars began to see the Quranic origin of Sufism and wrote serious works on it. This trend began with Louis Massignon, followed by such notable figures as Henry Corbin and Annemarie Schimmel. Today there are a number of academic scholars of Islam, following the example of these illustrious figures, who are making important contributions to the study of Sufism in European languages, studies which are both scholarly and authentic. Some of them also belong to various Sufi orders. After the Second World War other Sufi orders began to spread to the West and their Western followers, even if not academic scholars, have produced a number of valuable studies on Sufism. Moreover, a number of born Muslim scholars who know Sufism from within, now write in European languages and they have also made valuable contributions to the now large corpus of authentic works on Sufism in English, French, German, Spanish, Italian, and other Western languages.

The present anthology includes works from all these categories of writers. The editors have been very judicious in selecting texts that are authentic and yet represent different approaches to the study of Sufism as well as diverse aspects of the subject. Jean-Louis Michon has spent a lifetime in both the practice and the study of Sufism and there are few in the West who can match his knowledge of the subject. All those interested in authentic Sufism must be grateful to him and his co-editor for having prepared this anthology. Each of these essays reflects in its own way the perfume of the flowers of that garden which is Sufism, and at the same time draws the reader through Sufism to that Garden, and ultimately to the Supreme Garden of the Essence (*jannat adh-Dhāt*), whose vision and realization is the goal of human life.

Seyyed Hossein Nasr
Bethesda, Maryland, U. S. A.
December 2005/Dhu'l-qa'da 1426 AH

PREFACE

It is said that when the destitute wandering dervish Shamsi Tabrīz met Rūmī, who was already a renowned scholar of exoteric and esoteric sciences, that Shamsi seized Rūmī's books and threw them into a pool of water. He offered Rūmī a choice: either join him in companionship in a state completely focused on the Spirit alone, or, if he preferred, Rūmī could retrieve his books—mysteriously, they would not be damaged. In abandoning those precious volumes filled with religious doctrines and speculative spiritual ideas, Rūmī started upon his destined path to union with the Beloved.

With Rūmī, we have reason to pause and ask ourselves: What use is it, after all, to be reading books on Sufism? Ultimately, wouldn't we be better served by turning our eyes from the page and instead engaging our tongues in the direct invocation of the Lord of the Universe? Regrettably, in this day and age few will have the good fortune to have the personal guidance of a Shamsi Tabrīz. Instead, we often turn to books, and from them we can get several types of benefit according to our individual needs. Some will read for data, for facts about Sufism, and they will find these in abundance in this book, though there is no systematic ordering of the essays. But the most profound benefit that can be derived from reading books on religion comes about when expositions of spiritual doctrines or ideas become keys to direct intellection within the reader. This, we hope, will be the fullest benefit of these essays: that while learning about a particular aspect of Sufism, the reader may come across one or more "keys" which will unlock doors to inner certainties; these corroborations within ourselves we may call "direct intellection." Many keys to this kind of "inner proof" of a universal metaphysical truth can be found throughout this book, if the reader is properly receptive. Such readers will not necessarily be converted into Sufis, which would only be possible for Muslims in any case—they will simply access a level of intelligence that all too often remains dormant in our modern habits of thinking.

These particular essays have been collected for several reasons: First, they are a sampler of the thought and approach of writers who would consider themselves "traditionalists" or "perennialists." We will say more on this further on. Second, amongst these writers there are some who are so eminent as to seemingly eclipse the newer generation of traditionalist writers, and so we have purposely included some essays from this younger group. Next, there are a number of European writers on Sufism whose works have not been presented adequately to the English-reading public. We have translated three outstanding essays on Sufism and present them here for the first time in English. Finally, we have sought to show the impressive range of writings that have come from the traditionalists' approach to Sufism. Thus this collection includes some rather introductory and systematic surveys of Sufi doctrines, writings on historical topics, complex metaphysical examinations of specific Sufi practices or doctrines, and so on. Since the essays are organized in more or less alphabetical order by author, we would suggest that readers new to Sufism should begin with the article by William Stoddart and then move to other essays of specific interest.

We must begin our brief description of the traditionalist or perennialist school of thought with a qualification: These writers have nothing to do with various trends of political or nationalist thought that have sprung up over the years and that also go under the banner of "traditionalist." To avoid such confusion, which has now even extended into academic circles through a few undiscriminating commentators, some of our writers on spirituality have preferred to be called "perennialists." For our purposes here, it will suffice to say that though these writers adhere to no single credo, they all subscribe to certain common principles. Those of particular interest to us here are:

- The Absolute exists, and its Truth takes precedence over all contingent considerations.
- The Absolute is One, beyond its manifestations, but when deployed into the created universe it results in particular revelations adapted to the historical and cultural circumstances of various civilizations.
- The full scope of human consciousness, will, sentiment, and virtue is only realized when human beings have actu-

alized their spiritual potential. This potential is of critical importance to both individuals and societies, and a traditional framework is the means by which individuals and societies maintain and constantly renew their link with their divine origin.

- Many traditions—particularly those based upon a revealed scripture and its resulting formal practices and Law—will, over time, develop esoteric practices and doctrines beyond the exoteric framework of the religion. It is possible that in some cases the esoteric dimension of a given religion may be partially or "accidentally" influenced by other religions (e.g., the practices of some Sufis may have been influenced by some Buddhist practices), but the essential wellspring of each esoterism comes from its own tradition, to which it is inextricably attached. Although the observable forms and means are remarkably varied, all traditions—in many cases through a combination of both their exoteric and esoteric dimensions—meet the same universal needs of human nature. Esoterism, within whatever traditional framework, offers the fullest range of spiritual possibilities to those suited to its demands.

- Esoteric traditions, such as Sufism, often reveal universal spiritual principles more readily than the exoteric frameworks of their respective traditions. From the lofty heights of esoteric intellection or perception, the differences between various religious forms become resolved. At this level, the multitude of religious forms melt away to reveal the universal principles behind them. The analogy is often made of a mountain with various paths progressing up it from its base: at the lower levels no one path can be seen from another, but the closer and closer the different paths come to the summit, the more clearly do other paths appear to each other. Thus, at the level of their complex and different exoteric theologies, traditions will inevitably appear distant from each other; however, further up each traditional path of esoteric spiritual realization, seekers can more easily see that their own paths converge with others towards a single summit. Sufis who have climbed to such heights, such as Rūmī or Ibn ʿArabī, readily claim a unity with those of other faiths, which is understandable since their perception, and thus their writings, are situated closer to that summit than the writings of exoteric theologians. In the realm of principles, traditionalists certainly recognize the "transcendent unity of religions," meaning a single divine source for a multiplicity of religious forms, but it must be stressed that in the realm of actual practice all traditionalists reject syncretisms—all would insist, for example, that Sufism can only live within its orthodox Islamic framework, and that one cannot piece together an effective spiritual practice as one chooses from various traditions.

- The God-centered "tradition," the essential link that ties groupings of humanity to the Absolute, suffuses a civilization with ideas, symbols, arts, and customs that work together to allow 'true' human nature to shine forth. Thus, one who studies that link may choose to be called a "traditionalist" or one who recognizes the equally valid relationships of various civilizations with their divine origins might choose to be called a "perennialist." The terms are generally interchangeable and, as can be seen here, are not associated with such worldly ambitions as political agendas. The Spirit will always be of more interest to these traditionalists or perennialists, simply because its Truth takes precedence over all contingent considerations.

Because of their explicit or implicit acceptance of the above principles, it will not be surprising if all of the authors in this collection show certain similarities in their writings. We will see that even for those whose professional careers are centered around a study of Islam and Sufism, these authors never display a fascination with a given figure in Sufism simply because of his flamboyance or even because of his historical significance—the content of what that saint wrote or did will always be of ultimate interest to our traditionalist authors. We might be well served here with another analogy: A tradition, such as Islam and its esoterism, Sufism, can be likened to a receptacle, like a vase. Being part of the world of forms, this vase is observable, and so most people will be drawn immediately to its shape and decoration. Many will put the vase up on a shelf for display to show to best effect its antique patina, its exquisite shape, or its remarkable patterns. This is how many writers approach Sufism, as a remarkable artifact, of rare beauty or of great extrinsic value to historians and social scientists. Traditionalist writers on Sufism, on the other hand, will approach the vase, pick it up, and immediately see what it contains! This is because they have no doubt but that the content of this rare and beautiful receptacle is the Truth of the Absolute. They know that an authentic receptacle's *raison d'être* is to serve the needs of its content, which is the intrinsic value of the receptacle. Indeed, to finish with the analogy, Sufism has sometimes been defined as the taste (*dhawq*) of the divine Reality, and our authors would all hope that as they reverently pass around the receptacle of Sufi science that some, at least, will both learn about the form and experience a "taste." Such a "taste," of course, is the same as the "direct intellection" mentioned above. In short, this collection of essays is special in the Western study of Sufism because it shows a different approach. It is an approach that certainly appreciates, along with the current predominant ones, the beauty of the forms of Sufism and the appeal of its colorful personages; however, these essays go beyond an endless fascination with form: they always orient and reorient themselves to the intrinsic Beauty of the Truth that lies within the form and within the saints who have lived it.

So, what can traditionalists bring to a study of Sufism? They will necessarily look back to its Islamic origins and recognize that the broader tradition itself is the aquifer that feeds this particular fountain of sanctifying possibility. They will look into the ways in which Islamic esoterism, Sufism, goes beyond the exoteric religious framework. Each of the writers, without exception, will base much of his or her development of ideas upon metaphysics. Although the term "metaphysics," too, has been appropriated and misrepresented (in this case into a very dry category of philosophical speculation, where it offers little of interest to regular believers), metaphysics is the language of universal spiritual principles, just as mathematics is said to be the language of empirical sciences. The essays in this book turn often to fundamental principles that might, for example, demonstrate how the Incarnation of Christ and the descent of the Koran derive from similar divine actions; we may thus come to see that metaphysics can be very useful in helping us to understand diverse religious phenomena and that metaphysics is not as inaccessible as we may have previously thought. By the same token, many of these writers will also occasionally depart from formal Islamic or Sufic terminology and use, for example, a Hindu or Christian term to show parallels or to explain a concept that may have been developed more clearly in that other tradition. This is because these traditionalist writers are often as interested in esoterism as such as they are in its specific Sufi garb. Their interest in comparative mysticism is sometimes due to a strong attraction to one or more particular traditions, such as Sufism and its Islamic framework, but more often it seems that as a study of a particular mysticism progresses, the emerging universal principles are of even more interest to traditionalist writers. This is because of what those principles tell us about the very nature of God and about the nature of human "being." Finally, unlike many other scholars of Sufism, not one of these writers would presume to say that "Sufism is dead," and this for many reasons. It may bear mentioning that many, though not all, of the writers represented in this book are known to have practiced Sufism, with a few even having attained to the station of spiritual master, or *shaykh*. We will leave it to you, the reader, to judge whether or not Sufism is dead after you have read this book.

In closing, the editors wish to thank the many helpful staff at World Wisdom for their long and careful labor upon this volume. It has been the product of several years of work, and we thank you for helping us through it. We thank the various authors and publishers who have permitted us to excerpt materials from their books—details are given on the acknowledgments pages at the back of this book. Finally, we must thank our families, who have had to forego our complete attention all too often. Perhaps even more we must thank our spiritual 'families,' those who have been spiritual fathers, mothers, brothers, and sisters to us.

But let us return to Rūmī and his books for a moment. The story doesn't say this, but we know that Rūmī later would return to his books and to writing, for his incredible outpouring of inspired poetry followed his short time with Shamsi Tabrīz. We can assume that Rūmī found new depths in his readings of Sufi literature in this later period of his life. May we all be able to reach into that tempting pool of water and draw out the text that lies there, undamaged through Shamsi's assurance, and may we then return it to its proper place after we learn from it the promise, and perhaps even some of the secrets, of greater Fountains yet unexplored.

Roger Gaetani
January 2006

INTRODUCTION

Among the persons who have developed an interest in "comparative religion" many will have discovered that between the vast array of myths, dogmas, and rituals characterizing the various religions there exists a common denominator, a deep affinity resulting from the central point toward which all the sacred paths aim at leading their followers. And these same persons may also have recognized that, within the framework of Islam, Sufism represents this inner dimension, the way opened to those who aspire to reach the realm of the Divine Presence. This is why a good number of contemporary thinkers who are "seekers of Truth"—and all the contributors to the present anthology belong to that category—recognize Sufism as being not only the very heart of Islam, but also a key that gives access to the deepest meaning of other sacred traditions (specific references to this recognition may be found, *inter alia*, in the articles by Geoffroy, Lings, Macnab, Nasr, Shah-Kazemi, and Schuon).

To avoid any misinterpretation of what is implied by the words "Sufi" and "Sufism," it is important to note that both terms have been used since the first century of the *Hijra* (eighth century C. E.), when "Sufism" (in Arabic: *taṣawwuf*, the fact of wearing a garment made of wool—*ṣūf*—as an emblem of purity) was adopted to designate the quest for spiritual illumination, while "*ṣūfī*" was applied to characterize the person who had attained an obvious degree of proximity to God. This indicates that Sufism has always been embedded in the texture of the Islamic creed, representing an ideal mode of worship derived from the Quranic Revelation and from the customs and sayings (*sunna* and *ḥadīth*) of the Prophet Muhammad, and then transmitted without interruption throughout the centuries.

As a way of access to the divine love and wisdom, which are the universal components of mysticism, Sufism has given abundant proofs of its authenticity and its supernatural efficiency and fecundity. This is so from the very beginning of the Revelation, when Muhammad's Companions sat with him during night-watches filled with the recitation of the holy verses and the invocation of the divine Names, up to the present time when thousands and thousands of devotees affiliated with Sufi brotherhoods throughout all corners of the Islamic world aspire to the purification of their souls and follow the way of their saintly ancestors under the guidance of a spiritual master.

Sufism, then, has nothing to do with the sectarian movements which, mostly in the Western world, have used its name, fame, and even some of its psycho-spiritual practices to attract a naïve clientele with the promise of quick spiritual advancement without any religious obligation. It is gratifying to note that many publications now exist, notably translations of treatises on Sufism written in Arabic or Persian by the most eminent Sufi masters, which may constitute a counterweight to the fallacious hopes nurtured by those who would, according to a phrase appearing several times in the Qurān (e.g. 2:86), "purchase the life of this world at the cost of the Hereafter."

In order to provide a kind of introduction, especially intended for "non-initiates," to the variety of highly instructive lessons contained in this book, a brief account now follows of what constitutes the backbone of Sufism, namely the metaphysical and methodological foundations which since its origin have been the subject of meditation and aids to concentration and contemplation of the adepts of Sufism.

The Doctrine of Unity (*Tawḥīd*)

The dominant theme of the Quranic Revelation, divine Unity, is expressed by the testimony of faith—*shahāda*—which every Muslim repeats a number of times every day when performing the five canonical prayers and which he hopes to be able to utter at the moment of his death: "There is no god if not God (*Allāh*); Muhammad is the Envoy of God." The two formulas composing this testimony are strictly complementary: the first one proclaims the dogma of absolute monotheism (*tawḥīd*) and concerns only the transcendent Principle, whereas the second one introduces the Envoy, bearer of the heavenly Message, a link between the Principle and manifestation.

Proclaimed as the first of the five pillars of Islam, the *shahāda* is comparable to the apex of a pyramid whose basis would rest upon the four other ritual obligations (i.e., the five daily prayers, the fast of Ramadan, required almsgiving, and the pilgrimage to Mecca). It represents the emblem, the specific identification mark of the Islamic religion in its outer as well as inner forms and contents, and it constitutes a most frequent leitmotif and reference point in the commentaries of the theological and legal scholars, as well as in the inspired works of the Sufi masters.

According to the mystical interpretation, the lucid believer who testifies that "there is no god if not God" denies the reality of anything which does not possess its own sufficient reason; he is aware of the illusory character of contingent phenomena, of the outer world, of individual existence; he empties himself from pretension, becomes "poor" (Arabic: *faqīr*, Persian: *darwīsh*; both terms often used as synonyms of *ṣūfī*) and "submitted" (Arabic: *muslim*) to the sole Real existing by itself, whose supreme Name is *Allāh*, literally: "the God," unique, infinite, and absolute (concerning this Name, see the essay by Schaya).

Thus, it is only by his own obliteration that man can attain to the consciousness of the Real, or Truth (*al-Ḥaqq*), which is one of "the beautiful Names of God"; by realizing his own nothingness, fragility, and dependence, he perceives the Presence, the Power, and the other qualities of the self-sustaining Being. As aptly described by Junayd of Baghdad, the ninth century C.E. "Master of the Circle" (*Shaykh aṭ-Ṭā'ifa*): "The loss of his individual being completes the purity of his real being; in this state of absolute purity, his individual attributes are made absent, while this absence makes himself present . . ."

Universal Man (*al-Insān al-Kāmil*)

The second part of the *shahāda*, which complements the dogma of divine Unity, points out the medium that makes it possible for human beings to realize this Unity. This medium is Muhammad, God's Prophet and Envoy, "the intermediary" (*al-wāsiṭa*) chosen to be the receptacle of the Revelation. Whereas Muhammad is a model for the generality of Muslims, who strive to imitate his virtues and whom they like to call "the best of created beings," for the Sufis their relationship with this "friend of God" is even more intimate, being based on the fact that they view him as the perfect symbol and form of the Prime Intellect (*al-ʿAql al-awwal*), the very root and prototype of all creation, the original Light of which all particular intelligences are but a refraction. When offering prayers and salutations upon the Prophet, as prescribed in the Qurān, the *faqīr* is thus praying for the good of the whole creation and also for the recovery of his own pristine nature (on that subject, see the essay by Burckhardt).

The Way of Recollection (*Dhikr*)

The idea of a return to a primordial, paradisiacal state in which man, created in the image of God, played his full role as a "lieutenant (*khalīfa*) of God on earth," according to a recurrent Quranic expression, is a theme of reflection often proposed by the Qurān, the *hadīth*, and the teachings of the Sufi masters. In this Adamic condition, there was no place for the individual will, the human soul being naturally submitted to the Creator and thus celebrating His praise as spontaneously as the leaves of trees sway to the rhythm of the wind, or as joyfully as the birds herald with their chirping the coming of a new dawn. Even more, enlightened by the Spirit which God had breathed into her, the soul was in harmony with all creatures, knowing their names (i.e., their essences) without being enraptured by their mirage and drawn away from worshiping the one Truth. After his own transgression—the "original sin"—had left him bereft of this privileged status, man received good tidings that ways and means existed to compensate him for his loss. These paths to salvation are the sacred Traditions which have been bestowed on every human community in the course of history and, singularly, when the last heavenly Message was delivered through the descent of the Qurān.

Generally known as the "Book of God" (*Kitābu 'Llāh*), or as "the Collected Pages" (*al-Muṣḥaf*), the Qurān is often called *Dhikru 'Llāh*, which means "the recollection of God" and which is also one of the many names given to the Prophet Muhammad. Chapter 38 of the Holy Book (*Ṣād*) opens with the words "By the Qurān, bearer of recollection!", and it is a fact that the most repeated and pressing injunctions made to men are commands to remember God, mention Him often, invoke His Name a great deal, day and night, standing, sitting or lying on their side, with reverence, humility and attention . . .

For Sufis, these commands have not gone unheeded. Conscious of having been granted a rope of salvation through the Qurān, a mine of sacred formulas ready to unveil their secret meanings and offer their liberating gifts, Muslim mystics have developed a very rich and effective science and art of *dhikr*: invocation with the tongue, with the mind, with the heart, with the breath, with or without concomitant use of music, percussion, song and dance (for more details, see the essay by Michon).

However, the practice of invocation, in particular when it entails a rhythmic repetition of one of the divine Names, including the supreme Name *Allāh* or the pronoun *Huwa* ("He"), is not an exercise within everyone's capacity. Whether it is carried out during solitary retreats or in collective sessions, it requires from the participants some serious qualifications which are only acquired via a regular discipline of the body and soul, a scrupulous adherence to the common religious law, and a spiritual education entrusted to an authentic guide (*murshid*), a master who has himself followed the way (*ṭarīqa*) to enlightenment (for more on this, see the essay by Nasr).

The Initiatic Chain (*Silsila*)

"Whoever has no master (*shaykh*) has Satan as his master" say the Sufis, thereby dooming to failure those who dare undertake by their own means the travel to God. The conditions surrounding the selection and the reciprocal acceptance of a master and his disciple—the latter committing himself to his master "like the cadaver in the hands of the washer-of-the-dead"—and the brotherly and caring feelings expected to reign between the members of the Sufi orders have been amply described in the handbooks of Sufism. It will suffice here to mention the fact that all relevant practices of the Sufis tend to perpetuate the initiatic pact which was sealed at Hudaybiya when, on their way back from the "lesser holy war" against the Meccan unbelievers, Muhammad's closest Companions took a solemn oath with him to wage a "greater holy war" against their own inner enemies. Since that momentous event, a continuous chain of masters and disciples has carried to the core of the Islamic Community, in all regions and at all times, the esoteric teachings contained in the Quranic Revelation and the influence of blessedness (*baraka*) inherited from Muhammad.

Jean-Louis Michon
October 2005, Ramadan 1426

SUFI DOCTRINE AND METHOD*

Titus Burckhardt

At-Taṣawwuf

Sufism, *Taṣawwuf*,[1] which is the esoteric or inward (*bāṭin*) aspect of Islam, is to be distinguished from exoteric or "external" (*ẓāhir*) Islam just as direct contemplation of spiritual or divine realities is distinguishable from the fulfilling of the laws which translate them in the individual order in connection with the conditions of a particular phase of humanity. Whereas the ordinary way of believers is directed towards obtaining a state of blessedness after death, a state which may be attained through indirect and, as it were, symbolical participation in Divine Truths by carrying out prescribed works, Sufism contains its end or aim within itself in the sense that it can give access to direct knowledge of the eternal.

This knowledge, being one with its object, delivers from the limited and inevitably changing state of the ego. The spiritual state of *baqā'*, to which Sufi contemplatives aspire (the word signifies pure "subsistence" beyond all form), is the same as the state of *mokṣa* or

* Editors' Note: This article is a selection of three chapters from Burckhardt's classic text on Sufism, *An Introduction to Sufi Doctrine*, which is widely regarded as one of the finest treatments of the subject.

[1] The most usual explanation is that this word means only "to wear wool (*ṣūf*)," the first Sufis having worn, it is said, only garments of pure wool. Now what has never yet been pointed out is that many Jewish and Christian ascetics of these early times covered themselves, in imitation of St. John the Baptist in the desert, only with sheepskins. It may be that this example was also followed by some of the early Sufis. None the less "to wear wool" can only be an external and popular meaning of the term *Taṣawwuf*, which is equivalent, in its numerical symbolism, to *al-ḥikmat al-ilāhiyya*, "Divine Wisdom." Al-Bīrunī suggested a derivation of *ṣūfī*, plural of *ṣūfiya*, from the Greek *Sophia*, wisdom, but this is etymologically doubtful because the Greek letter *sigma* normally becomes *sīn* (s) in Arabic and not *ṣād* (ṣ). It may be, however, that there is here an intentional, symbolical assonance.

"deliverance" spoken of in Hindu doctrines, just as the "extinction" (*al-fanā'*) of the individuality which precedes the "subsistence" is analogous to *nirvāṇa*, taken as a negative idea.

For Sufism to permit of such a possibility it must be identified with the very kernel (*al-lubb*) of the traditional form which is its support. It cannot be something super-added to Islam, for it would then be something peripheral in relation to the spiritual means of Islam. On the contrary, it is in fact closer to their superhuman source than is the religious exoterism and it participates actively, though in a wholly inward way, in the function of revelation which manifested this traditional form and continues to keep it alive.

This "central" role of Sufism at the heart of the Islamic world may be veiled from those who examine it from outside because esoterism, while it is conscious of the significance of forms, is at the same time in a position of intellectual sovereignty in relation to them and can thus assimilate to itself—at any rate for the exposition of its doctrine—certain ideas or symbols derived from a heritage different from its own traditional background.

It may appear strange that Sufism should on the one hand be the "spirit" or "heart" of Islam (*rūḥ al-islām* or *qalb al-islām*) and on the other hand represent at the same time the outlook which is, in the Islamic world, the most free in relation to the mental framework of that world, though it is important to note that this true and wholly inward freedom must not be confused with any movements of rebellion against the tradition; such movements are not intellectually free in relation to the forms which they deny because they fail to understand them. Now this role of Sufism in the Islamic world[2] is indeed like that of the heart in man, for the heart is the vital center of the organism and also, in its subtle reality, the "seat" of an essence which transcends all individual form.

[2] This refers to Sufism in itself, not to its initiatic organizations. Human groups may take on more or less contingent functions despite their connection with Sufism; the spiritual elite is hardly to be recognized from outside. Again, it is a well-known fact that many of the most eminent defenders of Islamic orthodoxy, such as ʿAbd al-Qādir Jīlānī, al-Ghazzālī, or the Sultan Ṣalāḥ ad-Din (Saladin) were connected with Sufism.

Because orientalists are anxious to bring everything down to the historical level it could hardly be expected that they would explain this double aspect of Sufism otherwise than as the result of influences coming into Islam from outside and, according to their various preoccupations, they have indeed attributed the origins of Sufism to Persian, Hindu, Neoplatonic, or Christian sources. But these diverse attributions have ended by canceling one another, the more so because there is no adequate reason for doubting the historical authenticity of the spiritual "descent" of the Sufi masters, a descent which can be traced in an unbroken "chain" (*silsila*) back to the Prophet himself.

The decisive argument in favor of the Muhammadan origin of Sufism lies, however, in Sufism itself. If Sufic wisdom came from a source outside Islam, those who aspire to that wisdom—which is assuredly neither bookish nor purely mental in its nature—could not rely on the symbolism of the Qur'ān for realizing that wisdom ever afresh, whereas in fact everything that forms an integral part of the spiritual method of Sufism is constantly and of necessity drawn out of the Qur'ān and from the teaching of the Prophet.

Orientalists who uphold the thesis of a non-Muslim origin of Sufism generally make much of the fact that in the first centuries of Islam Sufi doctrine does not appear with all the metaphysical developments found in later times. Now in so far as this point is valid for an esoteric tradition—a tradition, that is, which is mainly transmitted by oral instruction—it proves the very contrary of what they try to maintain.

The first Sufis expressed themselves in a language very close to that of the Qur'ān and their concise and synthetic expressions already imply all the essentials of the doctrine. If, at a later stage, the doctrine became more explicit and was further elaborated, this is something perfectly normal to which parallels can be found in every spiritual tradition. Doctrine grows, not so much by the addition of new knowledge, as by the need to refute errors and to reanimate a diminishing power of intuition.

Moreover, since doctrinal truths are susceptible to limitless development and since the Islamic civilization had absorbed certain pre-Islamic inheritances, Sufi masters could, in their oral or written teaching, make use of ideas borrowed from those inheritances provided they were adequate for expressing those truths which had to be made accessible to the intellectually gifted men of their age and which were already implicit in strictly Sufic symbolism in a succinct form.

Such, for example, was the case as regards cosmology, a science derived from the pure metaphysic which alone constitutes the indispensable doctrinal foundation of Sufism. Sufi cosmology was very largely expressed by means of ideas which had already been defined by such ancient masters as Empedocles and Plotinus. Again, those Sufi masters who had had a philosophical training could not ignore the validity of the teachings of Plato, and the Platonism attributed to them is of the same order as the Platonism of the Christian Greek Fathers whose doctrine remains none the less essentially apostolic.

The orthodoxy of Sufism is not only shown in its maintaining of Islamic forms; it is equally expressed in its organic development from the teaching of the Prophet and in particular by its ability to assimilate all forms of spiritual expression which are not in their essence foreign to Islam. This applies, not only to doctrinal forms, but also to ancillary matters connected with art.[3]

Certainly there were contacts between early Sufis and Christian contemplatives, as is proved by the case of the Sufi Ibrāhīm ibn Adham, but the most immediate explanation of the kinship between Sufism and Christian monasticism does not lie in historical events. As ʿAbd al-Karīm al-Jīlī explains in his book *al-Insān al-Kāmil* ("Universal Man") the message of Christ unveils certain inner—and therefore esoteric—aspects of the monotheism of Abraham.

In a certain sense Christian dogmas, which can be all reduced to the dogma of the two natures of Christ, the divine and the human, sum up in a "historical" form all that Sufism teaches on union with God. Moreover, Sufis hold that the Lord Jesus (*Sayyidnā ʿĪsa*) is of all the Divine Envoys (*rusūl*) the most perfect type of contemplative saint. To offer the left cheek to him who smites one on the right is true spiritual detachment; it is a voluntary withdrawal from the interplay of cosmic actions and reactions.

[3] Certain Sufis deliberately manifested forms which, though not contrary to the spirit of the Tradition, shocked the commonalty of exoterists. This was a way of making themselves free from the psychic elements and mental habits of the collectivity surrounding them.

It is none the less true that for Sufis the person of Christ does not stand in the same perspective as it does for Christians. Despite many likenesses the Sufi way differs greatly from the way of Christian contemplatives. We may here refer to the picture in which the different traditional ways are depicted as the radii of a circle which are united only at one single point. The nearer the radii are to the center, the nearer they are to one another; none the less they coincide only at the center where they cease to be radii. It is clear that this distinction of one way from another does not prevent the intellect from placing itself by an intuitive anticipation at the center where all ways converge.

To make the inner constitution of Sufism quite clear it should be added that it always includes as indispensable elements, first, a doctrine, secondly, an initiation and, thirdly, a spiritual method. The doctrine is, as it were, a symbolical prefiguring of the knowledge to be attained; it is also, in its manifestation, a fruit of that knowledge.

The quintessence of Sufi doctrine comes from the Prophet, but, as there is no esoterism without a certain inspiration, the doctrine is continually manifested afresh by the mouth of masters. Oral teaching is moreover superior, since it is direct and "personal," to what can be gleaned from writings. Writings play only a secondary part as a preparation, a complement, or an aid to memory and for this reason the historical continuity of Sufi teaching sometimes eludes the researches of scholars.

As for initiation in Sufism, this consists in the transmission of a spiritual influence (*baraka*) and must be conferred by a representative of a "chain" reaching back to the Prophet. In most cases it is transmitted by the master who also communicates the method and confers the means of spiritual concentration that are appropriate to the aptitudes of the disciple. The general framework of the method is the Islamic Law, although there have always been isolated Sufis who, by reason of the exceptional nature of their contemplative state, no longer took part in the ordinary ritual of Islam.

In order to forestall any objection which might be raised on this account to what had already been said about the Muhammadan origin of Sufism, it must here be clearly stated that the spiritual supports on which the principal methods of Sufism are based, and which can in certain circumstances take the place of the ordinary ritual of Islam, appear as the very keystones of the whole Islamic symbolism; it is indeed this sense that they were given by the Prophet himself.

Initiation generally takes the form of a pact (*bayʿa*) between the candidate and the spiritual master (*al-murshid*) who represents the Prophet. This pact implies perfect submission of the disciple to the master in all that concerns spiritual life and it can never be dissolved unilaterally by the will of the disciple.

The different "branches" of the spiritual "family tree" of Sufism correspond quite naturally to different "paths" (*ṭuruq*). Each great master from whom the start of a specific branch can be traced has authority to adapt the method to the aptitude of a particular category of those who are gifted for spiritual life. Thus the various "paths" correspond to various "vocations" all of them orientated to the same goal, and are in no sense schisms or "sects" within Sufism, although partial deviations have also arisen from time to time and given birth to sects in the strict sense. The outward sign of a sectarian tendency is always the quantitative and "dynamic" manner in which propagation takes place. Authentic Sufism can never become a "movement"[4] for the very good reason that it appeals to what is most "static" in man, to wit, contemplative intellect.[5]

In this connection it should be noted that, if Islam has been able to remain intact throughout the centuries despite the changes in human psychology and the ethnic differences between the Islamic peoples, this is assuredly not because of the relatively dynamic character it possesses as a collective form but because from its very origin it includes a possibility of intellectual contemplation which transcends the affective currents of the human soul.

[4] In some *ṭuruq*, such as the Qādiriyya, the Darqāwiyya, and the Naqshbandiyya, the presence of "outer circles" of initiates in addition to the inner circle of the elite results in a certain popular expansion. But this is not to be confused with the expansion of sectarian movements, since the outer circles do not stand in opposition to exoterism of which they are very often in fact an intensified form.

[5] What is in these days usually called the "intellect" is really only the discursive faculty, the very dynamism and agitation of which distinguishes it from the intellect proper which is in itself motionless being always direct and serene in operation.

Sufism and Mysticism

Scientific works commonly define Sufism as "Muslim mysticism" and we too would readily adopt the epithet "mystical" to designate that which distinguishes Sufism from the simply religious aspect of Islam if that word still bore the meaning given it by the Greek Fathers of the early Christian Church and those who followed their spiritual line: they used it to designate what is related to knowledge of "the mysteries." Unfortunately the word "mysticism"—and also the word "mystical"—has been abused and extended to cover religious manifestations which are strongly marked with individualistic subjectivity and governed by a mentality which does not look beyond the horizons of exoterism.

It is true that there are in the East, as in the West, borderline cases such as that of the *majdhūb* in whom the Divine attraction (*al-jadhb*) strongly predominates so as to invalidate the working of the mental faculties with the result that the *majdhūb* cannot give doctrinal formulation to his contemplative state. It may also be that a state of spiritual realization comes about in exceptional cases almost without the support of a regular method, for "the Spirit bloweth whither It listeth." None the less the term *Taṣawwuf* is applied in the Islamic world only to regular contemplative ways which include both an esoteric doctrine and transmission from one master to another. So *Taṣawwuf* could only be translated as "mysticism" on condition that the latter term was explicitly given its strict meaning, which is also its original meaning. If the word were understood in that sense it would clearly be legitimate to compare Sufis to true Christian mystics. All the same a shade of meaning enters here which, while it does not touch the meaning of the word "mysticism" taken by itself, explains why it does not seem satisfactory in all its contexts to transpose it into Sufism. Christian contemplatives, and especially those who came after the Middle Ages, are indeed related to those Muslim contemplatives who followed the way of spiritual love (*al-maḥabba*), the *bhakti mārga* of Hinduism, but only very rarely are they related to those Eastern contemplatives who were of a purely intellectual order, such as Ibn ʿArabī or, in the Hindu world, Śrī Śaṅkarāchārya.[6]

[6] There is in this fact nothing implying any superiority of one tradition over

Now, spiritual love is in a sense intermediate between glowing devotion and knowledge; moreover, the language of the *bhakta* projects, even into the realm of final union, the polarity from which love springs. This is no doubt one reason why, in the Christian world, the distinction between true mysticism and individualistic "mysticism" is not always clearly marked, whereas in the world of Islam esoterism always involves a metaphysical view of things—even in its bhaktic forms—and is thus clearly separated from exoterism, which can in this case be much more readily defined as the common "Law."[7]

Every complete way of contemplation, such as the Sufi way or Christian mysticism (in the original meaning of that word), is distinct from a way of devotion, such as is wrongly called "mystical," in that it implies an active intellectual attitude. Such an attitude is by no means to be understood in the sense of a sort of individualism with an intellectual air to it: on the contrary it implies a disposition to open oneself to the essential Reality (*al-Ḥaqīqa*), which transcends discursive thought and so also a possibility of placing oneself intellectually beyond all individual subjectivity.

That there may be no misunderstanding about what has just been said it must be clearly stated that the Sufi also realizes an attitude of perpetual adoration molded by the religious form. Like every believer he must pray and, in general, conform to the revealed Law since his individual human nature will always remain passive in relation to Divine Reality or Truth whatever the degree of his spiritual identification with it. "The servant (i.e. the individual) always remains the servant" (*al-ʿabd yabqā-l-ʿabd*), as a Moroccan master said to the author. In this relationship the Divine Presence will therefore manifest Itself as Grace. But the intelligence of the Sufi, inasmuch as it is directly identified with the "Divine Ray," is in a certain manner withdrawn,

another; it shows only tendencies which are conditioned by the genius and temperament of the peoples concerned. Because of this bhaktic character of Christian mysticism some orientalists have found it possible to assert that Ibn ʿArabī was "not a real mystic."

[7] The structure of Islam does not admit of stages in some sense intermediate between exoterism and esoterism such as the Christian monastic state, the original role of which was to constitute a direct framework for the Christian way of contemplation.

in its spiritual actuality and its own modes of expression, from the framework imposed on the individual by religion and also by reason, and in this sense the inner nature of the Sufi is not receptivity but pure act.

It goes without saying that not every contemplative who follows the Sufi way comes to realize a state of knowledge which is beyond form, for clearly that does not depend on his will alone. None the less the end in view not only determines the intellectual horizon but also brings into play spiritual means which, being as it were a prefiguring of that end, permit the contemplative to take up an active position in relation to his own psychic form.

Instead of identifying himself with his empirical "I" he fashions that "I" by virtue of an element which is symbolically and implicitly non-individual. The Qur'ān says: "We shall strike vanity with truth and it will bring it to naught" (21:18). The Sufi 'Abd as-Salām ibn Mashīsh prayed: "Strike with me on vanity that I may bring it to naught." To the extent that he is effectively emancipated the contemplative ceases to be such-and-such a person and "becomes" the Truth on which he has meditated and the Divine Name which he invokes.

The intellectual essence of Sufism makes imprints even on the purely human aspects of the way which may in practice coincide with the religious virtues. In the Sufi perspective the virtues are nothing other than human images or "subjective traces" of universal Truth;[8] hence the incompatibility between the spirit of Sufism and the "moralistic" conception of virtue, which is quantitative and individualistic.[9]

Since the doctrine is both the very foundation of the way and the fruit of the contemplation which is its goal,[10] the difference between

[8] It will be recalled that for Plotinus virtue is intermediate between the soul and intelligence.

[9] A quantitative conception of virtue results from the religious consideration of merit or even from a purely social point of view. The qualitative conception on the other hand has in view the analogical relation between a cosmic or Divine quality and a human virtue. Of necessity the religious conception of virtue remains individualistic since it values virtue only from the point of view of individual salvation.

[10] Some orientalists would like artificially to separate doctrine from "spiritual experience." They see doctrine as a "conceptualizing" anticipating a purely

Sufism and religious mysticism can be reduced to a question of doctrine. This can be clearly expressed by saying that the believer whose doctrinal outlook is limited to that of exoterism always maintains a fundamental and irreducible separation between the Divinity and himself whereas the Sufi recognizes, at least in principle, the essential unity of all beings, or—to put the same thing in negative terms—the unreality of all that appears separate from God.

It is necessary to keep in view this double aspect of esoteric orientation because it may happen that an exoterist—and particularly a religious mystic—will also affirm that in the sight of God he is nothing. If, however, this affirmation carried with it for him all its metaphysical implications, he would logically be forced to admit at the same time the positive aspect of the same truth, which is that the essence of his own reality, in virtue of which he is *not* "nothing," is mysteriously identical with God. As Meister Eckhart wrote: "There is somewhat in the soul which is uncreate and uncreatable; if all the soul were such it would be uncreate and uncreatable; and this somewhat is Intellect." This is a truth which all esoterism admits *a priori*, whatever the manner in which it is expressed.

A purely religious teaching on the other hand either does not take it into account or even explicitly denies it, because of the danger that the great majority of believers would confuse the Divine Intellect with its human, "created" reflection and would not be able to conceive of their transcendent unity except in the likeness of a substance the quasi-material coherence of which would be contrary to the essential uniqueness of every being. It is true that the Intellect has a "created" aspect both in the human and in the cosmic order, but the whole scope of the meaning that can be given to the word "Intellect"[11] is not what concerns us here since, independently of this question, esoterism

subjective "experience." They forget two things: first, that the doctrine ensues from a state of knowledge which is the goal of the way and secondly, that God does not lie.

[11] The doctrine of the Christian contemplatives of the Orthodox Church, though clearly esoteric, maintains an apparently irreducible distinction between the "Uncreated Light" and the *nous* or intellect, which is a human, and so created faculty, created to know that Light. Here the "identity of essence" is

is characterized by its affirmation of the essentially divine nature of knowledge.

Exoterism stands on the level of formal intelligence which is conditioned by its objects, which are partial and mutually exclusive truths. As for esoterism, it realizes that intelligence which is beyond forms and it alone moves freely in its limitless space and sees how relative truths are delimited.[12]

This brings us to a further point which must be made clear, a point, moreover, indirectly connected with the distinction drawn above between true mysticism and individualistic "mysticism." Those who stand "outside" often attribute to Sufis the pretension of being able to attain to God by the sole means of their own will. In truth it is precisely the man whose orientation is towards action and merit—that is, exoteric—who most often tends to look on everything from the point of an effort of will, and from this arises his lack of understanding of the purely contemplative point of view which envisages the way first of all in relation to knowledge.

In the principial order will does in fact depend on knowledge and not *vice versa*, knowledge being by its nature "impersonal." Although its development, starting from the symbolism transmitted by the traditional teaching, does include a certain logical process, knowledge is none the less a divine gift which man could not take to himself by his own initiative. If this is taken into account it is easier to understand what was said above about the nature of those spiritual means which are strictly "initiatic" and are as it were a prefiguring of the non-human goal of the Way. While every human effort, every effort of the will to get beyond the limitations of individuality is doomed to fall back

expressed by the immanence of the "Uncreated Light" and its presence in the heart. From the point of view of method the distinction between the intellect and Light is a safeguard against a "luciferian" confusion of the intellectual organ with the Divine Intellect. The Divine Intellect immanent in the world may even be conceived as the "void," for the Intellect which "grasps" all cannot itself be "grasped." The intrinsic orthodoxy of this point of view—which is also the Buddhist point of view—is seen in the identification of the essential reality of everything with this "void" (*śūnya*).

12 The Qurʾān says: "God created the Heavens and the earth by the Truth (*al-Ḥaqq*)" (64:3).

on itself, those means which are, so to say, of the same nature as the supra-individual Truth (*al-Ḥaqīqa*) which they evoke and prefigure can, and alone can, loosen the knot of microcosmic individuation—the egocentric illusion, as the Vedantists would say—since only the Truth in its universal and supra-mental reality can consume its opposite without leaving of it any residue.

By comparison with this radical negation of the "I" (*nafs*) any means which spring from the will alone, such as asceticism (*az-zuhd*) can play only a preparatory and ancillary part.[13] It may be added that it is for this reason that such means never acquired in Sufism the almost absolute importance they had, for instance, for certain Christian monks; and this is true even in cases where they were in fact strictly practiced in one or another *ṭarīqa*.

A Sufi symbolism which has the advantage of lying outside the realm of any psychological analysis will serve to sum up what has just been said. The picture it gives is this: The Spirit (*ar-Rūḥ*) and the soul (*an-nafs*) engage in battle for the possession of their common son the heart (*al-qalb*). By *ar-Rūḥ* is here to be understood the intellectual principle which transcends the individual nature[14] and by *an-nafs* the psyche, the centrifugal tendencies of which determine the diffuse and inconstant domain of the "I." As for *al-qalb*, the heart, this represents the central organ of the soul, corresponding to the vital center of the physical organism. *Al-qalb* is in a sense the point of intersection of the "vertical" ray, which is *ar-Rūḥ*, with the "horizontal" plane, which is *an-nafs*.

Now it is said that the heart takes on the nature of that one of the two elements generating it which gains the victory in this battle. Inasmuch as the *nafs* has the upper hand the heart is "veiled" by her, for the soul, which takes herself to be an autonomous whole, in a

[13] Sufis see in the body not only the soil which nourishes the passions but also its spiritually positive aspect which is that of a picture or *résumé* of the cosmos. In Sufi writings the expression the "temple" (*haykal*) will be found to designate the body. Muḥyi 'd-Dīn ibn 'Arabī in the chapter on Moses in his *Fuṣūṣ al-Ḥikam* compares it to "the ark where dwells the Peace (*Sakīnah*) of the Lord."

[14] The word *rūḥ* can also have a more particular meaning, that of "vital spirit." This is the sense in which it is most frequently used in cosmology.

way envelops it in her "veil" (*ḥijāb*). At the same time the *nafs* is an accomplice of the "world" in its multiple and changing aspect because she passively espouses the cosmic condition of form. Now form divides and binds whereas the Spirit, which is above form, unites and at the same time distinguishes reality from appearance. If, on the contrary, the Spirit gains the victory over the soul, then the heart will be transformed into Spirit and will at the same time transmute the soul suffusing her with spiritual light. Then too the heart reveals itself as what it really is, that is as the tabernacle (*mishkāt*) of the Divine Mystery (*sirr*) in man.

In this picture the Spirit appears with a masculine function in relation to the soul, which is feminine. But the Spirit is receptive and so feminine in its turn in relation to the Supreme Being, from which it is, however, distinguished only by its cosmic character inasmuch as it is polarized with respect to created beings. In essence *ar-Rūḥ* is identified with the Divine Act or Order (*al-Amr*) which is symbolized in the Qur'ān by the creating Word "Be" (*kun*) and is the immediate and eternal "enunciation" of the Supreme Being: ". . . and they will question you about the Spirit: say: The Spirit is of the Order of my Lord, but you have received but little knowledge" (Qur'ān, 17:85).

In the process of his spiritual liberation the contemplative is reintegrated into the Spirit and by It into the primordial enunciation of God by which "all things were made . . . and nothing that was made was made without it" (St. John's Gospel).[15] Moreover, the name "Sufi" means, strictly speaking, one who is essentially identified with the Divine Act; hence the saying that the "Sufi is not created" (*aṣ-ṣufi lam yukhlaq*), which can also be understood as meaning that the being who is thus reintegrated into the Divine Reality recognizes himself in it "such as he was" from all eternity according to his "principial possibility, immutable in its state of non-manifestation"—to quote Muḥyi 'd-Dīn ibn 'Arabī. Then all his created modalities are revealed, whether they are temporal or non-temporal, as mere inconsistent reflections of this principial possibility.[16]

[15] For the Alexandrines too liberation is brought about in three stages which respectively correspond to the Holy Spirit, the Word, and God the Father.

[16] If it is legitimate to speak of the principial, or divine, possibility of every being, this possibility being the very reason for his "personal uniqueness," it

Rites

A rite is an action the very form of which is the result of a Divine Revelation. Thus the perpetuation of a rite is itself a mode of Revelation, and Revelation is present in the rite in both its aspects—the intellectual and the ontological. To carry out a rite is not only to enact a symbol but also to participate, even if only virtually, in a certain mode of being, a mode which has an extra-human and universal extension. The meaning of the rite coincides with the ontological essence of its form.

For people of modern education and outlook a rite is usually no more than an aid in promoting an ethical attitude; it seems to them that it is from this attitude alone and from nothing else that the rite derives its efficacy—if indeed such people recognize in rites any efficacy at all. What they fail to see is the implicitly universal nature of the qualitative form of rites. Certainly a rite bears fruit only if it is carried out with an intention (*niya*) that conforms to its meaning, for according to a saying of the Prophet, "the value of actions is only through their intentions," though this clearly does not mean that the intention is independent of the form of the action.[17] It is precisely because the inward attitude is wedded to the formal quality of the rite—a quality which manifests a reality both ontological and intellectual—that the act transcends the domain of the individual soul.

The quintessence of Muslim rites, which could be called their "sacramental" element, is the Divine Speech for which they provide a vehicle. This speech is moreover contained in the Qur'ān, the recitation of the text of which by itself constitutes a rite. In certain cases this recitation is concentrated on a single phrase repeated a definite number of times with the aim of actualizing its deep truth and its particular grace. This practice is the more common in Islam because the Qur'ān is

does not follow from this that there is any multiplicity whatever in the divine order, for there cannot be any uniqueness outside the Divine Unity. This truth is a paradox only on the level of discursive reason. It is hard to conceive only because we almost inevitably forge for ourselves a "substantial" picture of the Divine Unity.

[17] Rites of consecration are an exception because their bearing is purely objective. It is enough that one should be qualified to carry them out and that one should observe the prescribed and indispensable rules.

composed in great part of concise formulas with a rhythmical sonority such as lend themselves to litanies and incantations. For exoterism ejaculatory practices can have only a secondary importance; outside esoterism they are never used methodically, but within it they in fact constitute a basic method.

All repetitive recitation of sacred formulas or sacred speech, whether it be aloud or inward, is designated by the generic term *dhikr*. As has already been noted this term bears at the same time the meanings "mention," "recollection," "evocation," and "memory." Sufism makes of invocation, which is *dhikr* in the strict and narrow sense of the term, the central instrument of its method. In this it is in agreement with most traditions of the present cycle of humanity.[18] To understand the scope of this method we must recall that, according to the revealed expression, the world was created by the Speech (*al-Amr*, *al-Kalīma*) of God, and this indicates a real analogy between the Universal Spirit (*ar-Rūḥ*) and speech. In invocation the ontological character of the ritual act is very directly expressed: here the simple enunciation of the Divine Name, analogous to the primordial and limitless "enunciation" of Being, is the symbol of a state or an undifferentiated knowledge superior to mere rational "knowing."

The Divine Name, revealed by God Himself, implies a Divine Presence which becomes operative to the extent that the Name takes possession of the mind of him who invokes It. Man cannot concentrate directly on the Infinite, but, by concentrating on the symbol of the Infinite, attains to the Infinite Itself. When the individual subject is identified with the Name to the point where every mental projection has been absorbed by the form of the Name, the Divine Essence of the Name manifests spontaneously, for this sacred form leads to nothing outside itself; it has no positive relationship except with its Essence

[18] This cycle begins approximately with what is called the "historical" period. The analogy between the Muslim *dhikr* and the Hindu *japa-yoga* and also with the methods of incantation of Hesychast Christianity and of certain schools of Buddhism is very remarkable. It would, however, be false to attribute a non-Islamic origin to the Muslim *dhikr*, first because this hypothesis is quite unnecessary, secondly because it is contradicted by the facts, and thirdly because fundamental spiritual realities cannot fail to manifest themselves at the core of every traditional civilization.

and finally its limits are dissolved in that Essence. Thus union with the Divine Name becomes Union (*al-waṣl*) with God Himself.

The meaning "recollection" implied in the word *dhikr* indirectly shows up man's ordinary state of forgetfulness and unconsciousness (*ghafla*). Man has forgotten his own pre-temporal state in God and this fundamental forgetfulness carries in its train other forms of forgetfulness and of unconsciousness. According to a saying of the Prophet, "this world is accursed and all it contains is accursed save only the invocation (or: the memory) of God (*dhikru 'Llāh*)." The Qur'ān says: "Assuredly prayer prevents passionate transgressions and grave sins but the invocation of God (*dhikru 'Llāh*) is greater" (29:45). According to some this means that the mentioning, or the remembering, of God constitutes the quintessence of prayer; according to others it indicates the excellence of invocation as compared with prayer.

Other Scriptural foundations of the invocation of the Name—or the Names—of God are to be found in the following passages of the Qur'ān: "Remember Me and I will remember you . . ." or: "Mention Me and I will mention you . . ." (2:152); "Invoke your Lord with humility and in secret. . . . And invoke Him with fear and desire; Verily the Mercy of God is nigh to those who practice the 'virtues' (*al-muḥsinīn*), those who practice *al-iḥsān*, the deepening by 'poverty' (*al-faqr*) or by 'sincerity' (*al-ikhlāṣ*) of 'faith' (*al-īmān*) and 'submission' to God (*al-islām*)" (7:55, 56). The mention in this passage of "humility" (*taḍarru'*), of "secrecy" (*khufya*), of "fear" (*khawf*) and of "desire" (*ṭama'*) is of the very greatest technical importance. "To God belong the Fairest Names: invoke Him by them" (7:180); "O ye who believe! when ye meet a (hostile) band be firm and remember God often in order that ye may succeed" (8:45). The esoteric meaning of this "band" is "the soul which incites to evil" (*an-nafs al-ammāra*) and with this goes a transposition of the literal meaning, which concerns the "lesser holy war" (*al-jihād al-aṣghar*), to the plane of the "greater holy war" (*al-jihād al-akbar*). "Those who believe and whose hearts rest in security in the recollection (or: the invocation) of God; Verily is it not through the recollection of God that their hearts find rest in security?" (13:28).

By implication the state of the soul of the profane man is here compared to a disturbance or agitation through its being dispersed in multiplicity, which is at the very antipodes of the Divine Unity. "Say: Call on *Allāh* (the synthesis of all the Divine Names which is also transcendent as compared with their differentiation) or call on *ar-Raḥmān* (the Bliss-with-Mercy or the Beauty-with-Goodness intrinsic in God); in whatever manner ye invoke Him, His are the most beautiful Names" (17:110); "In the Messenger of God ye have a beautiful example of him whose hope is in God and the Last Day and who invokes God much" (33:21); "O ye who believe! invoke God with a frequent invocation (*dhikran kathīrā*)" (33:41); "And call on God with a pure heart (or: with a pure religion) (*mukhliṣīna lahu-d-dīn*) . . ." (40:14); "Your Lord has said: Call Me and I will answer you . . ." (40:60); "Is it not time for those who believe to humble their hearts at the remembrance of God? . . ." (57:16); "Call on (or: Remember) the Name of thy Lord and consecrate thyself to Him with (perfect) consecration" (73:8); "Happy is he who purifies himself and invokes the Name of his Lord and prayeth" (87:14, 15).

To these passages from the Qur'ān must be added some of the sayings of the Prophet: "It is in pronouncing Thy Name that I must die and live." Here the connection between the Name, "death," and "life" includes a most important initiatic meaning. "'There is a means for polishing everything which removes rust; what polishes the heart is the invocation of God, and no action puts so far off the chastisement of God as this invocation.'[19] The companions said: 'Is not fighting against infidels like unto it?' He replied: 'No: not even if you fight on till your sword is broken'"; "Never do men gather together to invoke (or: to remember) God without their being surrounded by angels, without the Divine Favor covering them, without Peace (*as-sakīna*) descending on them and without God remembering them with those who surround Him"; "The Prophet said: 'The solitaries shall be the first.' They asked: 'Who are the solitaries (*al-mufridūn*)?' And he

[19] According to the *Viṣṇu-Dharma-Uttara* "water suffices to put out fire and the rising of the sun (to drive away) shadows; in the age of Kali repetition of the Name of *Hari* (*Viṣṇu*) suffices to destroy all errors. The Name of *Hari*, precisely the Name, the Name which is my life; there is not, no, there surely is no other way." In the *Mānava Dharma-Śāstra* it is said: "Beyond doubt a brahmin (priest) will succeed by nothing but *japa* (invocation). Whether

replied: 'Those who invoke much'"; "A Bedouin came to the Prophet and asked: 'Who is the best among men.' The Prophet answered: 'Blessed is that person whose life is long and his actions good.' The Bedouin said: 'O Prophet! What is the best and the best rewarded of actions?' He replied: 'The best of actions is this: to separate yourself from the world and to die while your tongue is moist with repeating the Name of God'";[20] "A man said: 'O Prophet of God, truly the laws of Islam are many. Tell me a thing by which I can obtain the rewards.' The Prophet answered: 'Let your tongue be ever moist with mentioning God.'"

* * *

The universal character of invocation is indirectly expressed by the simplicity of its form and by its power of assimilating to itself all those acts of life whose direct and elemental nature has an affinity with the "existential" aspect of the rite. Thus the *dhikr* easily imposes its sway on breathing, the double rhythm of which sums up not only every manifestation of life but also, symbolically, the whole of existence.

Just as the rhythm inherent in the sacred words imposes itself on the movement of breathing, so the rhythm of breathing in its turn can impose itself on all the movements of the body. Herein lies the principle of the sacred dance practiced in Sufi communities.[21] This practice is the more remarkable since the Muslim religion as such is rather hostile both to dancing and to music, for the identification through the medium of a cosmic rhythm with a spiritual or divine

he carries out other rites or not he is a perfect brahmin." Likewise also the *Mahābhārata* teaches that "of all functions (*dharmas*) *japa* (invocation) is for me the highest function" and that "of all sacrifices I am the sacrifice of *japa*."

[20] Kabīr said: "Just as a fish loves water and the miser loves silver and a mother loves her child so also Bhagat loves the Name. The eyes stream through looking at the path and the heart has become a pustule from ceaselessly invoking the Name."

[21] According to a *ḥadīth*, "He who does not vibrate at remembrance of the Friend has no friend." This saying is one of the scriptural foundations of the dance of the dervishes.

reality has no place in a religious perspective which maintains a strict and exclusive distinction between Creator and creature. Also there are practical reasons for banishing dancing from religious worship, for the psychic results accompanying the sacred dance might lead to deviation. None the less the dance offers too direct and too primordial a spiritual support for it not to be found in regular or occasional use in the esoterism of the monotheistic religions.[22]

It is related that the first Sufis founded their dancing *dhikr* on the dances of the Arab warriors. Later, Sufi orders in the East, such as the Naqshabandis, adapted certain techniques of *hatha-yoga* and so differentiated their form of dance. Jalāl ad-Dīn Rūmī, who founded the Mevlevī order, drew the inspiration for the collective *dhikr* of his community from the popular dances and music of Asia Minor.[23] If the dances and music of the dervishes are mentioned here it is because these are among the best known of the manifestations of Sufism; they belong, however, to a collective and so to a rather peripheral aspect of *taṣawwuf* and many masters have pronounced against their too general

22 A Psalm in the Bible says: "Let them praise His Name in the dance: let them sing praises unto him with the timbrel and the harp." It is known that the sacred dance exists in Jewish esoterism, finding its model in the dancing of King David before the Ark of the Covenant. The apocryphal Gospel of the Childhood speaks of the Virgin as a child dancing on the altar steps, and certain folk customs allow us to conclude that these models were imitated in mediaeval Christianity. St Theresa of Avila and her nuns danced to the sound of tambourines. Mā Ananda Moyi has said: "During the *samkīrtana* (the "spiritual concert" which is the Hindu equivalent of the Muslim *samā*ʿ, or rather, of *ḥadra* or ʿ*imāra*) do not pay attention to the dance or the musical accompaniment but concentrate on His Name. . . . When you pronounce the Name of God your spirit begins to appreciate the *samkīrtana* and its music predisposes you to the contemplation of divine things. Just as you should make *pūjās* and pray, you should also take part in *samkīrtanas*."

23 An aesthetic feeling can be a support for intuition for the same reason as a doctrinal idea and to the extent to which the beauty of a form reveals an intellectual essence. But the particular efficacy of such a means as music lies in the fact that it speaks first of all to feeling, which it clarifies and sublimates. Perfect harmony of the active intelligence (the reason) and the passive intelligence (feeling or sensibility), prefigures the spiritual state—*al-ḥāl*.

use. In any case, exercises of this kind ought never to preponderate over the practice of solitary *dhikr*.

Preferably invocation is practiced during a retreat (*khalwa*), but it can equally be combined with all sorts of external activities. It requires the authorization (*idhn*) of a spiritual master. Without this authorization the dervish would not enjoy the spiritual help brought to him through the initiatic chain (*silsila*) and moreover his purely individual initiative would run the risk of finding itself in flagrant contradiction to the essentially non-individual character of the symbol, and from this might arise incalculable psychic reactions.[24]

[24] "When man has made himself familiar with *dhikr*," says al-Ghazzālī, "he separates himself (inwardly) from all else. Now at death he is separated from all that is not God. . . . What remains is only invocation. If this invocation is familiar to him, he finds his pleasure in it and rejoices that the obstacles which turned him aside from it have been put away, so that he finds himself as if alone with his Beloved. . . ." In another text al-Ghazzālī expresses himself thus: "You must be alone in a retreat . . . and, being seated, concentrate your thought on God without other inner occupation. This you will accomplish, first pronouncing the Name of God with your tongue, ceaselessly repeating: *Allāh, Allāh*, without letting the attention go. The result will be a state in which you will feel without effort on your part this Name in the spontaneous movement of your tongue" (from his *Iḥyā' 'Ulūm ad-Dīn*). Methods of incantation are diverse, as are spiritual possibilities. At this point we must once again insist on the danger of giving oneself up to such practices outside their traditional framework and their normal conditions.

SUFISM AND ISLAM

William C. Chittick

Sufism is the most universal manifestation of the inner dimension of Islam; it is the way by which man transcends his own individual self and reaches God.[1] It provides within the forms of the Islamic revelation the means for an intense spiritual life directed towards the transformation of man's being and the attainment of the spiritual virtues; ultimately it leads to the vision of God. It is for this reason that many Sufis define Sufism by the saying of the Prophet of Islam concerning spiritual virtue (*iḥsān*): "It is that thou shouldst worship God as if thou sawest Him, for if thou seest Him not, verily He seeth thee."

Islam is primarily a "way of knowledge,"[2] which means that its spiritual method, its way of bridging the illusory gap between man and God—"illusory," but none the less as real as man's own ego—is centered upon man's intelligence. Man is conceived of as a "theomorphic" being, a being created in the image of God, and therefore as possessing the three basic qualities of intelligence, free-will, and speech. Intelligence is central to the human state and gains a saving quality through its content, which in Islam is the *Shahāda* or "profession of faith": *Lā ilāha illā 'Llāh*, "There is no god but God"; through the *Shahāda* man comes to know the Absolute and the nature of reality, and thus also the way to salvation. The element of will, however, must also be taken into account, because it exists and only through it can man choose to conform to the Will of the Absolute. Speech, or communication with God, becomes the means—through prayer in general or in Sufism

[1] On the relationship between Sufism and Islam see Seyyed Hossein Nasr, *Ideals and Realities of Islam* (London, 1966), chapter 5; S.H. Nasr, *Sufi Essays* (London, 1972), pp. 32 ff; Titus Burckhardt, *An Introduction to Sufi Doctrine* (Lahore, 1959), chapter 1; and Frithjof Schuon, *Understanding Islam* (London, 1962), chapters 1 and 4.

[2] See Schuon, *Understanding Islam*, pp. 13 ff. and Nasr, *Ideals and Realities*, pp. 21 ff.

through quintessential prayer or invocation (*dhikr*)—of actualizing man's awareness of the Absolute and of leading intelligence and will back to their essence.[3]

Through the spiritual methods of Sufism the *Shahāda* is integrally realized within the being of the knower. The "knowledge" of Reality which results from this realization, however, must not be confused with knowledge as it is usually understood in everyday language, for this realized knowledge is "To know what is, and to know it in such a fashion as to be oneself, truly and effectively, what one knows."[4] If the human ego, with which fallen man usually identifies himself, were a closed system, such knowledge would be beyond man's reach. However, in the view of Sufism, like other traditional metaphysical doctrines, the ego is only a transient mode of man's true and transcendent self. Therefore the attainment of metaphysical knowledge in its true sense, or "spiritual realization," is the removal of the veils which separate man from God and from the full reality of his own true nature. It is the means of actualizing the full potentialities of the human state.

Metaphysical knowledge in the sense just described can perhaps be designated best by the term "gnosis" (*ʿirfān*), which in its original sense and as related to Sufism means "Wisdom made up of knowledge and sanctity."[5] Many Sufis speak of gnosis as being synonymous with love, but "love" in their vocabulary excludes the sentimental colorings usually associated with this term in current usage. The term love is employed by them because it indicates more clearly than any other word that in gnosis the whole of one's being "knows" the object and not just the mind; and because love is the most direct reflection in this world, or the truest "symbol" in the traditional sense, of the joy and beatitude of the spiritual world. Moreover, in Sufism, as in other traditions, the instrument of spiritual knowledge or gnosis is the heart,

[3] See Schuon, *Understanding Islam*, pp. 13 ff. and Nasr, *Ideals and Realities*, pp. 18 ff.

[4] René Guénon, "Oriental Metaphysics," *Tomorrow* (London), vol. 12, no. 1, p. 10; also in *The Sword of Gnosis* (Baltimore, 1974).

[5] G.E.H. Palmer, in the foreword to Schuon, *Gnosis: Divine Wisdom* (London, 1959), p. 8.

the center of man's being;[6] gnosis is "existential" rather than purely mental.

Rūmī indicates the profound nature of love (*'ishq* or *maḥabba*), a nature which can completely transform the human substance, by saying that in reality love is an attribute of God[7] and that through it man is freed from the limitations which define his state in the world.

> He (alone)[8] whose garment is rent by a (mighty) love is purged entirely of covetousness and defect.
> Hail, O Love that bringest us good gain—thou art the physician of all our ills,
> The remedy of our pride and vainglory, our Plato and our Galen (I, 22-24).

The interrelationship between love and knowledge is clearly expressed in the following passage:

> By love dregs become clear; by love pains become healing,
> By love the dead is made living. . . .
> This love, moreover, is the result of knowledge: who (ever) sat in foolishness on such a throne?
> On what occasion did deficient knowledge give birth to this love?
> Deficient knowledge gives birth to love, but (only love) for that which is really lifeless (II, 1530-1533).

[6] On the heart, which is the seat of the Intellect in its traditional sense, see Schuon, "The Ternary Aspect of the Human Microcosm," in *Gnosis: Divine Wisdom*, chapter 7.

[7] See *Mathnawī*, V, 2185, where Rūmī states this explicitly. He also says, "Whether love be from this (earthly) side or from that (heavenly) side, in the end it leads us yonder" (I, 111). The sources of quotations from Rūmī are indicated as follows: Roman numerals refer to the particular volume of the *Mathnawī* (R.A. Nicholson's translation [London, 1925-1940]) being cited. *Discourses* refers to *Discourses of Rūmī* [*Fīhi mā Fīhi*], translated by A.J. Arberry (London, 1961); and *Dīwān* to *Selected Poems from the Dīvāni Shamsi Tabrīz*, translated by R.A. Nicholson (Cambridge, 1898).

[8] The additions within parentheses are Nicholson's; those within brackets are my own.

In his commentary on these verses Nicholson recognizes that Rūmī does not differentiate between gnosis and love:

> Rūmī . . . does not make any . . . distinctions between the gnostic (*'ārif*) and the lover (*'āshiq*): for him, knowledge and love are inseparable and coequal aspects of the same reality.[9]

Rūmī describes the spiritual transformation brought about by love as follows:

> This is Love: to fly heavenwards,
> To rend, every instant, a hundred veils (*Dīwān*, p. 137).

> Love is that flame which, when it blazes up, consumes everything
> else but the Beloved (V, 588).

And therefore,

> When love has no care for him [the traveler on the spiritual path],
> he is left as a bird
> without wings. Alas for him then! (I, 31).

Sufism deals first and foremost with the inward aspects of that which is expressed outwardly or exoterically in the *Sharī'a,* the Islamic religious law. Hence it is commonly called "Islamic esotericism."[10] In the view of the Sufis, exoteric Islam is concerned with laws and injunctions which direct human action and life in accordance with the

[9] *Mathnawī*, vol. VII, p. 294. In Sufism, contrary to Hinduism for example, there is no sharp distinction between the spiritual ways of love and knowledge; rather, it is a question of the predominance of one way over the other. See the excellent discussion by Burckhardt, "Knowledge and Love," in *Introduction to Sufi Doctrine*, pp. 27-32. On the various dimensions of love in Sufism as manifested in the world, see Schuon, "Earthly Concomitances of the Love of God," in *Dimensions of Islam* (London, 1969), chapter 9.

[10] On esotericism and exotericism, see Burckhardt, *An Introduction to Sufi Doctrine*, chapter 1; and Schuon, *The Transcendent Unity of Religions* (London, 1953), chapters 2 and 3.

divine Will, whereas Sufism concerns direct knowledge of God and realization—or literally, the "making real" and actual—of spiritual realities which exist both within the external form of the Revelation and in the being of the spiritual traveler (*sālik*). The *Sharīʿa* is directly related to Sufism inasmuch as it concerns itself with translating these same realities into laws which are adapted to the individual and social orders.

Exotericism by definition must be limited in some sense, for it addresses itself to a particular humanity and a particular psychological and mental condition—even though its means of addressing itself is to some degree universalized and expanded through time and space to encompass a large segment of the human race. Esotericism also addresses itself to particular psychological types, but it is open inwardly towards the Infinite in a much more direct manner than exotericism, since it is concerned primarily with overcoming all the limitations of the individual order. The very forms which somehow limit exotericism become for esotericism the point of departure towards the unlimited horizons of the spiritual world. Or again, exotericism concerns itself with forms of a sacred nature and has for its goal the salvation of the individual by means of these very forms, whereas esotericism is concerned with the spirit that dwells within sacred forms and has as its goal the transcending of all individual limits.

With these points in mind it should be clear why the Sufis acknowledge the absolute necessity of the *Sharīʿa* and in general are among its firmest supporters.[11] They recognize that to reach the

[11] Sufism is also in a certain sense "opposed" to the *Sharīʿa*, although not in the way usually imagined. The spiritual Path is precisely a passing beyond or a penetrating into the forms of the *Sharīʿa*, and thus certain Sufis may at one time or another criticize the Divine Law, or rather those who follow it blindly, but only to warn them not to be limited and held back by it. The spiritual traveler must be able to pass to the inner essence of the Law, while at the same time following it on the individual and social planes. Deviations from Sufism have appeared when the Law has been ignored. On the equilibrium between esotericism and exotericism in Islamic civilization, see Nasr, *Ideals and Realities*, pp. 122 ff; and on a particular example during the Safavid period in Iran of opposition to Sufism caused by a rupture of this equilibrium, see Nasr, "Sūfism," *The Cambridge History of Iran*, vol. 4, edited

indwelling spirit of a doctrine or a sacred form (such as a rite or a work of art), one must first *have* that external form, which is the expression of the Truth which that form manifests, but in modes conformable to the conditions of this world. Moreover, the vast majority of believers are not capable of reaching the inner meaning that lies within the revealed forms, and so they must attain salvation by conforming to the exoteric dimension of the revelation.

Here it may be helpful to quote from Ibn ʿArabī. This great Andalusian sage of the seventh/thirteenth century (d. 1240) was the first to formulate explicitly many of the metaphysical and cosmological doctrines of Sufism. Rūmī, who lived a generation later than Ibn ʿArabī, was, as S.H. Nasr has pointed out,[12] certainly acquainted with Ibn ʿArabī's thought through the intermediary of Ṣadr al-Dīn Qunyawī. Qunyawī was Ibn ʿArabī's stepson and the foremost expositor of his school in the eastern lands of Islam and at the same time one of Rūmī's close friends and the leader of the prayers (*imām*) at the mosque where Rūmī prayed. In any case, the metaphysics which underlies Rūmī's writings is basically the same as that of Ibn ʿArabī—to the extent that certain later Sufis have called the *Mathnawī* "the *Futūḥāt al-Makkiyya* in Persian verse," referring to Ibn ʿArabī's monumental work. Therefore here, in the case of certain points of metaphysics where Ibn ʿArabī is much more explicit than Rūmī, I have taken the liberty of quoting Ibn ʿArabī's more theoretical and abstract formulations to make clear the underlying basis of Rūmī's doctrine.

To return to the subject at hand, Ibn ʿArabī points out that traditions have their exoteric and esoteric sides in order that all believers may worship to their capacities.

> The prophets spoke in the language of outward things and of the generality of men, for they had confidence in the understanding of him who had knowledge and the ears to hear. They took into account only the common people, because they knew the station of

by R. N. Frye (Cambridge, 1975), pp. 442-463.

[12] "Rūmī and the Sufi Tradition," *Studies in Comparative Religion*, vol. 8, 1974, p. 79. On Ibn ʿArabī, see Nasr, *Three Muslim Sages* (Cambridge, Mass., 1964), chapter 3.

> the People of Understanding. . . . They made allowances for those of weak intelligence and reasoning power, those who were dominated by passion and natural disposition.
>
> In the same way, the sciences which they brought were clothed in robes appropriate to the most inferior understandings, in order that he who had not the power of mystical penetration would stop at the robes and say, "How beautiful are they!", and consider them as the ultimate degree. But the person of subtle understanding who penetrates as one must into the depths after the pearls of wisdom will say, "These are robes from the King." He will contemplate the measure of the robes and the cloth they are made from and will come to know the measure of Him who is clothed in the robes. He will discover a knowledge which does not accrue to him who knows nothing of these things.[13]

In a similar vein Rūmī says the following:

> The perfect speaker is like one who distributes trays of viands, and whose table is filled with every sort of food,
>
> So that no guest remains without provisions, (but) each one gets his (proper) nourishment separately:
>
> (Such a speaker is) like the Quran which is sevenfold in meaning, and in which there is food for the elect and for the vulgar (III, 1895-1897).

Orientalists commonly speak of the derivation of Sufism from non-Islamic sources and of its historical development. From a certain point of view there has indeed been borrowing of forms of doctrinal expression from other traditions and a great amount of development.[14] But to conclude from this in the manner of many scholars that Sufism gradually came into being under the influence of a foreign tradition or from a hodgepodge of borrowed doctrine is to completely misunderstand

[13] Ibn ʿArabī, *Fuṣūṣ al-Ḥikam*, edited by A. Afifi (Cairo, 1946), pp. 204-205.

[14] Orientalists have proposed a variety of theories as to the "origin" of Sufism, which are well summarized in the introduction to R.A. Nicholson, *The Mystics of Islam* (London, 1914).

its nature, i.e., that in essence it is a metaphysics and means of spiritual realization derived of necessity from the Islamic revelation itself.[15]

For the Sufis themselves one of the clearest proofs of the integrally Islamic nature of Sufism is that its practices are based on the model of the Prophet Muhammad. For Muslims it is self-evident that in Islam no one has been closer to God—or, if one prefers, no one has attained a more complete spiritual realization—than the Prophet himself, for by the very fact of his prophecy he is the Universal Man and the model for all sanctity in Islam. For the same reason he is the ideal whom all Sufis emulate and the founder of all that later became crystallized within the Sufi orders.[16]

According to Sufi teachings, the path of spiritual realization can only be undertaken and traversed under the guidance of a spiritual master; someone who has already traversed the stages of the Path to God and who has, moreover, been chosen by Heaven to lead others on the Way.[17] When the Prophet of Islam was alive he initiated many of his Companions into the spiritual life by transferring to them the "Muhammadan grace" (*al-barakat al-Muḥammadiyya*) and giving them theoretical and practical instructions not meant for all believers. Certain of these Companions were in their own turn given the function of initiating others. The Sufi orders which came into being in later centuries stem from these Companions and later generations of disciples who received the particular instructions originally imparted by the Prophet. Without the chain (*silsila*) of grace and practice reaching back to the Prophet no Sufi order can exist.

[15] On the Islamic origin of Sufism, some of the proofs of which are briefly summarized here, see Nasr, *Ideals and Realities*, pp. 127 ff; Nasr, *Sufi Essays*, pp. 16-17; and Martin Lings, *A Sufi Saint of the Twentieth Century* (London, 1971), chapter 2.

[16] On the Sufi orders in their historical and social manifestation see J.S. Trimingham, *The Sufi Orders in Islam* (London, 1971).

[17] The absolute necessity for the spiritual master for entrance on the Sufi path is emphasized repeatedly in Rūmī's writings. On the significance of the master see Nasr, "The Sufi Master as Exemplified in Persian Sufi Literature," in *Sufi Essays*, chapter 4; and Schuon, "Nature and Function of the Spiritual Master," *Studies in Comparative Religion*, vol. 1, 1967, pp. 50-59.

> God's way is exceedingly fearful, blocked, and full of snow. He [the Prophet] was the first to risk his life, driving his horse and pioneering the road. Whoever goes on this road, does so by his guidance and guarding. He discovered the road in the first place and set up waymarks everywhere (*Discourses*, p. 232).

In the Sufi view of Islamic history, the very intensity of the spiritual life at the time of the Prophet did not permit a complete separation on the outward and formal plane between the exoteric and esoteric dimensions of the tradition. Both the *Sharīʿa* and the *Ṭarīqa* (the spiritual path) existed from the beginning. But only after gradual degeneration and corruption—the tendency of the collectivity to become increasingly diversified and forgetful—was it necessary to make certain formulations explicit in order to refute the growing number of errors and to breathe new life into a decreasing power of spiritual intuition.[18]

Rūmī was fully aware that on the collective level spiritual awareness and comprehension had dimmed since the time of the Prophet:

> Amongst the Companions (of the Prophet) there was scarcely anyone that knew the Quran by heart [which is not such a rare accomplishment in the Islamic world today, whereas it must have been common at the time of Rūmī], though their souls had a great

[18] "According to a very prevalent error . . . all traditional symbols were originally understood in a purely literal sense, and symbolism properly so called only developed as the result of an 'intellectual progress' or a 'progressive refinement' which took place later. This is an opinion which completely reverses the normal relationship of things. . . . In reality, what later appears as a super-added meaning was already implicitly present, and the 'intellectualization' of symbols is the result, not of an intellectual progress, but on the contrary of a loss by the majority of primordial intelligence. It is thus on account of increasingly defective understanding of symbols and in order to ward off the danger of 'idolatry' (and not to escape from a supposedly pre-existent, but in fact non-existent, idolatry) that the tradition has felt obliged to render verbally explicit symbols which at the origin . . . were in themselves fully adequate to transmit metaphysical truths" (Schuon, "The Symbolist Outlook," *Tomorrow*, vol. 14, 1966, p. 50).

> desire (to commit it to memory), Because . . . its kernel had filled (them) and had reached maturity (III, 1386-1387).

> It is related that in the time of the Prophet . . . any of the Companions who knew by heart one Sura [chapter of the Quran] or half a Sura was called a great man . . . since they devoured the Quran. To devour a maund of bread or two maunds is certainly a great accomplishment. But people who put bread in their mouths without chewing it and spit it out again can "devour" thousands of tons in that way (*Discourses*, p. 94).

If elaborated and systematized forms of Sufi doctrine were not present in early Islamic history, it is because such formulation was not necessary for the spiritual life. The synthetic and symbolic presentation of metaphysical truths found in the Quran and the *ḥadīth* (the sayings of the Prophet) was perfectly adequate to guide those practicing the disciplines of the *Ṭarīqa*. There was no need for detailed and explicit formulation. It was not until the third Islamic century/ninth Christian century in fact that the *Ṭarīqa* became clearly crystallized into a separate entity, at the same time that the *Sharīʿa* underwent a similar process.[19]

As for the similarities which exist between the formulation of Sufi doctrine and the doctrines of other traditions, in certain cases these *are* due to borrowings from other traditional sources. But here again it is a question of adopting a convenient mode of expression and not of emulating inner spiritual states; in any case such states cannot be achieved through simple external borrowing. It would be absurd to suppose that a Sufi familiar with the doctrines of Neoplatonism, for example, who saw that the truths they expressed were excellent descriptions of his own inner states of realized knowledge, would completely reject the Neoplatonic formulations simply because of their source.[20]

[19] See Lings, *A Sufi Saint of the Twentieth Century*, pp. 42 ff.

[20] According to the famous saying of ʿAlī, the representative *par excellence* of esotericism in Islam, "Look at what is said not at who has said it." Islamic civilization in general has always adopted any form of knowledge, provided it was in keeping with divine Unity (*tawḥīd*). See Nasr, *Ideals and Realities*, pp.

In Sufism, doctrine has no right to exist "for its own sake," for it is essentially a guide on the Path. It is a symbolic prefiguration of the knowledge to be attained through spiritual travail, and since this knowledge is not of a purely rational order but is concerned ultimately with the vision of the Truth, which is Absolute and Infinite and in its essence beyond forms, it cannot be rigidly systematized. Indeed, there are certain aspects of Sufi doctrine which may be formulated by one Sufi in a manner quite different from, or even contradictory to, the formulations of another. It is even possible to find what appears outwardly as contradictions within the writings of a single Sufi. Such apparent contradictions, however, are only on the external and discursive level and represent so many different ways of viewing the same reality. There is never a contradiction of an essential order which would throw an ambiguity upon the nature of the transcendent Truth.

Doctrine is a key to open the door of gnosis and a guide to lead the traveler on the Path. Thus, for different people, different formulations may be used. Once the goal of the Path has been reached, doctrine is "discarded," for the Sufi in question *is* the doctrine in his inmost reality and he himself speaks with "the voice of the Truth."

> After direct vision the intermediary is an inconvenience (IV, 2977).

> These indications of the way are for the traveler who at every moment becomes lost in the desert.
> For them that have attained (to union with God) there is nothing (necessary) except the eye (of the spirit) and the lamp (of intuitive faith): they have no concern with indications (to guide them) or with a road (to travel by).
> If the man that is united (with God) has mentioned some indication, he has mentioned (it) in order that the dialecticians may understand (his meaning).
> For a newborn child the father makes babbling sounds, though his intellect may make a survey of the (whole) world. . . .
> For the sake of teaching that tongue-tied (child), one must go outside of one's own language (customary manner of speech).

36 ff. and Nasr, *An Introduction to Islamic Cosmological Doctrines* (Cambridge, Mass., 1964), p. 5.

> You must come into (adopt) his language, in order that he may learn knowledge and science from you.
>
> All the people, then, are as his [the spiritual master's] children: this (fact) is necessary for the Pir [the master] (to bear in mind) when he gives (them) instruction (II, 3312 ff).

In his preface to the fifth book of the *Mathnawī* Rūmī summarizes the relationship between the exoteric law (the *Sharīʿa*), the spiritual wayfaring which the Sufis undergo (the *Ṭarīqa*), and the Truth which is Sufism's goal (the *Ḥaqīqa*). He says that the *Mathnawī* is:

> . . . setting forth that the Religious Law is like a candle showing the way. Unless you gain possession of the candle, there is no wayfaring [i.e., unless you follow the *Sharīʿa*, you cannot enter the *Ṭarīqa*]; and when you have come on to the way, your wayfaring is the Path; and when you have reached the journey's end, that is the Truth. Hence it has been said, "If the truths (realities) were manifest, the religious laws would be naught." As (for example), when copper becomes gold or was gold originally, it does not need the alchemy which is the Law, nor need it rub itself upon the philosopher's stone, which (operation) is the Path; (for), as has been said, it is unseemly to demand a guide after arrival at the goal, and blameworthy to discard the guide before arrival at the goal. In short, the Law is like learning the theory of alchemy from a teacher or book, and the Path is (like) making use of chemicals and rubbing the copper upon the philosopher's stone, and the Truth is (like) the transmutation of the copper into gold. Those who know alchemy rejoice in their knowledge of it, saying, "We know the theory of this (science)"; and those who practice it rejoice in their practice of it, saying, "We perform such works"; and those who have experienced the reality rejoice in the reality, saying, "We have become gold and are delivered from the theory and practice of alchemy: we are God's freedmen". . . .[21]
>
> The law is [theoretical[22]] knowledge, the Path action, the Truth attainment unto God.

[21] On the spiritual significance of alchemy see Burckhardt, *Alchemy: Science of the Cosmos, Science of the Soul* (London, 1967).

[22] It should be remembered that the original meaning of the Greek word *theôria* is "viewing" or "contemplation"; doctrine is therefore "a view of the mountain to be climbed."

THE VISION OF GOD ACCORDING TO IBN ʿARABĪ

Michel Chodkiewicz

"You shall not see Me!" (*lan taranī*). The divine reply to Moses' request (*arinī unẓur ilayka:* "Let me see, so that I can behold You" [Qurʾan 7:143]), seems final. It is no less categorical in its formulation than the one that Exodus gives in a parallel account (Ex. 33:18-23):[1] "Thou canst not see my face: for there shall no man see me, and live." Another verse seems, moreover, to extend to all creatures the impossibility of seeing the Face of God, as the Prophet of the Banū Isrāʾīl was informed: *lā tudrikuhu ʾl-abṣār wa huwa yudriku ʾl-abṣār,* "The looks do not reach Him but it is He who reaches the looks" (Qurʾan 6:103).

Despite their evident meaning, these two verses are interpreted in many ways within the Islamic tradition and, more often than one would expect, in a way which safeguards the possibility of vision. The *lan taranī* addressed to Moses, in particular, provokes numerous commentaries. The verse continues: "But look at the mountain; if it remains firm in its place, then you shall see Me. And when his Lord manifested Himself to the mountain, He reduced it to dust and Moses fell down, thunderstruck. When he came to himself he said, 'Glory be to You! I turn to You with repentance and I am the first of the believers.'" For Ṭabarī, the theophany at Sinai which reduces the mountain to dust and which even so, he says, "had only the strength of a little finger," demonstrates the fundamental inability of creatures to bear the vision of God, and the repentance of Moses testifies that

[1] For the biblical facts relating to the vision of God, see also Judges: 6: 22-23 and 13:22. Cf. also the article by Colette Sirat, "Un midrasch juif en habit musulman: la vision de Moïse sur le Mont Sinaï," *Revue de l'Histoire des Religions*, vol. CLXVIII, no. 1, 1965, pp. 15ff.

his request was presumptuous and unacceptable.[2] But another classic commentary, by Qurṭubī, whilst avoiding taking sides too explicitly, favors a very different opinion. For some people, he says, *lan tarānī* means: "you shall not see Me in this world." But, he adds, according to others, whose views Qāḍi 'Iyad has recorded, "Moses sees God and that is why he falls down in a swoon." Similarly, commenting on the verse which states that "the looks do not reach Him," Qurṭubī, who obviously tends towards an admission of the possibility of vision, sets out the arguments of those who defend this point of view: the ordinary look cannot reach God but God creates in certain beings—and such is certainly the case of the Prophet Muhammad—a look by which He can be seen. Besides, if the impossibility were definitive, would Moses, who is an Envoy, have had the audacity to ask God for an absurd favor? Concerning Muhammad, Qurṭubī relates the contradictory assertions of 'Ā'isha, on the one hand, and of Abū Hurayra and Ibn 'Abbās on the other, and favors the latter. The question, for him, is not to know *if* the Prophet saw God but to know *how* he saw Him: *bi'l-baṣar? aw bi-'ayni qalbihi?* With his physical eyes or with the eye of the heart?[3] However, the great theologian Fakhr ad-Dīn ar-Rāzī, Ibn 'Arabī's contemporary and correspondent, dismisses the possibility that Moses saw God, but affirms that vision is possible in principle.[4]

The position of the *mutakallimūn*—the theologians—on this question is generally left fairly open, at least if one discounts the case of the Mu'tazilites.[5] For the Ash'arites, it is rationally conceivable and scripturally established that "the looks" (*abṣār*) will see God in the future life. Does the Qur'an not assert: "On that day, there will be radiant faces which shall see their Lord" (75:22–23)? Did the Prophet

[2] Ṭabarī, *Jāmi' al-Bayān*, ed. Shakir, XIII, pp. 90-105.

[3] Qurṭubī, *Al-Jāmi li-Aḥkām al-Qur'an* (Cairo, 1938), VII, pp. 278-280 (on 7:143) and VII, p. 54 (on 6:103).

[4] Fakhr ad-Dīn ar-Rāzī, *Tafsīr* (Teheran, undated), XIV, pp. 227-234.

[5] We are summing up very briefly here a set of attitudes that, of course, present divergencies which it is not appropriate to list here. On the doctrine of the Ash'arite *kalām* concerning this subject see Daniel Gimaret, *La Doctrine d'al-Ash'arī* (Paris, 1990), second part, Ch. X, pp. 329-345.

not say: "you shall see your Lord just as you see the moon on the night of the full moon"?[6] Verse 6:103, according to which "the looks do not reach Him," cannot justify any conclusive objection. For some theologians, it is exclusively a question of this lower world and does not apply to the heavenly status of the chosen ones. For others, it is necessary to distinguish between *idrāk*, "all-embracing perception" (*ihāta*), effectively forever forbidden to the creatures, and *ruʾya*, vision itself, to which they have access but which will never exhaust the divine infinity. As for the vision of God here below, whilst it is ruled out by some, others reserve it for exceptional individuals: again, a saying of ʿĀʾisha's, according to which the Prophet did not see God at the time of his *miʿrāj*, comes up in the debate and also an equally categorical assertion of Ibn ʿAbbās' to the contrary, which relies in particular on two verses of the *Sūrat an-Najm* (Qurʾan 53:11, 13). Moreover, a *duʿaʾ** is attributed to the Prophet in which he addresses God in the following terms which are very similar to those of Moses: *asʾaluka ladhdhat al-naẓar ilā wajhika*, "I beg of You the joy of seeing Your face."[7]

If one now turns towards the spiritual masters who preceded Ibn ʿArabī, one finds there, too, many differences of interpretation, but this time they rely on spiritual experience rather than knowledge from books. A comparative clarification is taking place which is conveyed by the increased precision of the vocabulary. For Sahl al-Tustarī, in the ninth century, vision *stricto sensu* is the privilege of the elect in the heavenly abode: *kushūf al-ʿiyān fīʾl-ākhira*. But the men of God benefit in advance from the *kushūf al-qalb fīʾl-dunyā*, from the "lifting of the veil of the heart here below."[8] In his *Kashf al-Maḥjūb*, Hujwīrī relies on the words of Dhūʾn-Nūn, Junayd, and Abū Yazīd al-Bisṭāmī

[6] Bukhārī, *tawḥīd*, 24, pp. 1-5.

* Editors' Note: A prayer of personal supplication.

[7] Darimi, *ʿaqāʾid*, 303, pp. 11-12.

[8] On Tustarī, refer to the work by Gerhard Böwering, *The Mystical Vision of Existence in Classical Islam* (Berlin-New York, 1980), pp. 165-175. Niffarī's position regarding the possibility of vision here below seems to be more positive. See his *Mawāqif*, ed. A.J. Arberry (London, 1935) (see index for *ruʾyat Allāh*).

among others, to assert that God can be *contemplated* in this world and that this contemplation *resembles* vision in the future life.[9] To the notion of "unveiling" (root *k-sh-f*) that we have just come across, that of "contemplation" (root *sh-h-d*) is therefore added. I shall come back, with regard to Ibn ʿArabī, to the problems posed by the vocabulary of these authors who are careful to distinguish precisely between all modes of mystical knowledge.

In his famous *Risāla*, Qushayrī envisages three degrees in the progression towards knowledge of God: *muḥāḍara*, "presence," *mukāshafa*, "unveiling," and *mushāhada*, "contemplation."[10] These stages correspond to a standard model and, with the same or other names, one finds them almost everywhere in the literature of *taṣawwuf*. However, if one consults the great commentary of the Qurʾan of which Qushayrī is also the author, it confirms what the *Risāla* hinted at: that vision as such remains forbidden in this life. It is worth quoting what he writes about the incident at Sinai: "Moses came like one of those who are consumed by desire and lost in love. Moses came without Moses. He came when nothing of Moses remained in Moses." But, Qushayrī adds, it is under the sway of this amorous drunkenness that he had the audacity to ask for vision. It was refused him but, because of this state where he no longer had control over what he was saying, he was not punished for his boldness. Muhammad himself hoped for this supreme favor, without expressing his wish, however. But he was not granted his wish either, Qushayrī maintains.[11]

If we next examine the words of two other great Sufi contemporaries of the Shaykh al-Akbar, we notice that for them a direct perception of Divine Reality is definitely possible. But is it a question of anything other than what spiritual Christians called "an advance payment of beatitude," that is, of a still confused and imperfect vision? Najm ad-Dīn Kubrā describes the stages of contemplation, the last of

[9] Hujwīrī, *Kashf al-Maḥjūb*, trans. R.A. Nicholson (London, 1976, 6th ed.), pp. 329-333.

[10] Qushayrī, *Risāla* (Cairo, 1957), p. 40.

[11] Qushayrī, *Laṭāʾif al-Ishārāt*, ed. Ibrahim al-Basyuni (Cairo, undated), II, pp. 259-262.

which is the contemplation of the Unique Essence.[12] Rūzbihān Baqlī, in his *Tafsīr*,[13] concludes from the Qurʾanic text that Moses did not obtain vision. In another of his works, however, he too maintains that the *viator** can arrive at the point where his *sirr*, the secret center of his being, "is immersed in the ocean of the Divine Essence."[14]

There are, therefore, considerable differences amongst the authors whom I have cited. The very meaning of the word "vision" (*ruʾya*—not to be confused with *ruʾyā*, vision in a dream) remains, nevertheless, rather vague. Should one understand it literally as designating a perception identical to the apprehension of material objects by the organ of sight? Or is it on the contrary only necessary to retain the suggestion of an analogy, the relation between its two terms then remaining to be clarified? In the latter case, is there a radical difference in nature between "unveiling," "contemplation," and "vision"? *A contrario*, if these terms only express differences of degree—and since the highest contemplation seems accessible to some people who are neither Envoys nor Prophets—what does the *lan tarānī* addressed to Moses mean? The abrupt Qurʾanic phrase is variously understood but it evidently inspires a great deal of uncertainty.

The picture I have just drawn from a few examples is extremely scanty, leaving out many subtleties. I think, nevertheless, that it faithfully draws the outlines of the landscape which opens out around this Sinai where Moses, called by his Lord, is not satisfied with hearing Him and demands to see Him. Ibn ʿArabī is the heir of this long and complex tradition. He is, in particular, going to take up the rich vocabulary of spiritual phenomenology such as the men of the Way have gradually built up, without stinting nevertheless on inflecting the meaning or drawing out the significance. But above all, one is going to discover, disseminated in the immense body of his works, a teaching

[12] Najm ad-Dīn Kubrā, *Fawāʾiḥ al-Jamāl*, ed. F. Meier (Wiesbaden, 1957), paras. 42, 95, 97.

[13] Rūzbihān Baqlī, *Arāʾis al-Bayān* (Indian lithographed ed., 1315 AH), I, pp. 271-277.

* Editors' Note: Latin for "traveler."

[14] Rūzbihān Baqlī, *Mashrab al-Arwāḥ* (Istanbul, 1973), p. 215.

which, nourished by his intimate experience, illuminates the whole field of the knowledge of God, in all its forms and in all its degrees.

Before attempting to discern the essential points of his doctrine, it would be worthwhile going over the account of his own meeting with Moses, in the sixth heaven, as he relates it in Chapter 367 of the *Futūḥāt.* "You asked to see Him," he says to Moses. "Now, the Prophet of God has said: no-one will see God before he dies."[15] "That is so," replies Moses. "When I asked to see Him, He granted my wish and I fell down thunderstruck. And it was whilst I was struck down that I saw Him." "Were you dead, then?" "I was, in fact, dead."[16] One already notices here that, for the Shaykh al-Akbar, the *lan tarānī* is not, under certain conditions, an insurmountable obstacle.

But the issue of the vision of God and what it means for Ibn ʿArabī is not separable from an axiom which, in Akbarian doctrine, governs all methods of spiritual realization. In accordance with the *ḥadīth qudsī* often quoted by the Shaykh al-Akbar: "I was a hidden treasure and I loved to be known. . . ,"[17] God is known *because He wants to be known.* He is *only* known because He wants to be known and He alone determines the form and the extent of this knowledge. One must never lose sight of this point if one is concerned with correctly interpreting everything that Ibn ʿArabī writes on the steps of the Way and on the charismas that correspond to them. In fact his teaching, like that of all the great masters of the Islamic tradition, presents two complementary aspects and this polarity can be a source of confusion: in so far as it is metaphysical, it explains the principles and aims; in so far as it is initiatory teaching, it explains the means and therefore takes as point of departure the awareness that the ordinary man has of himself. Now, whatever his theoretical knowledge, the disciple, when he undertakes the *sulūk*, does not escape from the voluntarist illusion. He considers himself to be autonomous. He is *murīd*—willing, desiring. He still does not know that he is *murīd* because he is *murād*—willed,

[15] Ibn Māja, *fitan*, p. 33.

[16] *Al-Futūḥāt al-Makkiyya* (Bulaq, 1329 AH), III, p. 349.

[17] This *ḥadīth* does not appear in the canonic collections. For its use by Ibn ʿArabī, see for example, *Futūḥāt*, II, pp. 232, 327, 399; III, p. 267.

desired by Him whom he claims to reach by his own powers. The initiatory teaching, therefore, in order to be realistic, displays an apparent aspect that one could call Pelagian. Read without discernment, it risks giving the impression that by putting certain precise techniques into practice—such and such a form of invocation or type of retreat (*khalwa*)—specific results will definitely be obtained. The literature of the *ṭurūq*, in later times, unfortunately also contributes to reinforcing this impression, despite some rhetorical precautions. The Shaykh al-Akbar's work, so long as one does not make selective use of it, constantly warns against this naive and dangerous interpretation. The *ḥadīth qudsī*, the beginning of which I have already quoted, is perfectly clear about this: "I therefore created the creatures and I made Myself known by them and it is *through Me* that they have known Me (*fa-bī ʿarafūnī*)."

At the core of the vocabulary of spiritual experience, there is, therefore, in the Shaykh al-Akbar's doctrine, a term which is its key: *tajallī* (a word that, for Arab Christians, designates the Transfiguration of Christ on Mount Tabor), which can be translated, according to the context, as "epiphany" or "theophany." It had already been used in the works of the Sufi authors whom I have mentioned but one finds it constantly in Ibn ʿArabī's writings. Moreover, it is directly linked to the verse with which this paper begins: the Divine Manifestation which reduces the mountain to dust and strikes Moses down is expressed in the Qurʾan by the verb *tajallā*. *Tajallī* is a divine act and it is by virtue of this divine act that man can attain a direct perception of God, whatever degree or form that may take.

The Akbarian doctrine of theophanies is complex.[18] I would merely like to recall here the essential features, commencing by quoting some lines which appear at the beginning of a chapter of the *Futūḥāt* which is precisely devoted to the Pole (*quṭb*) whose "initiatory dwelling-place" is the phrase of verse 7:143, "and when his Lord manifests on the mountain":

[18] There are many references to texts of Ibn ʿArabī's relating to the idea of *tajallī* in the work of Souad Hakim, *Al-Muʿjam aṣ-Ṣūfī* (Beirut, 1981), pp. 257-267.

> God—there is nothing Apparent but He in every similar and every contrary
> In every kind and every species, in all union and all separation
> In everything that the senses or the intellect perceive
> In every body and every form.[19]

These lines express synthetically what many others explain in detail: that is, that theophanies which proceed from the divine name *aẓ-Ẓāhir*, the Apparent[20] never cease, even if men do not know it,[21] since the universe is only the theatre where they are shown and our look, wherever it may turn, only meets with them. If this world is varied, if it is perpetually changing, it is because God does not appear twice in the same form, nor in the same form to two beings.[22]

But the perfect gnostic (*al ʿārīf al-kāmil*) recognizes God in all these forms, unlike other men who only recognize Him when He presents Himself to them in the form of their *iʿtiqād*, the mental image that they make of Him.[23] This *ʿārīf kāmil* himself, however, even if he perceives the perpetual succession of theophanies, even if he distinguishes one from the other and knows *why* they are produced, does not know *how* they are produced for that is a secret which belongs only to the Essence.[24] This has already been pointed out by Henri Corbin and Toshihiko Izutsu[25] and I shall not dwell on it, my intention being limited to determining the effects of the doctrine of the *tajallīyat* on the faculty given to man to "grasp" God—and on this

19 *Futūḥāt*, IV, p. 591.

20 Ibid., I. p. 166.

21 Ibid., I. p. 498.

22 An oft-repeated statement. See, for example, Ibid., IV, p. 19.

23 Ibid., III, pp. 132-1333.

24 Ibid., II. p. 597. Ibn ʿArabī points out that the secret of *kayfiyya* is unknown even to the prophets and the angels.

25 Cf. Henri Corbin, *L'imagination Créatrice dans le Soufisme d'Ibn ʿArabī* (Paris, 1958), Part Two; Toshihiko Izutsu, *Sufism and Taoism* (Tokyo, 1983), chap. 11.

point I think it moreover necessary to correct Corbin's interpretation somewhat.

First of all, a double distinction between theophanies is essential, according to their origin on the one hand and according to their form on the other. The first is standard: it is the one which establishes a hierarchy between the theophanies of the divine acts, those of the attributes, and those of the Essence.[26] One already finds it in the works of authors whom I have cited, for example Najm ad-Dīn Kubrā and Rūzbihān Baqlī. The second, although it did not escape the masters of the past, finds its most precise and complete formulation in Ibn ʿArabī. *Tajallī* can appear in a sensible form or in an imaginal form. It can also be a manifestation transcending all form. When the Prophet declares, "I have seen my Lord in the most beautiful of forms"[27] it is evidently a question of a *tajallī fī ʿālam al-khayāl*, in the imaginal world where "spirits take bodies and bodies become spirits." When Ibn ʿArabī describes his own vision of Divine Ipseity and even adds in the margin a diagram showing the figure in which the *Huwiyya* appeared to him,[28] there too it is a question of a theophany taking place in this intermediary world (*barzakhī*), which he also calls "Land of Truth" (*arḍ al-haqīqa*).[29]

But nothing would be more contrary to the Shaykh al-Akbar's thought than to believe that this imaginal world constitutes the *nec plus ultra.** By insisting on the importance for Ibn ʿArabī of the notion

26 *Futūḥāt*, I, p. 91.

27 On this *ḥadīth* of disputed authenticity, cf. H. Ritter, *Das Meer der Seele* (Leiden, 1956), pp. 445ff. Cf. also Jīlī, *Insān Kāmil* (Cairo, 1963), chap. 42.

28 This vision, which occurred on the night of Wednesday 4th of the month of *rabī ath-thānī* in the year 627, is described in *Futūḥāt*, II, p. 449 (27th *fasl* of chap. 198) but the diagram which accompanies the account has not been reproduced by the editor. It appears in the 1293 AH edition, II, p. 591, and is reproduced by Asin Palacios, *El Islam Cristianizado* (Madrid, 1931), p. 105, by Corbin, *L'imagination*, p. 175, and by A.A. Affifi, *The Mystical Philosophy of Ibnu'l-ʿArabī* (Cambridge, 1939), p. 114.

29 This is specifically the title of chapter 8 of the *Futūḥāt* which is a description of this "imaginal world."

* Editors' Note: That is, the highest or ultimate world.

of the *ʿālam al-khayāl*, Corbin filled a serious gap in previous studies. By paying too much attention to this discovery, he was led to overestimate its importance and reduced the field of perceptions of the divine to the domain of formal theophanies. Many of Ibn ʿArabī's works overrule this limitation which would prohibit all access to the absolute nakedness of the Divine Essence: forms, be they tangible or imaginal, are created and cannot confine the uncreated. The highest knowledge is beyond every image; it requires what Meister Eckhart calls *entbildung.** If the perception of the *tajallī ṣuwarī* or *barzakhī* represents, relative to the blindness of the majority of human beings in their earthly condition, a considerable privilege, it remains very imperfect. If, under different names—most often *mushāhada*—it occupies an important place in the account of the spiritual experience of Ibn ʿArabī himself or other *awliyāʾ*, it is because theophany, when it is formal, can, up to a point, be described. Speaking of a famous contemporary Sufi, ʿUmar Suhrawardī, Ibn ʿArabī emphasizes several times that his *tajallī* was *only barzakhī* for otherwise he would not have maintained that it was possible to look at God and hear Him at the same time.[30] "When He (God) allows Himself to be gazed upon, He does not speak to you," he wrote in another passage, "and when He speaks to you, He does not allow Himself to be seen *unless it is a question of a theophany in a form*":[31] this wording obviously implies the possibility of a supraformal theophany.

* Editors' Note: *Entbildung* is a term coined by Eckhart, meaning "deimagining." It refers to the process of stripping away the images that one has of Ultimate Reality, permitting one to perceive It through a means free of the mundane imagination, thus purifying one's contemplation of all forms. Of course, stripping away all such images would require a stripping away of the mundane self that generates them.

[30] Ibid., I, p. 609; III. p. 213.

[31] Ibid., I, p. 397. Corbin's position, which excludes all informal contemplation, is defined in particular, in *L'imagination*, Part Two, chap. 4 ("La Forme de Dieu"). It is based on a very selective reading of Ibn ʿArabī and of Jīlī (see, on the latter, chap. 41 and chap. 62 of *Insān Kāmil* where he refers to verse 7:143).

Some important information about this can be found in the "Book of Theophanies," of which Osman Yahya has compiled an excellent critical edition accompanied by a commentary by Ibn Sawdakīn, which transcribes the explanations which he received from Ibn ʿArabī's own mouth, and by an anonymous commentary, the *Kashf al-Ghayāt*, sometimes attributed to ʿAbd al-Karīm al-Jīlī but which is probably not his work.[32] Chapters 70, 71, and 72 describe successively the theophanies of "red light," "white light," and "green light" and the meetings that the Shaykh al-Akbar had at each of these stages: with ʿAlī ibn Abī Ṭālib in the first, then with Abū Bakr, and finally with ʿUmar. Here we are at the closest to the mystery of the Essence which is symbolized by the "radiant light (*an-nūr ash-shaʿshaʿānī*) by which one apprehends but which cannot itself be apprehended" because of its blinding brilliance.[33] The red light, the *Kashf al-Ghayāt* tells us, is only a reflection of this light of the Essence in the immensity of the *khayāl muṭlaq*, and it is still only a question here of a *ruʾya mithāliyya*, of a vision in imaginal form. The white light represents a more elevated degree than the red and green for, Ibn ʿArabī tells Ibn Sawdakin, "the color white is the only one which includes all the others. . . . Its rank is that of the Name of Majesty [*Allāh*] amongst the other Names and that of the Essence amongst the attributes."[34] But Abū Bakr, however, who is standing in this white light, has his face turned towards the west—the place of occultation of light—for the west is "the mine of secrets": thus it is clearly pointed out to us that it is beyond the highest formal theophanies, beyond created lights, that

[32] *Kitab at-Tajallīyāt* (Teheran, 1988). The vocabulary of the *Kashf al-Ghayāt* presents significant differences from that of Jīlī. The text makes no reference, besides, to other works by Jīlī, contrary to the latter's custom.

[33] Ibid., pp. 420-421. The Prophet said of this light: *Nūrun annā arāhu*, "It is a light, how should I see it?" (Muslim, *īmān*, p. 291; Tirmidhī, *Tafsīr* S. 53:7). On this *ḥadīth* see *Futūḥāt*, IV, pp. 38-39.

[34] Ibid., p. 425. Cf. also the *Kashf al-Ghayāt*, p. 429. Note that, in the vision mentioned in note 28, the Divine Ipseity appears to Ibn ʿArabī as a figure of white light on a background of red light.

the uncreated light of the Divine Essence is revealed to him who turns towards the "occidental" darkness.[35]

All vision assumes a commensurateness (*munāsaba*) between that which sees and that which is seen. Between the divine infinity and the limitedness of the creature, this *munāsaba* is evidently lacking and all possibility of "seeing God" other than in an indirect way, in the forms in which He manifests His names, seems then to be excluded.[36] If *mushāhada* is like that, the contemplation accessible to mortals is not even an "advance payment" of the beatific vision promised to the elect who will see God "like the moon on the night of the full moon": it is only a very imperfect prefiguration of it. That is what the definition that Ibn ʿArabī gives of it seems to confirm: contemplation, he says, is indeed vision (*ruʾya*), but a vision which is preceded, on the part of he who sees, by a knowledge of what he is going to see. It is then strictly limited since the contemplator refuses to recognize the theophany as such if it presents itself other than in conformity to his previous conception, with his *iʿtiqād*. Vision *stricto sensu*, on the contrary, presupposes the absence of this preliminary conditioning of which the contemplator is the prisoner. It receives all theophanies without subjecting them to the test of *recognition*, without referring them to a previous model.[37] One may note, however, that Ibn ʿArabī, despite these very rigorous technical definitions, does not feel obliged to respect the distinction thus established between *mushāhada* and *ruʾya* and, on many occasions, employs one or the other word indifferently. Nevertheless, the context allows one, as we shall see, to clear away the apparent ambiguities and contradictions.

When Ibn ʿArabī writes that "theophany only occurs in the forms of beliefs (*iʿtiqādāt*) or needs (*ḥājāt*),"[38] or again that "the Theophany

[35] On the symbolism of the west in Ibn ʿArabī, see *Futūḥāt*, I, pp. 67, 68, 71; II, p. 121; III, p. 287; *Kitāb al-Intisār*, printed in *Rasāʾil Ibn al-ʿArabi* (Hyderabad, India, 1948), 2 vols., p. 4.

[36] *Futūḥāt*, IV, p. 38.

[37] Ibid., II, p. 567.

[38] Ibid., II, pp. 277–278 and III, p. 119. The episode of the Burning Bush illustrates, for Ibn ʿArabī, the theophany "in the form of one's needs": because

of the Essence can only take place in the form of mental images and conceptual categories (*maʿqūlāt*),"[39] these remarks only apply to contemplation taken in its limited sense. But he also says, "God has servants whom he has allowed to *see* Him in this life without waiting for the future life";[40] now, to describe what, this time, is indeed vision, he often uses the terms *shuhūd* and *mushāhada.* This is the case in a passage of the *Futūḥāt* where, speaking of the *muqarrabūn* (those who are brought close), a term which for him designates the highest degree of sainthood, he states that they are in perpetual contemplation and never come out of it although "the tastes of it are varied."[41]

How can such people overcome the obstacle which the total absence of proportion between God and man presents? "The looks do not reach Him" states the Qurʾan. Although he often has recourse to the traditional distinction between "interior sight" (*baṣīra*) and "exterior sight" (*baṣar*), Ibn ʿArabī overlooks it here; what he retains is the fact that the Qurʾan uses the plural *abṣār* and not the singular *baṣar.*[42] The multiplicity inherent to the creature cannot in fact grasp the One. It follows that "it is God's look which reaches God and sees Him and not yours."[43] "He is the One who sees, He who is seen, and that by which He is seen."[44]

Therein resides the paradox of vision. Only he who has lost everything, he whose contemplation is free from all form, attains to

Moses is seeking fire, it is in the form of fire that God manifests Himself to him (cf. *Fuṣūṣ al-Ḥikam,* ed. A.A. Affifi [Beirut, 1946], pp. 212-213).

39 *Futūḥāt,* II, p. 606.

40 Ibid., IV, p. 38.

41 Ibid., III, p. 104. This chapter 328 forms part of the series of 114 *manāzil* ("spiritual abodes") which, as I have shown in a recent book (*Un Océan sans Rivage* [Paris, 1992], chap. III; an English translation of this work has been published by SUNY Press in 1993), correspond to the *sūras* of the Qurʾan in reverse order. Chapter 328 corresponds to *sūra* 56 and the terms which are used there (*sābiqūn, muqarrabūn,* etc.) are taken from this *sūra.*

42 *Futūḥāt,* IV, pp. 37-38.

43 Ibid., IV, p. 2.

44 Ibid., IV, p. 38.

the Being in His absoluteness. Nothing remains of "he who has lost everything" (*al-muflis*): in contradistinction to formal theophanies, which are compatible with the subsistence (*baqā'*) of the creature, this *tajallī* which is beyond forms implies the annihilation (*fanā'*) of the one to whom it is granted.[45] It prevents by that very fact all appropriation of vision—and that is the true sense of the *lan tarānī*: the grammatical "second person" has no place besides the divine "I." "The Essential Divine Reality is too elevated to be contemplated . . . whilst there remains a trace of the creatural condition in the eye of the contemplator."[46] This extinction of the contemplator in the most perfect contemplation has a logical consequence which may, however, seem strange: in this *mushāhada*—or to give it its real name, this *ru'ya*—there is neither joy, nor knowledge.[47] This is a logical consequence, in fact, since "joy" and "knowledge" would imply a reflexive action, a turning back on oneself which is incompatible with the *sine qua non* of vision of God. But would it not then be a question of a sort of coma of which one would ill understand that it constituted a privilege?

Ibn 'Arabī gives a reply to this in several of his works:[48] joy and knowledge are the fruits of *mushāhada* but these fruits cannot be garnered except on coming out of the contemplative state. For, corresponding to every true *mushāhada* (otherwise it would only be "a drowsiness of the heart," *nawmat al-qalb*) there is necessarily a "witness" (*shāhid*). This witness, who takes over the evidence of

[45] Ibid., III, p. 105 and IV, p. 191. Such is also the position of Qāshānī in a short unedited letter (*Risāla fī Qawlihi ta'ālā: Arinī Unẓur Ilayka*), MS Yahya Ef. 2415, folios 14–15.

[46] *Kitāb al-Fanā' fi'l-Mushāhada* (*Rasā'il*), p. 2. Note that this treatise is a complement to chapter 286 of the *Futūḥāt* which corresponds, in the order of the *manāzil*, to *sūra* 98 and whose theme is taken from the first two words (*lan yakun*) of this *sūra* (*Un Océan sans Rivage*, chap. V).

[47] *Kitāb al-Tarājim* (*Rasā'il*), p. 42. See also *Futūḥāt*, IV, p. 55.

[48] See *Futūḥāt*, chap. 266; *Kitāb al-Tarājim*, p. 16; *Kitāb Wasā'il as-Sā'il*, ed. M. Profitlich (Fribourg, 1973), pp. 43-45; see also Badr al-Habashi's *Kitāb al-Inbāh*, ed. Denis Gril, in *Annales Islamologiques*, XV, 1979, p. 106, para. 8.

the vision and authenticates it (allusion to Qurʾan 11:17, *wa yatlūhu shāhidun minhu*), is "the trace left in the heart of the contemplator by the contemplation."[49] Having regained consciousness, like Moses after the *tajallī* which struck him down, the individual then delights in this supreme knowledge whose price is precisely the unconditional submission to the mortal splendor of theophany. "No one will see his Lord before he dies," the Prophet said.[50] But he also said: "Die before you die."[51] And that is why Ibn ʿArabī, echoing this *ḥadīth*, unhesitatingly wrote in the *Kitāb al-Tajalliyāt*:[52] "Demand vision and do not be afraid of being struck down!"

Are there any favored places or times for this vision? God is free to manifest Himself when He wishes, to whom He wishes, how He wishes. But He has let His servants know the surest of ways that lead to Him. It is only given to the creature to see God through God's eye. Now, a well-known *ḥadīth qudsī* teaches us, with reference to the servant whom God loves: "When I love him, I am his hearing by which he hears, *his look by which he sees. . . .*"[53] We are told that this servant approaches God by supererogatory acts. But, the *ḥadīth* specifies: "He does not approach Me through something which I love more *than with the acts that I have prescribed for him.*" These prescribed acts, the *farāʾiḍ*, are therefore above all those which may lead to vision, and the reason for this is that they already represent a form of death since the will of the servant plays no part in them: it is God alone who determines their moments and their forms.[54] But, among these obligatory

[49] *Iṣṭilāḥāt aṣ-Ṣūfiyya* (*Rasāʾil*), no. 60. This definition is taken up by Qāshānī, amongst others, in a work of the same title (Cairo, 1981, pp. 153-154) and by Jurjānī in his *Taʿrīfāt* (Cairo, 1357 AH), p. 114.

[50] Cf. note 15.

[51] Tirmidhī, *qiyāma*, 25. On this theme of "initiatory death," see *Futūḥāt*, II, p. 187; III, pp. 223, 288.

[52] Chapter 100, p. 517.

[53] Bukhārī, *tawādu*. Ibn ʿArabī has included this *ḥadīth* in his *Mishkāt al-Anwār* and quotes it and comments on it many times (*Futūḥāt*, I, p. 406; III, p. 68; IV, pp. 20, 24, 30, 65, 312, 321, etc.).

[54] That is why, for Ibn ʿArabī (cf. in particular *Futūḥāt*, IV, pp. 24, 449), the

acts, there is one which holds a particular importance: the ritual prayer (*aṣ-ṣalāt*) which is, as the Prophet said, *miʿrāj al-muʾmin*, the "spiritual ascension of the believer." For Ibn ʿArabī, this ritual prayer is the favored place for the highest theophanies. These theophanies, always new, appear hierarchically in a harmonic relation to the different positions prescribed for the believer. I have shown elsewhere[55] that some replies formulated in enigmatic terms to Tirmidhī's well-known questionnaire would be elucidated once one understood that they refer to the *ṣalāt*. The mysterious sessions (*majālis*) during which God speaks correspond to the *julūs*, the sitting position, which symbolizes stability, vigilance, and permanence (*baqāʾ*): conditions which are all necessary to hear the divine discourse but which exclude vision. But those to whom God thus speaks (the *muḥaddathūn*) and who, in this respect, are "behind a veil" are also in another respect *ahl ash-shuhūd*, people of contemplation.

They are so when the conditions required to hear God disappear and are replaced by their opposite: annihilation, which tears the veil and of which the symbol is *sujūd*, prostration. Do not let the word "symbol" mislead us. For most people prostration is most certainly nothing more than a gestural representation of this annihilation which must leave all the space to the One without second. For some, this symbol is operative and for them what Ibn ʿArabī writes in the *Tanazzulāt Mawsiliyya*[56] is verified: "your rising up is in your abasement." When their body crashes against the earth, they arrive at the summit of the "Sinai of their being." And, there, the *lan tarānī* resounds in the void; there is no longer anyone to hear it.

closeness acquired by the accomplishment of obligatory acts (*qurb al-farāʾiḍ*) is more perfect than that obtained by the accomplishment of supererogatory acts (*qurb an-nawāfil*). It is to the former that the case of the *muqarrabūn* corresponds (ibid., II, p. 104) for whom "contemplation is perpetual" and who see "the multiplicity in the One and separation in union." On this subject, see *Un Océan sans Rivage*, pp. 144ff. and my translation of the *Ecrits Spirituels* by Emir ʿAbd al-Qādir (Paris, 1982), note 84, pp. 202-204.

55 *Un Océan sans Rivage*, pp. 136ff.

56 *Tanazzulāt Mawsiliyya* (Cairo, 1961) (under the title *Laṭāʾif al-Asrār*), p. 103.

APPROACHING SUFISM*

Éric Geoffroy

A Reality Without a Name

Many Muslims are suspicious of Sufism for the sole reason that the terms *Ṣūfī* and *taṣawwuf* are not found in the Koran and may not have existed during the lifetime of the Prophet. In their eyes, it is a question of a "blameworthy innovation." Ibn Khaldūn, who himself was not a Sufi, replied that at the time of the Prophet it was not necessary to give a particular name to Islam's interior path. The new religion was then being lived in its fullness, the exoteric along with the esoteric, because the Companions of Muhammad were witnessing the model of "realized" man in the Prophet. This spiritual companionship (*ṣuḥba*) was able to concentrate within itself all of the spiritual benefit that the Prophet's entourage drew from him. In this proximity to the luminous prophetic source, terminology and doctrine didn't have a place. A shaykh of the tenth century affirmed that "Sufism once [at the time of the Prophet] was a reality without a name; it is now a name without a reality."[1] For Shiblī, who was one of the great masters of Baghdad and one who loved a paradox, the fact that Sufis were given a name resulted from the fouling of their own egos. If they had been really transparent, devoid of their own attributes, no name could have been attributed to them.

The doctrine and terminology of *taṣawwuf* took their essential form in the ninth century, during the time of the "collecting" or "codification" (*tadwīn*) of Islamic doctrine, which from then on was formed into different sciences. These (i.e. the "fundamentals of law," the "fundamentals of religion," "comparative law," "terminology of *ḥadīth*," and "Koranic commentary") did not exist during the time of

* Editors' Note: This essay is a translation of an excerpt from the book *Initiation au Soufisme* by Éric Geoffroy. The chapter from which it is taken was titled "Approaches," thus the title for the essay in this volume.

[1] Hujwirī in *Kashf al-Maḥjūb.*

the Prophet any more so than did "Sufism." The term *salafī*, which designates modern Muslims who claim to be like the first believers (*salāf*) and who reject all doctrinal, and notably mystical, contributions, emerged over the course of centuries and does not have any greater claim to scriptural support.[2] It is therefore a duty for contemporary Muslims to remember to bring to Sufism a respect similar to the one that they show for the other disciplines of Islam.

The Science of Spiritual States

If Sufism does have a place within the domain of Islamic sciences, this doesn't mean that it has any less of its own specific character. Being of a subtle essence, it has been called since its beginnings the "knowledge of hearts" or the "knowledge of spiritual states" as opposed to the formal disciplines such as the law. Being the "knowledge of the inner" (*ʿilm al-bāṭin*), as opposed to exoteric knowledge (*ʿilm aẓ-ẓāhir*), it proposes an alternative and paradoxical explanation of the world, which most often is incomprehensible to exoterists. The Prophet Moses, representing the Law, experiences this at his own expense when he meets Khaḍir, the enigmatic character who appears to some saints in order to initiate them.[3] Following his example, Sufis are content with making "allusion" (*ishāra*) to the spiritual realities to which they have access.

Sufism distinguishes itself once again by its supra-rational—not irrational—character, whereas theology and law rely on discursive reason and dialectical thought. Sufis do not reject the other disciplines of Islam, but they use them as a springboard, explaining that the word *ʿaql*, which means "reason" or mind, also means "shackle." Because the spiritual world does not obey the laws of duality, it is indeed by the union of opposites that the Sufi realizes the divine Unicity.

Sufi knowledge rests on spiritual inspiration and "unveiling." The works of Ibn ʿArabī, along with the orisons and poems of many other masters, are considered to be inspired directly by God or indirectly by

[2] This observation comes from Sufi shaykhs, but equally from contemporary Muslim scholars (Cf. the work of M.S.R. Būtū, *As-Salafīyya* [Damascus, 1988]).

[3] See the Koran, 18:65-82.

the Prophet. It is necessary here to distinguish inspiration (*ilhām*) from revelation (*waḥy*), which only prophets receive, even if Sufis should present the former as the successor of the latter. As for "unveiling" (*kashf*), it constitutes for Sufis the principal mode of access to the supra-sensible world. As the fruit of an exacting discipline, it permits the raising of the veils that the world of the senses (*mulk*) throws over man, which then allows him to reach the world of the spirit (*malakūt*), or even the world of the Divine (*jabarūt*). Often described as a bolt of lightning that illuminates the consciousness and imposes itself upon the latter through its intense flashing and clarity, this "unveiling" leads to the vision of certainty (*yaqīn*) and to the direct perception (*ʿiyān*) of spiritual realities and dissipates the doubt associated with the speculative sciences. Notably, it has its foundation in the Koranic verse 50:22: "Thou wast heedless of this; now have We removed from thee thy veil, and piercing is thy vision this day." Al-Ghazzālī (d. 1111) was the first to insist on "unveiling" as a method of cognition but it has reappeared so frequently in *taṣawwuf* that one can speak of it as "Sufi epistemology."[4]

The knowledge bestowed by divine Grace (*al-ʿilm al-wahbī*) eludes the usual coursings of the reason. It distinguishes itself from knowledge acquired through individual effort (*al-ʿilm al-kasbī*), and can by this fact come upon an unlettered, simple farmer or craftsman because he knows nothing of the pretensions and the ratiocinations peculiar to many humans. In Sufism, these unlettered people figure among the greatest saints. *Taṣawwuf* has also been defined, notably by Ibn Khaldūn, as "the knowledge that comes directly from God" (*al-ʿilm al-ladunī*), in reference to verse 18:65: "We taught him [Khaḍir] a knowledge [emanating] from Us."

Even in its most speculative dimension, Sufism cannot be reduced to a theoretical philosophy. Obviously, the aspirant can derive more benefit from his master's presence than from the reading of any mystical treatise. Sufism is above all a matter of "tasting" (*dhawq*). When one of his disciples informed him that some criticized Sufism because it didn't depend on argumentation, Ibn ʿArabī gave him this answer: "If someone enjoins you to prove the existence of the 'knowledge of divine

[4] A. Knysh, *Islamic Mysticism* (Leyden, 2000), p. 311.

secrets,' demand that they in turn prove the smoothness of honey. He will answer you that this is a question of a gustatory knowledge. Reply to them that it is the same for Sufism."[5] It is in that same sense that one must understand this Sufi adage: "Only the one who has tasted knows." Sufism is a path of awakening, a path destined to develop the higher states of consciousness of being; it begins with daily life, with the world of forms, and with rites.

The Initiatic Way

Though it is of an intuitive nature, the Sufi experience rests on rules and proven methods. Far from pertaining to some "natural mysticism," it rests upon an initiation. Under a master's direction, the aspirant follows an interior journey that must lead him to climb the ladder of the universal hierarchy of Being, just as the Prophet was carried at the time of his nocturnal Ascent (*miʿrāj*) up to the divine Presence.

This initiatic path proceeds from the Koran, which defines itself as a "guidance" (*hudā*). Beginning with the first *sūra*,* the *Fātiḥa*, the believer asks God to guide him on the "straight path" (*aṣ-ṣirāṭ al-mustaqīm*). But Sufis frequently invoke this verse: "As for those who strive [spiritually] in Us, surely We shall guide them to Our paths: God is with those who search for excellence" (Koran 29:69). To define the initiatic Way, masters use the geometric symbol of the circle. The circle represents the divine Law (*Sharīʿa*). Most men remain within this limit all their lives, which is to say that they are content with an exterior observance of the religion. Only some undertake the initiatic journey that will convey them to the center, where they have access to the interior Reality (*Ḥaqīqa*) of the divine message and, beyond, of all manifested things.

[5] Ibn ʿArabī, *Tadbīrāt al-Ilahiyya* (Leyden, 1917), pp. 114-115.

* Editors' Note: A *sūra* is one of the 114 chapters of the Koran.

"As many paths (*ṭarīqa*; pl. *ṭuruq*) as [there are] sons of Adam":
One can travel a path toward the Real (*al-Ḥaqq*),
God, from any authentic spiritual tradition.

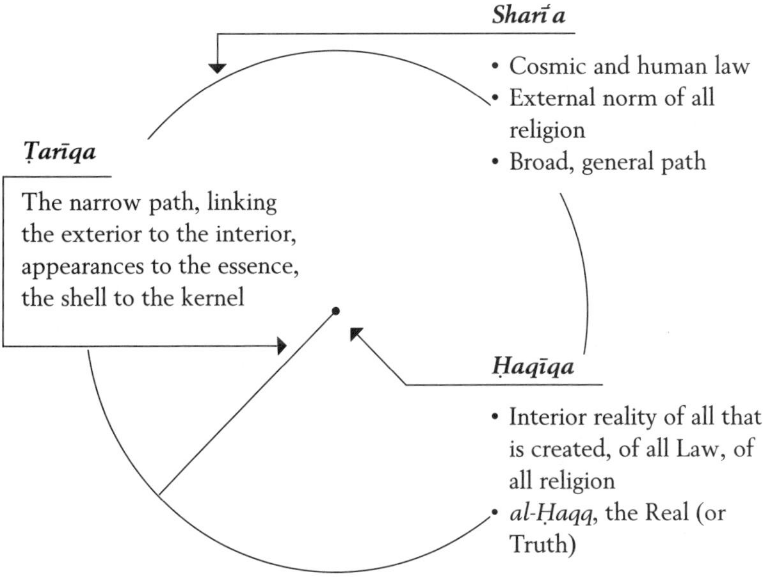

Etymologically, the terms *Sharīʿa* and *Ṭarīqa* each mean "path." The *Sharīʿa* is the "broad path," marked out by the prophets, that all Muslims must follow—it being understood that for Islam every kingdom and every community follows its own *Sharīʿa* here below. The *Ṭarīqa* designates the "narrow path" to which only those who have some predisposition are called. It is the path of the Sufis and it is for this reason that they perceive themselves as the spiritual elite (*al-khāṣṣa*). In this sense, they distinguish themselves from the commonality of believers (*al-ʿāmma*) who will only know God in the world beyond, after their death. Propelled by Love, the Sufis seek to know God in this world: through the "initiatic death" they anticipate the meeting.

Reality is immutable, but it is obvious that man can have access to It only while following the *Sharīʿa*: in Islam as in all other traditions, it would not be possible to have authentic esoterism without exoterism. The symbol of the circle not only shows the intrinsic orthodoxy of Sufism in relation to the religion that is its support, but it also explains why Sufi masters see in Sufism the heart, the "kernel" of Islam.

As the Sufi progresses on the Way, he ascends a double ladder, one of "initiatic stations" (*maqām*; pl. *maqāmāt*) and one of "spiritual states" (*ḥāl*; pl. *aḥwāl*). The former, which are the fruits of spiritual discipline (*mujāhada*), remain secured for the one who has attained them; the latter are divine favors which are granted to the mystic without his having caused them and which therefore assume a fluctuating and elusive character. Through his spiritual work, the initiate can "master" this ephemeral state and can transform it into a "station," the goal being to dominate his *ḥāl* and not the other way around. Sufis assign to the term *maqām* this scriptural origin: "There is no one among us who hath not a designated station (*maqām*)" (Koran 37:164). The first to have evoked an initiatic gradation, in ten stages, was the Imam ʿAlī,[6] but more often one attributes the formulation of the stations and states of the Way to Dhū'n-Nūn al-Misrī (d. 859).

Among the stations are "repentance," "renouncement," "destitution before God," "endurance," and "contentment." Among the states: "desire for God," "love," "contemplation," "proximity to God," and "intimacy." In regard to the ambivalent character of human consciousness, certain states or stations are presented in pairs which are at once opposed and complementary: "the fear of God" is coupled with "hope" placed in Him, "constriction" with "dilation," etc. These classifications remain "schematic," as René Guénon reminds us,[7] because the number and the order of the stations and states vary considerably from one author to another. Some Sufis are able to make out "one thousand stations" or "innumerable stations." The initiatic Path, indeed, is not exempt from optical illusions: "Every time that I thought I had come to the end of the Path," confesses Abū Yazīd al-Bisṭāmī, "it was made known to me that this was the beginning of it."[8] In the

[6] As-Sarrāj, *Lumaʿ*, p. 130.

[7] *Initiation et realisation spirituelle* (Paris, 1980), p. 195.

[8] Sulamū, *Tisʿa Kutub* (Beirut, 1993), p. 381.

same way, what one Sufi defines as a "station" can be considered a "state" by another. Therefore, it is necessary to take a nuanced view of the opposition between these two forms because they are interdependent. Anṣārī Harawī groups the two together under the term "dwelling places" (*manāzil*). At a certain degree of initiation, the Sufi is freed from duality; for him "there is no longer state nor station."[9] When touching upon this subject, Ibn ʿArabī speaks of "non-station" (*lā maqām*), which is exclusively a domain of divine grace.[10]

In a more immediate way, all masters put the accent on the sincerity and purity of intention (*ṣidq, ikhlāṣ*) required of the aspirant. The latter will have to track down within the recesses of his soul any traces of self-satisfaction toward himself and toward the works of devotion that he accomplishes. The difficulty resides in the fact that while he hasn't reached a certain level of contemplation, he perceives himself as adoring God, as being sincere, etc. To get out of this labyrinth he must endeavor to subdue the self-awareness of the soul.

To this end, the aspirant will first have to practice "trusting self-abandonment in God" (*tawakkul*), a major station and a cardinal virtue. He will thus perceive that it is God who "wants" (*murīd*) that His servant should come closer to Him. Whatever may be the asceticism to which he gives himself over, whatever may be his degree of spiritual aspiration, the disciple must never forget that first he "is wanted" by God (*murād*), and that it is love alone that provides him with energy.[11] Within this relationship, two complementary paths exist: the "traveler" (*sālik*) progresses in a conscious way, while the one "overjoyed in God" (*majdhūb*), is drawn into Him and traverses the path in a lightning-like way, as if distanced from himself. The latter is generally considered to be inferior to the former because he rarely has the capacity to help others to accomplish this journey. It is the role of the spiritual guide to make the novice share in his own experience.

9 Ibn ʿAbbād, *Al-Rasāʾil al-Kubrā* (Fes, 1902), letter no. 14.

10 *Futūḥāt Makkiyya*, cited by D. Gril, *Les Voies d'Allah* (Paris, 1996), p. 100.

11 Cheikh Khaled Bentounès, *Le Soufisme, coeur de l'islam* (Paris, 1996), p. 72.

Goals of the Sufi

According to their various spiritual experiences, Sufis assign several goals to their discipline. Fundamentally, the Sufi wants to react against the spiritual degeneration that has affected humanity, and therefore himself as well, since the creation of the world. While following the initiatic Path, he recovers the state of "union" that was his in the spiritual world, and at every moment he renews the Pact (*mīthāq*) sealed between God and men before the incarnation on earth.[12] More conscious than others of this contract, the Sufi attempts to regain his initial purity while fighting against bodily and worldly attachments.

For this purpose, the Koran and the Prophet frequently put the believer on guard against the snares that his carnal soul (*nafs*) sets for him. Echoing the Prophet's words, "Man's fiercest enemy is the carnal soul that lies hidden within him," one of the earliest masters defined Sufism as a discipline "leaving no part for the ego." Such are the foundations of the "greater holy war" (*al-jihād al-akbar*), extolled by the Prophet, and the different forms of struggle against the passions of the soul to which Sufis have dedicated themselves throughout the centuries.

Purifying the Soul

Sufis agree on the necessity of devoting oneself to the purification of the soul (*tazkiyat an-nafs*), which is the only way that can bring about the emergence of a noble character (*khuluq*) and the proper inward and outward attitude (*adab*) in a human being. In doing this their intention is to follow the model of the Prophet: "Surely thou art endowed with a tremendous character (*khuluq*)," says the Koran addressing the Prophet (68:4). The noble virtues (*akhlāq*, pl. of *khuluq*) that Sufis endeavor to acquire are therefore the same as those of Islam, but Sufis give them particular weight by bringing them to life within themselves; thus these virtues are transmuted into initiatic stations. This type of Sufism, it goes without saying, has been accepted by the general body of *ʿulamāʾ*. In this perspective, it represents one of the three parts of the religion, along with the dogma (*ʿaqīda*) and the Law (*Sharīʿa*). He who travels the Path would not try therefore to experiment with supernatural

[12] See the Koran, 7:172.

phenomena but would try instead to ascertain the truth of the Law and to perfect his submissiveness to God.

Knowing God

Other Sufis, going further, considered purification to be just a means and not an end in itself, since its goal is to arrive at the knowledge of God in order to better adore Him. "They have not appreciated God equal to His true measure" (Koran 6:91). According to al-Qushayrī, this verse means "They did not know God in His true measure." The doctrinal seeds of "knowledge," of gnosis (*maʿrifa*), are present in the first masters, and it may be that it is necessary to see in this the beginning of a Neoplatonic influence which would later provide Sufism with conceptual tools. According to Maʿrūf al-Karkhī (d. 815), who was regarded as the founder of the Sufi school of Baghdad, Sufism consists in "seizing upon Divine Realities (*ḥaqāʾiq*) and forsaking all that comes from creatures (*khalāʾiq*)." During this same period, al-Bistāmī affirms that the "knower," the gnostic, "flies towards God, while the ascetic only walks," and Ruwaym says that "the hypocrisy of gnostics is better than the sincerity of aspirants [who aspire only to purification]."[13] Knowledge is a mirror, adds Ruwaym, in which the gnostic sees God revealing Himself. Dhūʾn-Nūn insists on this direct grasping of God: "How did you (come to) know your Lord?" someone asked him. "I knew my Lord through Himself."[14]

Inspiration and unveiling are indispensable for he who wants to clear a path towards this God who appears as "the Light of the heavens and the earth" (Koran 24:35). It is for this reason that all Sufis sought to make room in themselves for the "radiation" (*tajallī*) of this light. Unblocking human nature from its opacity, just as the sun drives away darkness,[15] this theophany reveals God to the heart of man. As-Sarrāj observes that the simple believer sees by the light of God, while the gnostic sees by God Himself.[16] Later, Ibn ʿArabī would explain how

[13] Al-Qushayrī, *Risāla*, pp. 315-316.

[14] Ibid., p. 315.

[15] Cf. Koran, 92:2.

[16] *Lumaʿ*, p. 41.

multiplicity is spread from its start in Unicity through a succession of uninterrupted theophanies that take innumerable forms. The Sufi thus sees God in all being, in every manifested thing. Unlike the ascetic, he does not reject the world, because to him it is illuminated by the divine Presence. "Beings were not created so that you would see them, but so that you would see their Master in them," said Ibn ʿAṭāʾ Allāh.[17] Again and again the Koran encourages man to decipher the "signs" (*āyāt*), to contemplate God by contemplating His Manifestation. "We shall show them Our signs in the universe and in themselves until they see that it is the Truth [God]" (Koran 41:53).

Uniting Oneself With God, or "Extinguishing Oneself" in Him?

The ultimate goal of the mystical life cannot be to know God but to be united with Him. However, in Islam one cannot speak of a *via unitiva* in the same sense as in Christian theology. From the point of view of the central dogma of *tawḥīd*, which focuses only on "the divine Unicity," the very concept of "union" with God is eminently paradoxical. Indeed, union presumes the coming together of two entities, of two substances. Now, the profession of faith (*shahāda*) of Islam affirms: "There is no god but God." For the Sufi, this negative assertion actually means: "Only God is," since that which is created, the contingent, vanishes in the face of the Absolute.

Therefore the Sufi doesn't live in a state of union, strictly speaking, since in Islam there is no continuity of substance between God and creation. His goal is "extinction in God" (*fanāʾ*). Removed from the various solicitations of the world, the initiate then knows the intoxication of immersion in the divine Presence. Being completely unaware of himself as subject-consciousness, he becomes a mirror in which God contemplates Himself. One can illustrate this state, which is accompanied by a temporary withdrawal from the perceptible world, by an example:

> One day Junayd was at home with his wife when Shiblī entered. His wife wished to veil herself again, but Junayd told her: "He is

[17] *La Sagesse des maîtres soufis*, translated from the Arabic (to French) by É. Geoffroy (Paris, 1998), p. 51.

> not aware of your presence, remain as you are." Junayd spoke for a moment with Shiblī, and the latter began weeping. Junayd then said to his wife: "Veil thyself now, for Shiblī has just come out of his state of absence."[18]

This state paradoxically opens up the horizons of Knowledge, for man can only have access to divine realities when his ego no longer interposes itself in his contemplation, that is to say when divine Being shows through in him.[19]

This experience of extinction in God, which is the essential paradigm of the mystical life in Islam, transmutes the exoteric "testimony" (*shahāda*) of Islam into contemplation (*mushāhada*). It was validated by exoteric scholars, who saw in it the interior realization of the fundamental dogma of the divine Unicity. However, *fanā᾽* was interpreted by Sufis in a variety of ways. Cultivating the paradox, some, upon coming out of their ecstasy, let it be thought that they had really been experiencing union with God (*ittiḥād*) or, worse in the eyes of Islam, the incarnation of God in themselves (*ḥulūl*). This is not, however, what they would profess on the dogmatic plane in their moments of lucidity. The jurists of Islam obviously didn't take such nuances into consideration.

Dying to Oneself, and Living Again Through Him

In order to react against the slippery slope made use of by the "intoxicated" mystics, other Sufis, called "temperate," emphasized that in the ecstatic state of *fanā᾽* man always had to keep a glimmer of lucidity, especially as this state, being paroxysmal but still transient, was only the prelude to a more complete experience, that of *baqā᾽*: having burnt away his individual attributes, the initiate "subsists" henceforth in and by God so that it is the divine Attributes that now act in him. According to a *ḥadīth qudsī* frequently cited by Sufis, God

[18] Junayd, *Enseignement spirituel*, translated by R. Deladrière (Paris, 1983), p. 197.

[19] See, for example, Ansāri, *Chemin de Dieu*, translated by S. de Laugier of Beaurecueil (Paris, 1985), p. 120; Ibn ʿArabī, *Le Livre de l'extinction dans la contemplation*, translated by M. Vâlsan (Paris, 1984), pp. 48-49.

becomes "the ear with which he hears, the sight through which he sees, the hand with which he grasps, and the foot with which he walks." In the first phase, the one of *fanāʾ*, a person doesn't see anything outside of God; in the second, the one of *baqāʾ*, he sees Him in everything. After the intoxication of immersion in God comes the soberness that allows the initiate to be with God and with the world at the same time. Letting God do with him as He will, he achieves his ontological servitude (*ʿubūdiyya*) while at the same time putting himself at the service of men.

This double experience of *fanāʾ/baqāʾ* is so essential in Sufism that Junayd thought that it is this experience alone which defines it. "*Taṣawwuf*," he said, "is summed up thus: the Real [or, the 'Truth,' i.e. God] makes you die to yourself, and causes you to come alive again through Him."[20] This theme is the transposition onto a mystical plane of the Koranic verse: "All that is on [earth] is passing away (*fān-in*). There remaineth (*yabqā*) but the Countenance of thy Lord of Majesty and Munificence" (Koran 55:26-27). The initiatic death, as implied by the experience of *fanāʾ/baqāʾ*, is a response to the Prophet's injunction: "Die before dying!" Specifically, it is inscribed in the example of Muhammad, he who "has been sent" among men to guide them.

Extending the dogma of the divine Unicity and the spiritual "tasting" of *fanāʾ*, some Sufis explained that God is One in the sense that He alone possesses Being: in manifesting creatures, He endowed them with an existence emanating from His Being, but this has only an ontological content that is relative, or even non-existent. Many exoteric scholars have fought against this metaphysical formulation, which is known as the "oneness of Being" (*waḥdat al-wujūd*) because it has seemed to them to deny divine transcendence.

For all those that travel the path of Sufism, purification is therefore an obligatory part of the passage: the initiate must consider the miasmas of his ego as just so much darkness that stops him from receiving the light of gnosis or from being united with the divine. Similarly, for the men and women who follow *taṣawwuf*, they aspire to live Islam fully, in all its dimensions, and not only by adhering to its dogma or law. In no case can Sufism be assimilated into some other mysticism or

[20] Al-Qushayrī, *Risāla*, p. 280.

into some other esoterism that is either similar or dissimilar to Islam. If some Sufis, in reaction to the authoritarian formalism of jurists, have adopted antinomic and provocative attitudes, they have always remained—except for some notable "deviations"—within the sphere of Islam.

THE PROPHETIC MODEL OF THE SPIRITUAL MASTER IN ISLAM[1]

Denis Gril

There is considerable literature in Islam on master and disciple, particularly in Sufism where the relation between the two plays a central role in the spiritual Path. The precise rules of this spiritual companionship (*ṣuḥba*) were only codified bit by bit, but they largely replicate the reciprocal relationship of the Prophet and his Companions. Thus the basis of the duties that bind the master and disciple together are to be found not only in the prophetic tradition (*Sunna*) but in the very text of the Koran, which evokes some aspects of the prophetic function simply by its transmission of the Revelation. Shihāb ad-Dīn ʿUmar as-Suhrawardī (d. in Baghdad in 632/1234) dedicated some writings to spiritual mastership (*mashyakha*) and to the rules of etiquette (*adab*, pl. *ādāb*) which must be observed by masters and disciples and by the latter between themselves. These writings perfectly illustrate the primordial place of the prophetic model in the exposition of these rules.[2] In this essay we will therefore look into the Koran and the *Sunna* to see how, for later Muslim spirituality, the figure of the spiritual master is based upon the person of the Prophet.

[1] Michel Chodkiewicz shows in a communication titled "Le modèle prophétique de la sainteté en islam," published in *Sociétés et cultures musulmanes d'hier et d'aujourd'hui*, the Newsletter of AFEMAN, no. 10, 1996, pp. 505-518, that there cannot be holiness nor therefore spiritual masterhood without identification with the prophetic model. Our approach is complementary since it has above all as its point of departure scriptural data, mainly *Sūrat al-Aḥzāb*, whose importance for our topic M. Chodkiewicz has highlighted.

[2] Cf. Suhrawardī, *ʿAwārif al-Maʿārif* (Beirut, 1966), chap. 10, pp. 83-102 and chaps. 51-55, pp. 403-442, partial translation in A. Popovic and G. Veinstein, *Les voies d'Allāh. Les ordres mystiques dans le monde musulman des origines à aujourd'hui* (Paris, 1996), pp. 547-568, translated by D. Gril.

Every master is a spiritual father to his disciple, a parent in the realm of the spirit. To speak of a "father" in regard to the Prophet might seem inappropriate. The Koran does not affirm this in *Sūrat al-Aḥzāb* (*The Factions*), many verses of which concern the person of the Prophet and his wives: "Muhammad is not the father of any man among you, but the messenger of God and the Seal of the prophets" (33:40). The absence of male descendants, which was a disgrace among the Arabs, was compensated therefore by the supreme election: the prophetic mission and especially the privilege of bringing the latter to its conclusion. Let us notice that *khātam* means the seal as well as the ring on which it is fixed. If the ring symbolizes the cycle, the seal represents the beginning as well as the end. The negation of the Prophet's fatherhood in the flesh puts all the more value on the spiritual kinship that unites every believer to the Prophet.

Another passage at the beginning of the same *sūra* abolishes the fatherhood by adoption that bound the Prophet to his freedman Zayd, and concludes: "The Prophet is closer (*awlā*) to the believers than they are to their own souls and his wives are (as) their mothers" (33:6). The expression *awlā* has been commented on in various ways. First of all let us recall that one reading not retained in the canonical version but transmitted by Ḥasan al-Baṣrī and Qatāda specified: "closer . . . to their own souls and he is a father to them."[3] This verse includes a legal meaning: the Prophet's wives, mothers of the believers, will not be allowed to remarry after his death (Cf. 33:53). This rule has generally been taken in Sufism to also apply to the master's wife: she cannot be remarried to a disciple, except with express permission of the master before his death.[4] This proximity also results on the legal plane in the fact that the Prophet and, after him, the *imām* of the Community, become the heir of those who don't have one. Indeed "closer" (*awlā*) is the superlative of *walī*, literally "close," and thus friend, legal guardian, heir, patron, or client and, finally, holy.

[3] Cf. Ṭabarī, *Jāmiʿ al-Bayān* XXI, 77.

[4] This is the case with Abū ʿAbdallah al-Qurashī and his disciple Abūʾl-ʿAbbās al-Qastallā. See the *Risāla* of Safī ad-Dīn Ibn Abīʾl-Manṣūr (Cairo, 1986), p. 112.

On another plane, the prophetic proximity recalls, analogically, those verses in which God says of Himself and of man: "And We are nearer to him than (his) jugular vein" (50:16), and also of the dying: "And We are nearer unto him than ye are, but ye see not" (56:85). The prophetic presence in all believers therefore brings them closer to the transcendent divine presence. The following verse from *Sūrat al-Aḥzāb* suggests in effect that it is in his supra-temporal reality that the Prophet is called upon here:

> And when We sealed with the prophets their alliance, with you, with Noah, Abraham, Moses, and Jesus the son of Mary, We sealed with them a solemn alliance (33:7).

The enumeration of prophets limits itself here to the main phases of the prophetic cycle in which the Prophet holds the first place, that of Adam. One can comfortably interpret this substitution as an allusion to his antecedence and to his paternity on the plane of the Spirit, which coincides with the posteriority of his function as Seal. Several *ḥadīths*, to which we will return later, confirm this interpretation, which was made explicit beginning in the third/ninth century and developed later in the sixth-seventh/twelfth-thirteenth centuries. Antecedently, as a spiritual entity, the Prophet is the father in spirit (*al-ʾab ar-rūḥī*) of humanity, just as Adam is their father of clay (*al-ʾab aṭ-ṭīnī*).

The proximity that binds the believers to the Prophet is also that of *walāya*, the tie of tutelage, of protection, of aid and inheritance that connects *walī* to *walī*, since the word designates the mentor as well as the protégé, the protector as well as the dependent. This protective tie and aid or vassalage between tribes is transposed by the Koran into an allegiance to God alone, then through a line of descent to the Prophet and the body of believers. At the close of the cycle of existence, the *walāya* necessarily comes back to its origin: God Himself.[5] The Prophet, who is qualified with *awlā*, the elative form of *walī*, is the vehicle *par excellence* of this reconnection to God through faith,

[5] Let us just cite as an example these verses: "My Protector (*waliyya*) is God who hath sent down the Book, and He taketh the saints into His protection (*yatawallā*)" (7:196); "Thy sole protector is God, and His Messenger, and

which then communicates itself to all believers so that they may come back to God once again. The bond of master to disciple constitutes a particular form of this *walāya*, which is all the stronger for its goal of moving the aspirant back toward God. So the term *awlā*, and the root *W-L-Y* from which it derives proclaim, through the person of the Prophet, some of the functions of the master, who is the Prophet's heir and spiritual son and who, in his turn, becomes a spiritual father to his disciples.

Sūrat al-Aḥzāb defines the Prophet's mission thus:

> O Prophet! Lo! We have sent thee as a witness and a bearer of good tidings and a warner. And as a summoner unto Allāh by His permission, and as a luminous lamp. (33:45-46).

There are many functions that designate the Prophet as a guide through the Hereafter and towards God, and by which a master, on the inward and initiatic plane, can be considered as the Prophet's direct heir:

(1) The Prophet is the "witness" in this world and in the other for or against mankind, just as the master sees through his disciple with his inward eye. This witnessing, especially in its eschatological dimension, also implies intercession. As we will later see, the next world has stations through which the Prophet helps conduct souls.

(2, 3) The Prophet, following the Koran, gives tidings of Paradise and warns against hell. In initiatic terms, the master raises the disciple's aspiration toward the higher degrees of being and helps him escape the snares of the world and the individual soul.

(4) The transmission of the Revelation, the instituting and the application of the Law, the fighting for the triumph of faith and the submissiveness of the soul, all converge on what in the end constitutes the Prophet's highest mission: to call men to God "with His permission" (*bi-idhni-hi*), for the Prophet and the master are only the heralds of God and who alone guide men toward Him. The "permission" received from God and the Prophet, and then from master to master

those who believe" (5:55); "There (in the afterlife) the only holding fast (*walāya*) is to God, the Real; He Himself is Best for reward, and best for consequence" (18:44).

through the initiatic chain, guarantees the regularity of its transmission and the efficacy of the summons that emanates from God. It is this "permission" which makes possible that descent of the Spirit through which the son becomes a father.

(5) Having achieved extinction, effaced in its function as herald, the inner being of the Prophet thus reflects the divine light all the more strongly and refracts it onto the cosmos. One may be familiar with the many developments of the notion of the Light of Muhammad—the symbol of the Reality of Muhammad—at the origin of the universe. The lamp (*sirāj*), as the sun is called in the Koran, represents above all the spreading out of the divine light towards created beings. The master, projecting the divine and prophetic light onto the disciple's heart, vivifies this heart and causes it to be reborn into a new life.

Also in this *sūra*, the Prophet's wives are asked to choose between the desire for this world, and thus to leave the Prophet, and the desire for God, His Prophet, and the next world, and thus to dedicate themselves completely to them, without expecting anything from the life of this world (Cf. 33:28-29). In the context of the Revelation, this passage concerns only the Prophet's wives. Not only are they presented as models to women believers but also to male believers,[6] and everything that is said of them in these verses can transpose itself onto the initiatic plane. The relationship between the master and the disciple can be considered indeed as the marriage of the spirit and the soul; in pledging itself to the former, the soul is bound totally to it and to God, while giving up the life of this world. Of all the women affected by this verse, the Prophet had no children with any of them, but he elevated their souls, thus making of them the "mothers of the believers." Thus, increasing the quality of spouses and other functions related to marriage and childbirth are added to spiritual fatherhood.

The *Sūrat al-Aḥzāb* also invites believers to show towards the Prophet and his wives some rules of decorum (*adab*) which the disciple must also observe vis-à-vis his master:

[6] As shown in verse 35 where, after the passage on the Prophet's wives, the main virtues and forms of worship are enumerated as accomplished by both men and by women (e.g. "humble men and humble women," "modest men and modest women," etc.).

> O ye who believe! Enter not the dwellings of the Prophet for a meal without waiting for the proper time, unless permission be granted you. But if ye are invited, enter, and, when your meal is ended, then disperse. Linger not for conversation. Lo! that would cause annoyance to the Prophet, who would be ashamed of telling you (to go), but God is not ashamed of the truth. When ye ask of them (the wives of the Prophet) anything, ask it of them from behind a curtain. That is purer for your hearts and for their hearts. It is not for you to cause any annoyance to the Messenger of God, nor that ye should ever marry his wives after him. Lo! that in Allah's sight would be an enormity (33:53).

One doesn't enter such a sacred place without having been called there. This rule of *adab* underscores first the importance of spiritual election, then that of being given permission while on the path, particularly since it is here a question of nourishment, that is to say, symbolically, of knowledge. One can only receive such things according to the measure of one's spiritual degree. Arrogating to oneself a restricted knowledge would be a cause for disqualification. In the same way, the veil put between believers and their spiritual mothers preserves the intimacy of the life of the Prophet and his family. Too much familiarity would risk upsetting them while making the hearts forget the spiritual dimension of the beings who are present. The first verses of the *Sūrat al-Ḥujurāt* (*The Apartments*, 49:1-7) also recall the respect with which believers must address the Prophet.[7] Any violation in this regard could seriously compromise the posthumous development of the person, in other words his spiritual progression, because it would break the interior link by which the Prophet nourishes or sustains him spiritually. Now, it is essential that the one who receives this spiritual influx (*madad*) not reflect upon the secret—and in reality, divine—ways by which it is transmitted to him. One can thus understand the necessity of the veil interposed between the Companions and their "mothers" who had to participate along with the Prophet in the spiritual nurturing of their children. The title of the *Sūrat al-Ḥujurāt* makes allusion, as does the *Sūrat al-Aḥzāb*, to the Prophet's intimate life, the "apart-

[7] This passage is notably commented upon by Suhrawardī in his *ʿAwārif al-Maʿārif*, chapter 51. See note 1 above.

ments" actually being those of his wives. The favor of being allowed to enter there must be accompanied by an attitude of respect and outward and inward reverence because the Prophet is intimately present in every believer: "And know that the Messenger of God is among you (or: 'in you,' *fī-kum*)" (49:7).

Several verses suggest that this Prophetic presence is none other than that of God. In the following verse only the context of the Divine Transcendence permits us to distinguish between the pronouns: "We have sent thee as a witness and a bearer of good tidings and a warner, that ye (mankind) may believe in God and His Prophet, that ye may assist and honor him and that ye may glorify Him morning and evening" (48:8-9). Does not the following verse, which is the basis of the initiatic pact, strongly affirm that God appears in a certain manner in the person of the Prophet: "Those who seal the pact with you do actually make it with God. The hand of God is over their hands" (48:10)? This is not at all a matter of divinizing the Prophet or the spiritual masters who came after him, but merely of showing that the Koran and sometimes the Prophet himself affirm the identity of a presence that is essentially none other than that of God. A *ḥadīth* shows this clearly:

> Abū Saʿīd ibn al-Muʿallā recounts: I was praying in the mosque, when the Prophet called me. I didn't answer him (right away), but when the prayer was over, said to him: "I was praying, O Messenger of God." "Doesn't God say," he objected, "'Respond to God and the Messenger when *he* calls you'?" (8:24)[8]: Then he said to me: "I am going to teach you the *sūra* that is the greatest *sūra* of the Koran before you leave the mosque." He took me by the hand. When he began to leave, I asked him: "Didn't you tell me that you were going to teach me the *sūra* that is the greatest *sūra* of the Koran?" "'Praise

[8] Here is the entire verse: "O ye who believe, respond to God and the Messenger when he calleth you unto that which will give you life; and know that God cometh in between a man and his own heart, and that He it is unto Whom ye will be gathered." This shows that the heart, through the effect of the Divine Will, has difficulty grasping the identity of the two presences, the recognition of which, however, assures the resurrection of the heart and the gathering of all that is scattered in it.

> be to God, the Lord of the worlds.'[9] It is the 'Seven Divided-between-two'[10] and the Magnificent Koran that was given to me." (Cf. Koran 15:87.)[11]

One sees at work here the Prophet's pedagogy which prepares his disciple to understand simultaneously the deep significance of the *Fātiḥa*, which is the synthesis of the Koran, and the reality of the Prophet, the Word of God, to which one must respond as if to God Himself. It may be that this *ḥadīth* is the origin of the tenet that recommends that the disciple not fulfill supererogatory prayers in the presence of the master, unless of course the latter were explicitly to invite the disciple to do so or were to set an example for him to follow.

While the primary function of the spiritual master is to guide men toward God, the Koran seems to deny this role to the Prophet: "Thou guidest not whom thou lovest, but it is God who guidest whom He will" (28:56). Other verses indeed affirm the identity between Divine and prophetic guidance, as is expressed by the following one that comes after a passage on the modes of the revelation: "Thus have We inspired in thee a Spirit by Our command. Thou knewest not what the Scripture was, nor what the Faith, but We have made it a light whereby we guide whom we will of Our servants. And thou verily dost guide unto a straight path" (42:52). The revelation of the Spirit therefore follows a process of descent through five phases: Emanation of the Spirit, teaching, illumination, divine guidance, prophetic guidance. Initiation could be described as a process parallel to this, except that it is a process of ascent and under the master's direction from the start.

[9] That is to say, the *Fātiḥa*, the first *sūra* of the Koran, thus the Companion's astonishment.

[10] That is to say, the seven verses of the *Fātiḥa*, shared, according to a tradition, between God and man.

[11] Qurṭubī, *Jāmiʿ Aḥkām al-Qurʾān* I, 108, according to Bukhāri, *Ṣaḥīḥ*, *tafsīr* 1, VI, 20.

To receive the influx of the Spirit and the divine Word, the heart must be purified. This inner purification (*tazkiya*) is therefore one of the Prophet's first functions and a preparatory phase for the receipt of the sacred knowledge: "We have sent unto you (or: 'in you') a messenger from among you, who reciteth unto you Our verses, purifieth you (*yuzakkīkum*), and teacheth you the Scripture and wisdom, and teacheth you that which ye knew not" (2:151). That which man does not know and which he cannot come to know by himself alone is direct knowledge, revealed to the prophets, and inspired in the saints. Access to this knowledge which is taught by God presupposes not only purification and renunciation of all pretension, but also absolute trust and obedience. It is a long and difficult path, the last stages of which al-Khaḍir, the prototype of the master, teaches to Moses.[12] When teaching this knowledge to men through the Revelation, the Prophet was only retransmitting that which he had himself received from the time of the Angel's first appearance:

> Recite in the name of thy Lord Who created—
> Created man from a clot.
> Recite: And thy Lord is the Most Generous,
> Who hath taught by the *Qalam* (Pen).
> Taught man that which he knew not (96:1-5).

In order to receive this word and to transmit it, the Prophet had to be purified and had to purify himself, as he was commanded to do by the verses revealed, according to the tradition, immediately after those above: "Arise, and warn! Thy Lord magnify. Thy garments purify" (74:2-4). This function of purification, which is divine in its principle ("God doth purify whom He will" [4:49 or 24:21]), is carried out by the Prophet in many ways, particularly through the intermediary of alms, the vehicle of forgiveness and grace:

> Take alms of their wealth, wherewith thou mayst purify them and mayst make them better.[13] Pray that upon them may descend grace;

[12] See the Koran, 18:60-82.

[13] The first verb (*tuṭahhiru-hum*) expresses the idea of a purification that is

> thy prayer is a comfort for them, and God is All-hearing, All-knowing. Know they not that it is God Who accepteth repentance from His servants and taketh alms? (9:103-104).

Spiritual masters and saints in general have become the heirs of this utilization of wealth as a means for the purification of souls of disciples and people in general.[14] A revelation instituted the obligation of almsgiving before all interviews with the Prophet, regardless of how short: "O ye who believe! When ye hold conference with the Messenger, offer an alms before your conference. That is better and purer for you" (58:12). This rule, soon abrogated because it was too burdensome for the believers, was initially aimed at limiting the number of questions that ceaselessly deluged the Prophet, but it equally sets off the sacred character of his person, the intermediary between men and God. Indeed, alms are received by God before coming into the hands of their human recipients. The Sufis didn't forget this revelation, and it is a frequently observed practice to bring alms or a gift when paying a visit to one's master.

While interceding for his companions and for the whole of humanity, the Prophet, who is a "Mercy for the worlds," (21:107) manifests an aspect that is not only paternal but also maternal, for "mercy" (*raḥma*) is derived from the same root[15] as the "womb" (*raḥm*).[16] The last verse of the *Sūrat at-Tawba* (*Repentance*), which is filled with narration of the Prophet's last battles, assigns to him two

both physical and spiritual. The second (*tuzakkī-him*), translated above by "to purify," evokes purity or excellence of the inner order.

[14] See our study "De l'usage sanctifiant des biens en islam," in *Revue de l'Histoire des Religions*, 215-1/1998, pp. 59-89.

[15] Translator's Note: The "root" in question refers to the basic linguistic root from which both of the Arabic terms are derived. This is not at all to say that the similarity between the two terms is limited solely to a shared linguistic origin.

[16] See the *ḥadīth*: "The family relationship (*raḥm* or *raḥim*, that is to say, issuing from the womb) is a ramification of the Most Merciful (*ar-Raḥmān*). God says: The one who remains bound to you, I remain bound to him; the

divine qualities, compassion and mercy, as well as an attitude towards believers that one also finds amongst all spiritual masters:

> Now there has come to you a Messenger from among yourselves; grievous to him is your suffering; full of concern is he for you, and towards the believers compassionate, merciful (9:128).

A figure of mercy, and a war leader—this is how the Prophet appears to us. The coming together of these two aspects in him is explained by the meaning of this "combat." It is aimed at raising God's Word over all other words, according to the definition of "combat" in the path of God. Indeed, the eternal outcome of this combat is of relatively little importance; that which matters is the inner disposition of the combatant. We cannot give here all of the Koranic passages that reveal the spiritual dimension of this combat. Let us just recall the *Sūrat al-Fatḥ*, "the Victory" or "the Reconquest," which foretells the taking of Mecca by the Prophet. Besides the verse on the treaty already mentioned above, three mentions are made of the descent of the Divine Presence (*sakīna*) into the hearts of the believers, which is accompanied by the armies of the heavens and the earth (48:4, 18, 26) for a cosmic and interior struggle that must succeed in the reconquest of the Center. It is through analogy with this major event in the life of the Prophet and his Companions that in Sufism one calls *fatḥ* the reconquest of the heart or the illumination that gives access to the higher degrees of the initiation.

There are, therefore, hardly any qualities and functions of the spiritual master that the Koran does not attribute to the Prophet. This is all the more evident in a verse of the *Sūrat al-Aḥzāb* which encompasses everything that the master must be for the disciple: "Ye have indeed in the Messenger of God a beautiful example for anyone whose hope is in God and the Last Day, and who invokes God frequently" (33:21).

one who breaks with this bond, I break with him" (Bukhārī, *Ṣaḥīḥ*, *adab* 13, VIII, 7).

The Koran teaches the Companions how to behave towards their spiritual father. As a counterpart, it invites the latter to turn first towards the humblest among them, those who consecrate themselves entirely to God; these are the models of those who will later be called "the poor in God" (*al-fuqarā' ilā 'Llāh*). Indeed, they realize by their poverty and their indigence the perfection of servitude and have truly taken the Prophet as their guide towards God. The Koran reproaches the Prophet for an instance in which he preferred the company of rich Qurayshites whom he wanted to attract to Islam, and in so doing for forsaking one of God's servants:

> Keep thyself content with those who invoke their Lord morning and evening, in desire of His Countenance; and let not thine eyes turn away from them, desiring the adornment of the life of this world; and obey not him whose heart We have made neglectful of Our remembrance, who followeth his own passion and who hath gone beyond all bounds (18:28).

Is one not able to visualize in this scene the master in the midst of his disciples, as well as the test that this company can sometimes be? Through the gaze that the shaykh always keeps on his disciples, he protects them, educates them, and opens the eye of the heart to their inner vision.

A question arises here: in *taṣawwuf*, as in every initiatic path, no one can follow the way if it is not under the direction of a master and no one can become a master if he has not received the permission (*idhn*) of a master that authorizes him to direct those who aspire to "the first death and the second birth." Thus, whose disciple was Muhammad? Could he have been without a master other than God Himself? God certainly instructed him through the Revelation, taught him that which he knew not, and commanded him to call people to God. Muslim scholars generally distinguish between two forms of revelation: one received directly by the Prophet, the other through the intermediary of the Archangel Gabriel and which was destined to be transmitted to mankind. Thus, in order to transmit, the Prophet must have received. This supposes the presence of a master, or in other words a mediator, who would be both a link to and a veil between him and God so that the Divine Transcendence would be preserved.

The first verses to be revealed remind the Prophet of his double birth. Of his carnal birth: "He created man from a clot" in the womb. And of his spiritual birth: "Who taught by the *Qalam*." The "supreme *Qalam*" is the symbol of the Spirit and can be identified with Jibrīl (Gabriel), the Archangel of the Revelation, the faithful or uncorrupted Spirit (*ar-rūḥ al-'amīn*), for it transmits fully and faithfully the "deposit" that is entrusted to it (*'amāna*). Indeed Gabriel projects God's Word into the Prophet's heart "with the permission of God," just as the Prophet calls people to God "with the permission of God." Masters do likewise, for they have been confirmed in this same mission by the permission of their own masters.[17] This succession of transmissions explains why in some initiatic chains Gabriel is included between God and the Prophet.

In this respect Gabriel fulfills the role of spiritual father for the Prophet. His paternity evidently appears in the Koranic narration of the Annunciation to Mary:

> She placed a veil between her and (her people); and We sent unto her Our Spirit that took for her the form of a man without fault. She said to him: "I take refuge in the All-merciful from thee, if thou dost fear God." He replied: "I am but a messenger come from thy Lord, to give thee a son most pure" (19:17-19).

One can see in these three persons the model of the spiritual father: In Gabriel one sees the disciple who is receptive to the Word of God. In Mary and in the future master who must be born, Jesus, one sees the incarnation of the Word of God. The master is the way, and Jesus powerfully affirms this. As for Muhammad, he receives the order to say:

> This is my way: I call unto God with sure knowledge, I and whosoever followeth me. Glory be to God, and I am not of those who associate (false gods with God) (12:108).

[17] See Suhrawardī, *'Awārif al-Ma'ārif*, chap. 51, p. 404, on the parallel between the projection of the divine Word by Gabriel and the inspiration of the master on the subject of spiritual direction of the disciple.

The prophetic tradition relating the circumstances of the first revelation explains how Gabriel brought forth Muhammad's birth into prophethood. To those who ask how revelation comes to him, the Prophet answers:

> Sometimes it comes to me like the ringing of a bell and this is the most taxing on me. When it leaves me, I retain it. Sometimes the angel presents himself to me; he speaks to me and I retain what he tells me.

This last sentence calls to mind the Annunciation. The following tradition, reported by ʿĀʾisha, specifies that the Revelation first came to the Prophet in the form of a holy vision in a dream. (One will find further below an example of the importance of dreams in the Prophet's relation with his Companions.) There has always been a parallel in Sufism between the Prophet's retreats in the cave on Mount Hira following the visitation of Gabriel, and the Sufi's spiritual retreat in isolation (*khalwa*) in the anticipation of illumination (*fatḥ*). Gabriel appears to the Prophet and commands him three times: "Recite!" (*iqraʾ*). Each time, the Prophet replies: "I don't know how to recite"; Gabriel presses so strongly against him that Muhammad thinks that he is going to die, until finally he manages to recite. Could one not interpret these three successive applications of pressure as births, each one into a new world, each an escape from what would correspond spiritually to the three darknesses of the womb that envelope the fetus (Cf. Koran 39:6)? Through this process of birthing, Muhammad is born to a new existence, as a prophet.

In this triple application of pressure, a mode of training and initiatic transmission has also been perceived.[18] Its arduous aspect represents spiritual combat (*mujāhada*) and the education or the improvement of the soul (*taʾdhīb an-nafs*). The embrace or grasp of the Archangel is also aimed at communicating the luminous strength of the Spirit to bear the Revelation. An anecdote illustrates how masters can reproduce in their own way the action of Gabriel: In a gathering, some

[18] See ʿAbdallāh ibn Abī Jamra (d. 699/1299), *Bahjat an-Nufūs* (Cairo, 1355 AH, reproduced in Beirut, 1979), I, 15 (a partial commentary of Bukhārī).

doctors of the Law were attacking a shaykh with questions in order to find some fault in him. The shaykh catches sight of a simple illiterate shepherd who is attending the debate, clasps him against himself, and suddenly the shepherd starts answering all of the objections in the place of the master. This done, the shaykh again hugs the shepherd, who once more becomes as ignorant as before. The latter protests:

> "Master, when *fuqarā'* give something, they don't take it back!" "Certainly," replies the shaykh, "but you are not bound to this way" (*laysa laka nisba fī hadhā 'l-sha'n*).

The shaykh's behavior is intended to make the doctors of the Law understand that true knowledge is drawn out much more directly by the prophetic model than from exoteric learning. He then withdraws the knowledge that had been transmitted for an instant to the shepherd, meaning that one cannot bear such knowledge if one has not been prepared for it through the initiation and that this necessitates being bound to a master.

Finally, according to Ibn Abī Jamra, the embrace of Gabriel and the revelation that follows it correspond to the two phases of every spiritual progression: stripping away (*takhallī*) followed by "dressing in finery" (*taḥallī*).

One could push the comparison still farther: the presence of Jibrīl at the side of the Prophet throughout his mission evokes a shaykh's tie with the master who trained him. Indeed, the Archangel continues to appear to the Prophet in a great number of circumstances outside of the context of the Revelation, just as a master does not stop receiving guidance from his own shaykh, even when the latter has died, or from other shaykhs in his initiatic chain: the link with the father or the ancestors is never broken.

It now remains to see to what extent the relations between the Prophet and his Companions, as depicted in the *Sunna*, can be interpreted in terms of the master-to-disciple relationship.

First of all, the Prophet reveals the reality of his inner principial being to some Companions. The Koran alludes to this, as we have seen. In most cases, the Prophet does respond to a Companion who inquires of him when he became a prophet. The answer rises to another level in order to awaken the disciple's mind to a higher perception of reality, as we see here:

> I was already the servant of God and the Seal of the prophets when Adam was still between clay and water. I will tell you where it is proclaimed: the plea of my father Abraham, the prophecy of my brother Jesus, and the vision that my mother had.[19]

In another tradition the Prophet summarizes his existence thus: "I was the first man to be created and the last raised up to be a prophet."[20] However, the life and the mission of the Prophet are not interrupted by his death, any more than are those of a spiritual father. He announces his role as intercessor in several traditions. One of these is the long *ḥadīth* on intercession, in which on the Day of Judgment people come before the successive prophets until they come before Muhammad, who intercedes for the whole of mankind.[21] What is the relationship between intercession and spiritual mastership? Besides the aspect of mercy attached to this function, the Prophet appears in other traditions as the guide or the ferryman of souls to the afterworld. When his young servant Anas ibn Mālik asks him to intercede for him on the Day of Resurrection, he replies to him:

> "I shall do it." Once more, Anas asks: "Where will I find you?" "Search for me first on the *Ṣirāṭ*" (the bridge that passes above Hell and leads to Paradise). "And if I don't find you on the *Ṣirāṭ*?" "Search for me by the Balance" (where actions and works will be weighed). "And if I don't find you by the Balance?" "Search for me by the Pool,"(from which the Prophet will quench the thirst of the believers) "for I cannot fail to be found at these three places."[22]

[19] Ibn Saʿd, *Tabaqāt al-Kubrā* (Cairo, 1358 AH), I, 130. Several versions are also reported in the *Musnad* of Aḥmad Ibn Ḥanbal. The plea of Abraham makes allusion to Koran 2:129, and Jesus' prophecy to 61:6. While delivering Muhammad, his mother sees a light come out of his breast and illuminate the castles of Syria.

[20] Ibid. I, 130.

[21] See Bukhārī, *Ṣaḥīḥ*, *tawḥīd* 36, IX, 179-180.

[22] Tirmidhī, *Jāmiʿ*, *qiyāma* 9 and Ibn Ḥanbal, *Musnad*, III, 296.

This tradition gives real meaning to the expression "the way of the Hereafter" by which masters define *taṣawwuf.* The object of the quest is here the Prophet, who recounts the main stages of an eschatological and initiatic journey for his companion. The three places can represent, respectively, the salvation of the soul through its shunning the causes of perdition, its sanctification through its works, and its access to the knowledge symbolized by the providing of water. All through the period of his preaching, the Prophet always kept his Companions in the eschatological anticipation that: "I will precede you to the Pool."[23] Each person will be able to understand this expression according to the desire and the aspiration of his own soul. Close to the "Banner of Praise,"[24] another eschatological "place," the Prophet will praise God with praises till then unknown and which will be inspired in him by God. This is an allusion to a new and higher knowledge of God within him, or the knowledge of God by God. Being the ferryman to the great beyond, the master, because he is himself identified with the Way, is the one that a seeker readies himself to find in order to conclude a journey that otherwise inevitably remains unfinished.

Most certainly this dimension of the Prophet's teaching can elude those who would content themselves with just consulting the *Sīra* (i.e. traditional biography of the Prophet), which relates the main events of his life. In particular, the period in Medina appears to be an uninterrupted succession of battles, leaving little room for spiritual teachings. But it is precisely during this period that the most powerful moments are those when the Companions throw themselves, full of longing for the great beyond and for the meeting with God and the Prophet, into combat in the pursuit of martyrdom. According to the Koran, the Prophet transmits to them the longing for and anticipation of resurrection—being their spiritual father, he prepares them for their rebirth.

He also prepares them for his own death by teaching them that the only legacy that he will leave will be knowledge.[25] We know the

[23] Bukharī, *fitan* 1-2, IX, 58-59.

[24] See Aḥmad ibn Ḥanbal, *Musnad* I, 281 (in another version of the "*ḥadīth* of intercession").

[25] See Abū Dāwūd, *Sunan*, *'ilm* 1, no. 3641, III, 317: "The sages are the heirs

importance of this notion of prophetic inheritance in the symbolism of holiness. The Prophet puts this into practice by bequeathing concise spiritual wills (*waṣiyya*) to several Companions, condensing into these the essentials of a spiritual teaching. He gives the following advice to Muʿādh ibn Jabal whom he sends to Yemen: "The last charge," [said Muʿādh ibn Jabal,] "given to me by the Messenger of God, when I already had a foot in the stirrup, was this: 'Behave with good character toward people, O Muʿādh ibn Jabal.'"[26] In just a few words the Prophet recalls the essence of the Law, the Way, and essential Reality. Character (*khulq* or *khuluq*), the inner mold of man, is indeed reflected in his outer behavior. Each of the commandments of the Law puts this character to the test, particularly in relations with others. *Taṣawwuf* has been defined as the acquisition of a noble character (*makārim al-akhlāq*), which proceeds from the divine Attributes.

The Prophet himself affirms that he has been sent "to perfect noble characters"[27] and is endowed, according to the Koran, with "a magnificent character" (68:4), which ʿĀʾisha says is identified with the Koran itself.[28] One can see, therefore, that the Prophet is inviting Muʿādh to follow what seems to be moral advice, but on the path of perfection.

One may wonder if the Prophet and his closest Companions devoted themselves to specific rites that were distinct from those practiced by the generality of believers, just as in *taṣawwuf* one invokes the Name or divine names (*dhikr*) according to precise rules. Now, during this period and for the generations that followed, the *dhikr par excellence* seems to have been the recitation of the Koran in evening prayer (*qiyām al-layl*). It is said of those that practice this

of the prophets and the prophets have left them an inheritance of neither *dinar* nor *dirhem*, but they left them an inheritance of knowledge. He who takes it, receives a great portion."

[26] Mālik, *Muwattaʾ*, *ḥusn al-khuluq* 1, III, 94-95.

[27] Mālik, *Muwattaʾ*, *ḥusn al-khuluq* 8, II, 97, and Ibn Ḥanbal, *Musnad* II, 381.

[28] "Do you not read the Koran? His character was the Koran," was her reply to he who asked her about the Prophet's character. See Ibn Ḥanbal, *Musnad* VI, 54, 91.

prayer that they are "a group (*ṭā'ifa*) of those that are with you" (73:20). To be fully with the Prophet implied, therefore, the practice of this rite. His regular practice had first been called *wird*, a term that would later come to designate the set of daily recitations characteristic of every initiatic path: "He who did not recite his *wird* at night, but who recites it between the dawn prayer and the one at midday, it is as if he had recited it at night."[29] Night is a special time for receiving the Word of God, which came down in its totality during the "Night of the Destiny." The Prophet encouraged the best of his Companions to await this interior and cosmic event, which is renewed every year, through such praying at night.

Incontestably, the Prophet transmitted a specific teaching to some of his Companions. Sufis most often cite this sentence of Abū Hurayra to justify the existence of an esoteric teaching destined just for a few: "I have retained from the Messenger of God, on him be God's grace and peace, two vessels. One I have divulged, but if I were to divulge the other, they would cut my throat."[30] One also finds in the *Sunna* modes of transmission in which gestures count more that words; these modes remind us of the way in which masters transmit initiatic knowledge and power to their disciples. Abū Hurayra, the Companion who reported the most *ḥadīths*, complains one day to the Prophet that he forgets many of the Prophet's words. The latter then asks him to open up his cloak (*ridā'*), and then makes a gesture of drawing water (as from a well) from within, using his hands. He then asks Abū Hurayra to pull the garment back in or to put it back on. "After that," recounted the latter, "I never again forgot anything."[31] Sometimes the Prophet would join such gestures to his words. One day, employing a maieutic method recalling the one of Gabriel, he clasps his young cousin 'Abdallāh Ibn 'Abbās to him while making this prayer: "O my God, teach him the Book."[32] After this, Ibn 'Abbās became the interpreter *par excellence* of the Koran.

[29] Ibn Ḥanbal, *Musnad* I, 32, 53. For another version with *juz'* instead of *wird*, see Wensinck, *Concordance et indices de la tradition musulmanes*, I, 459.

[30] Bukhārī, *'ilm*, 42, I, 40.

[31] Ibid.

[32] *Ivi* I, 29; in a version "wisdom" v. 34.

Food also plays a role in this type of transmission. Abū Hurayra speaks of this subject in an anecdote that could have happened between a master and a disciple:

> By God—there is no god other than God—, I used to suffer so much from hunger that I would press my liver against the earth or would put a stone on my abdomen (to relieve the pangs). Pushed by hunger, I positioned myself one day at the door of the mosque. Abū Bakr came out. I asked him about a verse from God's Book only so that he might then offer me something to calm my hunger, but he passed on and didn't do anything about it. 'Umar came out. I asked him the same thing with the same intent, but he passed on and didn't invite me. Abū'l-Qāsim (the Prophet), grace and peace be upon him, in turn came out. When he saw me, he smiled and knew what was troubling my soul and was showing on my face. He said to me: "Abū Hirr!" (the familiar diminutive form of Abū Hurayra's name). "Here I am for thee, O Messenger of God" (i.e. "at your service"). "Follow me!" I followed him. He went into his house, asked permission for me to enter and invited me in. There was a bowl of milk there. "Where did this milk come from?" he asked. "Some man or woman must have offered it to you," I answered him. He called out "Abū Hirr!" "Here I am for thee, O Messenger of God." "Go find the 'People of the Bench' and bring them here."[33]
>
> The People of the Bench were the "lodgers" of Islam. They had neither goods nor family. When alms were sent to the Prophet, he would give these to them and wouldn't take any for himself. If he received a gift, he would share it with them. This worried me and I said to myself, "How can this milk be enough for the People of the Bench? I have more right than anyone else to drink a mouthful of this milk in order to regain my strength."
>
> When the Prophet would give me such an order, it was I who would take the food to them. I despaired of this milk, therefore, because it was necessary for me to obey God and His messenger. I

[33] *Ahl aṣ-ṣuffa*: the poorest of the Companions, one of whom was Abū Hurayra. They lived in a retreat in the mosque while dedicating themselves to the worship of God. They have been considered as the model of the first Sufis.

went to call them, they came and asked permission to enter. The Prophet invited them in and they sat down in the room.

"Abū Hirr!" called the Prophet to me. "Here I am for thee, O Messenger of God." "Take the bowl and give it to them to drink." I took it. I had hardly passed it to one of them when he drank his fill and returned it to me. I continued (passing it around) thus until (I came to) the Prophet, grace and peace be upon him. All had satisfied their thirst. The Prophet took the bowl, held it in his hand, looked at me and, smiling, said: "Abū Hirr!" "Here I am for thee, O Messenger of God." "Only thou and I remain." "That is true," I replied. "Sit and drink!" Which I did. He repeated: "Drink!" and continued to repeat it until I had finished by saying to him: "By He who sent thee according to the Truth, I am not able to swallow any more!" "Show it to me!" I gave him the bowl. He praised God, pronounced His name and drank the rest.[34]

This Prophetic tradition deserves a developed commentary. Let us stick with the most important points for our subject:

• First, the hunger. Although it certainly is not entirely by their own volition, the People of the Bench lead, as does the Prophet, an extremely ascetic life by necessity, but also by choice. Some masters will consider hunger as one of the fundamental rules of the Way along with silence, the prayer vigils at night, and isolation.

• Abū Bakr and 'Umar, who are hardly ordinary Companions, did not discern the state of Abū Hurayra. The master himself knows the state of his disciple, outwardly and inwardly.

• The relationship of Abū Hurayra with the Prophet bears the imprint of both familiarity, or even of complicity, and of reverence. The expression, "Here I am for thee" (*labbay-ka*) testifies to this and brings to mind the formula said by pilgrims to God, and punctuating here the four parts of the narration.

[34] Bukhārī, *riqāq* 17, VII, 119-120 and an excerpt in *isti'dhān* 14; *Musnad*, II, 515.

• The student-disciples are often a test and the Prophet here uses the other *fuqarāʾ* to this end. By putting Abū Hurayra, nearly dead of hunger, in the service of others, he instills in him one of the fundamental virtues: to favor the other above oneself.

• One finds in this anecdote the hagiographical theme of the incredulous, or at least disquieted, disciple who thus enhances the miraculous outcome of history and the divine grace that always grants more than could be anticipated.

• This milk, as other traditions attest, symbolizes knowledge.[35] It also underscores the master's maternal solicitude for his disciple to whom he provides the food and water of his knowledge according to the disciple's measure. Here, that measure is so great that only the Prophet can finish the bowl.

Let us add that the image of the nursing master is not rare among the People of the Way.[36] It recalls the state of infancy of the disciple whose nursing assumes that he will be born again to a new existence. One has seen that the Prophet prepared his Companions for the passage from this world to the other. Now, there is an intermediate state (*barzakh*) between every world, which corresponds to the world of dreams and dream-visions within the perceptual order. For prophets, this kind of vision is an integral part of prophethood.[37] This is because it reveals the higher realities within the world of forms. For believ-

[35] Cf. the *ḥadīth* in which the Prophet recounts: "'Whilst I was sleeping, someone brought me some milk. I drank so much that I saw it coming out again through my nails. Then I gave the rest to ʿUmar to drink.' 'How do you interpret that, O Messenger of God?' asked ʿUmar. 'Knowledge,' he replied" (Bukhārī, *Ṣaḥīḥ*, *ʿilm* 22, I, I, 31).

[36] Let us mention the case of a contemporary master who speaks to a disciple whose master has died and who is hesitating to attach himself to the other master: "When one of the breasts is dry, the child takes the other."

[37] "The vision of the prophets is a revelation" (Bukhārī, *wuḍūʾ* 5, *adhān* 161).

ers, this kind of vision is a participation in prophethood[38] and allows the Prophet in particular, or the master, to decipher the disciple's state more clearly. A tradition reports that after the dawn prayer, the Prophet once asked his Companions: "If anyone amongst you has had a vision this past night, tell it to me so that I may interpret it." Thereafter, in order not to unveil what had to remain hidden, he only interpreted visions when someone requested this of him.[39]

ʿAbdallāh ibn ʿUmar recounts that he heard his companions relate their visions to the Prophet:

> I also wanted to have a vision myself to tell to the Prophet. I was then a young unmarried man and used to sleep in the mosque. In a dream I saw myself carried by two angels toward the Fire, which appeared to me to be constructed like a well with a lip and mounts (for the pulley). Some people whom I knew were there. I began to cry out: "I take refuge in God against the Fire, I take refuge in God against the Fire." Another angel joined (the other two) and said to me, "You need not be afraid." I related this vision to Ḥafṣa (sister of ʿAbdallāh and wife of the Prophet). She reported it to the Prophet who exclaimed: "How excellent a man ʿAbdallāh would be if he spent the night in prayer!"[40]

Sālim (who reported the *ḥadīth* upon the authority of Ibn ʿUmar) adds: "After that, ʿAbdallāh only slept very little each night."[41]

In this narration, the Prophet appears to do very little. In one version, it is not even he but the angel who incites the young Companion to spend the night in prayer. Yet, by inducing the desire to have a dream, he initiates the process of an inner journey within his disciple in which the latter, after a quasi-descent into hell, understands how the ascent must come about: through the word of God, which itself

[38] "The 46th part of prophecy" (Cf. Wensinck, *Concordance* I, 343, II, 205).

[39] Cf. Nabhānī, *Al-Anwār al-Muḥammadiyya min al-Mawāhib al-Laduniyya* (Beirut, 1312 AH), p. 475.

[40] In another version of the *ḥadīth*, it is the angel who says this to ʿAbdallāh: Cf. Bukhārī, *taʿabir*, commentary of Ibn Hajar al-Asqālānī, *Fatḥ al-Bārī*, XII, 351-353.

[41] Bukhārī, *Faḍāʾil Aṣḥāb an-Nabī* 19, V, 31, *tahajjud* 2, and *Musnad* II, 146.

has come down to man. The master didn't act directly, but he had prepared his disciple to receive this word and to understand its eschatological urgency through experiencing the threat by himself and by internalizing it. In addition, as the master or the father, the Prophet preaches more by example than by speaking: He himself spends his nights in prayer, as the Koran had ordered him to do (cf. 73:1-20). Through the dream, the disciple has reached a new world; through the recitation of the Koran he rises degree by degree; the Revelation is a way of rebirth and inner resurrection to which the master is the door and the guide.

One could develop this symbolism of the second birth further. Let us recall in conclusion the Prophet's participation in this spiritual childbirth. In his supra-temporal reality, he is born of the Mother of the Book (*umm al-kitāb*), which is why he is called *ummī*, which signifies "illiterate" but which also means, etymologically and symbolically, "connected to his mother." Being born from it, he receives knowledge from it and manifests mercy from it. Within the heart of the night, by spending it in prayer, he leads his disciples to be born again within their mother and, along with her, to let themselves be impregnated by the Spirit. Being a spiritual father, he also has all the qualities of a mother. Like Jesus, a child of the divine Word, he, too, is for those whom he helps to be reborn, similar to a midwife, as is Gabriel. He nourishes them with the milk of divine knowledge and educates them with the rigor and solicitude of a father. It is undoubtedly for this reason that the term "spiritual father" is generally prevalent, which, however, is not sufficient to express everything that a master is for his disciple.

This portrait of Muhammad is not what one discerns most immediately upon reading the *Sunna* and the *Sīra*. It is indisputable that throughout his life he never stopped transmitting and teaching. He was in this sense and in this domain very much like Jesus, much more than he generally appears. The demands he made upon his close Companions were just as rigorous and his predictions of the times to come were just as urgent. Certainly, he also prepared them all to conquer lands and to establish therein an order founded on a sacred law, and this combat was for him the means of accomplishing his mission and reforming the souls of his adepts. At the same time that he was foretelling to them the fall of empires, he was above all shaping them to await a kingdom that is not of this world, announcing to them that the coming of Jesus to the world was close at hand.[42] Not all of his Companions followed equally upon this way, as the Koran says about those archers who through desire of booty had failed their duty and brought about the defeat of the Muslims at the Battle of Uhud: "Among you are some that desire this world and others that desire the Hereafter" (3:152). For the former, Muhammad is the transmitter of the Word, the founder of a religion, a law, and a community; for the latter, he is all this but also that by which all began and all will finish, whether it is a question of the world or the disciple's soul.

[42] The Koran emphasizes the parallel between Jesus and Muhammad by calling the disciples of the former "auxiliaries" (*anṣār*) of their master, a term which evokes combat and the Anṣār of Medina; Cf. Koran 3:52 and 61:14.

ḤAQĪQA AND *SHARĪʿA* IN ISLAM*

René Guénon

Islamic Esoterism

Of all traditional doctrines, perhaps Islamic doctrine most clearly distinguishes the two complementary parts, which can be labeled exoterism and esoterism. In Arabic terminology, these are the *sharīʿa*, literally the "great way," common to all, and the *ḥaqīqa*, literally the "inward truth," reserved to an elite, not because of some arbitrary decision, but by the very nature of things, since not all men possess the aptitudes or "qualifications" required to reach knowledge of the truth. To express their respective "outward" and "inward" natures, exoterism and esoterism are often compared to the "shell" (*qishr*) and the "kernel" (*lubb*), or to the circumference and its center. The *sharīʿa* comprises everything that in Western languages would be called "religious," and especially the whole of the social and legislative side which, in Islam, is essentially integrated into the religion. It could be said that the *sharīʿa* is first and foremost a rule of action, whereas the *ḥaqīqa* is pure knowledge; but it must be well understood that it is this knowledge that gives even the *sharīʿa* its higher and deeper meaning and its true *raison d'être*, so that even though not all those participating in the religion are aware of it, the *ḥaqīqa* is nevertheless its true principle, just as the center is the principle of the circumference.

But this is not all, for esoterism comprises not only the *ḥaqīqa*, but also the specific means for reaching it, and taken as a whole, these means are called the *ṭarīqa*, the "way" or "path" leading from the *sharīʿa* to the *ḥaqīqa*. If we return to the symbol of the circumference and its center, we can say that the *ṭarīqa* is represented by the radius that runs from the former to the latter. And this leads us to the following: to

* Editors' Note: This article comes from two chapters of Guénon's writings on Sufism, published in the collection *Insights into Islamic Esoterism and Taoism* (Sophia Perennis, 2001).

each point on the circumference there corresponds a radius, and all the radii, which are indefinite in number, terminate in the center. It can thus be said that these radii are so many *ṭuruq* (plural of *ṭarīqa*) adapted to the beings "situated" at the different points on the circumference according to the diversity of their individual natures. This is why it is said that "the ways to God are as numerous as the souls of men" (*aṭ-ṭuruqu ila 'Llāhi ka-nufūsi bani Adam*). Thus the "ways" are many, and differ all the more among themselves the closer they are to their starting-point on the circumference; but their end is one, as there is only one center and one truth. Strictly speaking, the initial differences are effaced along with "individuality" itself (*al-innīya*, from *ana*, "I"); in other words, when the higher states of the being have been attained, and when the attributes (*ṣifāt*) of the creature (*'abd*, "slave")—which are really limitations—disappear (*al-fanā'*, "extinction"), leaving only those of Allah (*al-baqā'*, "permanence"), the being becoming identified with the latter [Divine attributes] in his "personality" or "essence" (*adh-dhāt*).

Esoterism, considered thus as comprising both *ṭarīqa* and *ḥaqīqa*, namely means and end, is designated in Arabic by the general term *taṣawwuf*, which can only be translated precisely as "initiation"—a point to which we will return later. Although *taṣawwuf* can be applied to any esoteric and initiatic doctrine, regardless of the traditional form to which it belongs, Westerners have coined the [derivative] term "Sufism" to designate Islamic esoterism; but, apart from being completely conventional, this term has the unfortunate disadvantage of inevitably suggesting by its "ism" suffix, the idea of a doctrine proper to a particular school, whereas this is not the case in reality, the only schools in question being the *ṭuruq*, which basically represent different methods, without there being any possibility of a fundamental difference of doctrine, for "the doctrine of Unity is unique" (*at-tawḥīdu wāḥid*). As for the derivation of the terms *taṣawwuf* and "Sufism," they obviously come from the word *ṣūfī*, and here it must first be said that no one can ever call himself a *ṣūfī*, except from pure ignorance, for he proves thereby that he is not truly so, this quality necessarily being a secret (*sirr*) between the true *ṣūfī* and Allah; one can only call oneself a *mutaṣawwuf*, a term applied to anyone who has entered upon the initiatic "way," whatever the "degree" he may have reached; but the *ṣūfī*, in the true sense of the term, is only the one who has reached the supreme degree.

Some have sought to assign the most diverse origins to the Arabic word *ṣūfī*; but this question is undoubtedly unsolvable from our present position, and we freely admit that the word has too many proposed etymologies, of equal plausibility, for only one to be true; in reality, we must rather see herein a purely symbolic name, a sort of "cipher," which, as such, requires no linguistic derivation strictly speaking; and this is not unique, for one can find comparable cases in other traditions. As for the so-called etymologies, these are basically only phonetic resemblances, which, moreover, according to the laws of a certain symbolism, effectively correspond to relationships between various ideas which have come to be grouped more or less as accessories around the word in question. But given the character of the Arabic language (a character which it shares with Hebrew), the primary and fundamental meaning of a word is to be found in the numerical values of the letters; and in fact, what is particularly remarkable is that the sum of the numerical values of the letters which form the word *ṣūfī* has the same number as *al-Ḥikmatuʾl-ilahiya*, "Divine Wisdom." The true *ṣūfī* is therefore the one who possesses this Wisdom, or, in other words, he is *al-ʿārif bi'Llāh*, that is to say "he who knows through God," for God cannot be known except by Himself; and this is the supreme or "total" degree of knowledge or *ḥaqīqa*.[1]

[1] In a work on *taṣawwuf*, written in Arabic, but from a very modern perspective, a Syrian writer so ill acquainted with us as to mistake us for an "orientalist," has taken it into his head to address a rather singular reproach to us: having somehow read *as-Sūfia* in place of *Ṣūfī* (in a special issue of *Cahiers du Sud* in 1935 on "Islam and the West"), he imagined that my calculation was inexact; wishing then to make the calculation himself according to his own lights, he managed, by way of several errors in the numeric value of the letters, to arrive (this time as equivalent to *aṣ-Ṣūfī*, which is still wrong) at *al-ḥakīm al-ilahī*, without, moreover, perceiving that, one *ya* being equal to two *ha*'s, these words form exactly the same total as *al-ḥakma al-ilahiya*! We know well enough that academic teaching of the present day is ignorant of the *abjad* [the alphabet], and is only familiar with the simple grammatical order of the letters; but just the same, when someone undertakes to treat

From the preceding, we can draw several important consequences, the foremost being that "Sufism" is not something that was "added" to Islamic doctrine as an afterthought and from outside, but, on the contrary, is an essential part of it, since without it, Islamic doctrine would be manifestly incomplete, and, what is more, incomplete "from above," that is to say in regard to its very principle. The completely gratuitous supposition of a foreign origin—Greek, Persian, or Indian—is in any case formally contradicted by the fact that the means of expression of Islamic esoterism are intimately linked with the very constitution of the Arabic language; and if there are incontestable similarities with doctrines of the same order existing elsewhere, these can be explained quite naturally and without recourse to hypothetical "borrowings," for, truth being one, all traditional doctrines are necessarily identical in their essence, whatever the diversity of the forms in which they are clothed. As regards this question of origins, it is of little importance whether the word *ṣūfī* and its derivatives (*taṣawwuf*, *mutaṣawwuf*) have existed in the language from the beginning or have appeared at some later juncture, this being a great subject for discussion among historians; the thing may well have existed before the word, or under another name, or even without it having been found necessary to give it one. In any case—and this ought to settle the matter for anyone not regarding things merely from the outside—tradition expressly indicates that esoterism, as well as exoterism, proceeds directly from the very teaching of the Prophet, and, in fact, every authentic and regular *ṭarīqa* possesses a *silsila* or "chain" of initiatic transmission that ultimately goes back to him through a varying number of intermediaries. Even if, subsequently, some *ṭuruq* really did "borrow," or, better said, "adapt," certain details of their particular methods, this has a very secondary importance, and in no way affects what is essential; and here again similarities may equally well be explained by the possession of the same knowledge, especially as regards the "science of rhythm" in its

these questions, such ignorance passes beyond the acceptable limits. Be that as it may, *al-ḥakīm al-ilahī* and *al-ḥakma al-ilahiya* have basically the same meaning; but the first of these two expressions has a somewhat unusual character, while the second, as we have indicated, is, on the contrary, completely traditional.

various branches. The truth is that "Sufism" is as Arab as the Koran itself, in which it has its direct principles; but in order to find them there, the Koran must be understood and interpreted according to the *ḥaqāʾiq* (plural of *ḥaqīqa*) which constitute its deepest meaning, and not simply by the linguistic, logical, and theological procedures of the *ʿulamā aẓ-ẓāhir* (literally the "doctors of the outward") or doctors of the *sharīʿa*, whose competence extends only to the exoteric realm. It is a question here of two clearly different domains, and this is why there can never be any contradiction or any real conflict between them; it is moreover obvious that one cannot in any way oppose exoterism and esoterism, since on the contrary the second finds its foundation and point of departure in the first, and since they are really no more than the two aspects or the two faces of one and the same doctrine.

We should also point out that contrary to an opinion only too widespread among Westerners, Islamic esoterism has nothing in common with "mysticism." The reasons for this are easy to understand given everything we have explained so far. First of all, mysticism seems to be unique to Christianity, and it is only through erroneous assimilations that one can pretend to find more or less exact equivalents of it elsewhere. Some outward resemblances, in the use of certain expressions for example, are undoubtedly the cause of this error, but they can in no way justify it in light of differences that bear on everything essential. Since by very definition mysticism pertains entirely to the religious domain, it arises purely and simply from exoterism; and furthermore, the end toward which it tends is assuredly far from being of the order of pure knowledge. On the other hand, the mystic could have no method since he has a "passive" attitude and, as a result, limits himself to receiving what comes to him spontaneously as it were and with no initiative on his part. Thus there cannot be any mystical *ṭarīqa*, and such a thing is even inconceivable, for it is basically contradictory. Moreover, the mystic, always isolated by the very fact of the "passive" nature of his "realization," has neither *shaykh* nor "spiritual master" (who, of course, has absolutely nothing in common with a "spiritual director" in the religious sense), neither does he have a *silsila* or "chain" through which the "spiritual influence" would have been transmitted to him (we use this expression to render as exactly as possible the meaning of the Arabic word *baraka*), the second of these two things being moreover an immediate consequence of the first. The regular transmission of the "spiritual influence" is what essentially characterizes "initiation," and even what properly constitutes it, and that is why we have used this word above to translate *taṣawwuf*. Islamic esoterism, like all true esoterism, moreover, is "initiatic" and cannot be anything else; and even without entering into the question of the difference of goals, which in any case results from the very difference in the two domains to which they refer, we can say that the "mystical way" and the "initiatic way" are radically incompatible by reason of their respective characters, and we might also add that in Arabic there is no word by which one can translate "mysticism" even approximately, so much does the idea expressed thereby represent something completely foreign to the Islamic tradition.*

In its essence, initiatic doctrine is purely metaphysical in the true and original meaning of this term; but in Islam, as in other traditional forms, it also includes a complex ensemble of "traditional sciences" by way of more or less direct applications to various contingent realms. These sciences are as if suspended from the metaphysical principles on which they depend and from which they derive, and draw from this attachment (and from the "transpositions" which it permits) all their real value; they are thereby an integral part of the doctrine itself, although to a secondary and subordinate degree, and not more or less artificial and superfluous accretions. There seems to be something here that is particularly difficult for Westerners to understand, doubtless because their own environment offers no point of comparison in this regard; nevertheless there were analogous Western sciences in antiquity and the Middle Ages, but these are entirely forgotten by modern men, who ignore the true nature of things and often are not even aware of their existence. Those who confuse esoterism with mysticism are especially prone to misunderstand the role and the place of these sciences, which clearly represent a knowledge as far removed as can be from the preoccupations of the mystics, so that the incorporation

* Editors' Note: This question of terminology regarding the term "mysticism," as it is often understood in the West, and its application to Sufism is treated in some depth in the selection in this volume by Titus Burckhardt (see the section "Sufism and Mysticism" in the article "Sufi Doctrine and Method").

of these sciences into "Sufism" constitutes for them an undecipherable enigma. Such is the science of numbers and of letters, of which we gave an example in the interpretation of the term *ṣūfī*, and which, in a comparable form, can be found only in the Hebrew *Kabbala*, by virtue of the close affinity of the languages which are the vehicles of expression for these two traditions, languages of which only this science can give the most profound understanding. Such are also the various "cosmological" sciences which are included in part in what is called "Hermeticism"; and in this connection we must note that alchemy is taken in a "material" sense only by the ignorant, for whom symbolism is a dead letter, those very people whom the true alchemists of the Middle Ages stigmatized as "puffers" and "charcoal burners," and who were the true precursors of modern chemistry, however unflattering such an origin may be for the latter. Likewise astrology, another cosmological science, is in reality something entirely other than the "divining art" or the "science of conjecture" which alone is what modern people see in it. Above all it has to do with the knowledge of "cyclical laws" which play an important role in all traditional doctrines. Moreover, there is a certain correspondence between all these sciences which, since they proceed from essentially the same principles, may be regarded as various representations of one and the same thing from a certain point of view. Thus, astrology, alchemy, and even the science of letters do nothing but translate the same truths into the languages proper to different orders of reality, united among themselves by the law of universal analogy, the foundation of every symbolic correspondence; and, by virtue of this same analogy, these sciences, by an appropriate transposition, find their application in the realm of the "microcosm" as well as in that of the "macrocosm," for the initiatic process reproduces in all its phases the cosmological process itself. To have a full awareness of all these correlations, it is necessary to have reached a very high degree in the initiatic hierarchy, a degree which is called that of "red sulfur" (*al-Kebrīt al-aḥmar*); and whoever possesses this degree may, by means of the science known as *sīmiyā* (a word that must not be confused with *kīmiyā*), and by operating certain mutations on letters and numbers, act on the beings and things that correspond to these in the cosmic order. *Jafr*, which according to tradition owes its origin to Sayyidnā ʿAlī himself, is an application of these same sciences to the prevision of future events; and this application, in which the cyclical laws to which we alluded just now naturally intervene, exhibits all the rigor of an exact and mathematical science for those who can understand and interpret it (for it possesses a kind of "cryptography," which in fact is no more astonishing than algebraic notation). One could mention many other "traditional sciences," some of which might seem even stranger to those who are not used to such things; but we must content ourselves with this, and restrict ourselves to generalities, in keeping with the scope of this exposition.

Finally, we must add one last observation of capital importance for understanding the true character of initiatic doctrine: this doctrine has nothing to do with "erudition" and could never be learned by the reading of books in the manner of ordinary or "profane" knowledge. The writings of the greatest masters themselves can only serve as "supports" for meditation; one does not become a *mutaṣawwuf* simply by having read them, and in any case they remain mostly incomprehensible to those who are not "qualified." Indeed, it is necessary above all to possess certain innate dispositions or aptitudes which no amount of effort can replace; then, it is necessary to have an attachment to a regular *silsila*, for the transmission of the "spiritual influence" that is obtained by this attachment is, as we have already said, the essential condition, failing which there is no initiation, even of the most elementary degree. This transmission, which is acquired once and for all, must be the point of departure of a purely inward work for which all the outward means are no more than aids and supports, albeit necessary, given that one must take the nature of the human being such as it actually is into account; and it is by this inward work alone that a being, if capable of it, will ascend from degree to degree, to the summit of the initiatic hierarchy, to the "Supreme Identity," the absolutely permanent and unconditioned state beyond the limitations of all contingent and transitory existence, which is the state of the true *ṣūfī*.

The Shell and the Kernel (*Al-Qishr Wa Al-Lubb*)

Al-Qishr wa al-Lubb [The Shell and the Kernel], the title of one of Muḥyi 'd-Dīn ibn al-ʿArabī's numerous treatises, expresses in symbolic form the relationship between exoterism and esoterism, likened respectively to the casing of a fruit and to its interior part, the pith or kernel.[2] The casing or shell (*al-qishr*) is the *sharīʿa*, that is, the external religious law which is addressed to all and which is made to be followed by all, as indicated moreover by the meaning of "great way" that is associated with the derivation of its name. The kernel (*al-lubb*) is the *ḥaqīqa*, that is to say truth or essential reality, which, unlike the *sharīʿa*, is not within reach of everyone but reserved for those who know how to discern it beneath outward appearances and how to attain it through the exterior forms which conceal it, protecting and disguising it at the same time.[3] In another symbolism, *sharīʿa* and *ḥaqīqa* are also designated respectively as the "[outer] body" (*al-jism*) and the "marrow" (*al-mukh*),[4] of which the relationship is exactly the same as that of shell and kernel; and one could no doubt find still other symbols equivalent to these.

Whatever the designation used, what is referred to is always the "outward" (*aẓ-ẓāhir*) and the "inward" (*al-bāṭin*), that is, the apparent and the hidden, which, moreover, are such by their very nature and not owing to any conventions or to precautions taken artificially, if not arbitrarily, by those who preserve traditional doctrine. This "outward" and this "inward" are represented by the circumference and its center, which can be looked upon as the cross-section of the fruit evoked by the previous symbol, at the same time that we are brought back to the image, common to all traditions, of the "wheel of things." Indeed, if one looks at the two terms in question according to their universal sense and without limiting them by applying them to a particular traditional form, as is most often done, one could say that the *sharīʿa*,

[2] Let us point out incidentally that this symbol of the fruit has a relationship with the "cosmic egg," and thus with the heart.

[3] One might remark that the role of exterior forms is related to the double meaning of the word "revelation," since such forms simultaneously manifest and veil the essential doctrine, the one truth, just as a word inevitably does for the thought it expresses; and what is true of a word in this regard is also true of any formal expression.

[4] One may recall here the "substantive marrow" of Rabelais, which also represents an interior and hidden meaning.

the "great way" traveled by all beings is nothing other than what the Far-Eastern traditions call the "current of forms," while the *ḥaqīqa*, the one and immutable truth, resides in the "invariable middle."[5] In order to pass from one to the other, thus from the circumference to the center, one must follow one of the radii, that is, a *ṭarīqa*, or, one might say, the "footpath," the narrow way which is followed by very few.[6] Furthermore, there are besides a multitude of *ṭuruq*, which are all radii of the circumference taken in the centripetal sense, since it is a question of leaving the multiplicity of the manifested to move toward principial unity; each *ṭarīqa*, starting from a certain point on the circumference, is particularly adapted to those beings who find themselves at that point, but whatever their point of departure, they all tend equally toward one unique point,[7] all arrive at the center and thus lead the beings who follow them to the essential simplicity of the "primordial state."

The beings who presently find themselves in multiplicity are forced to leave it in order to accomplish any realization whatsoever; but for most of them this multiplicity is at the same time the obstacle that stops them and holds them back; diverse and changing appearances prevent them from seeing true reality, so to speak, as the casing of a

[5] It is noteworthy that in the Far-Eastern tradition one finds very clear equivalents to these two terms, not as two aspects, exoteric and esoteric, of the same doctrine, but as two separate teachings, at least since the time of Confucius and Lao Tzu. In fact, one might say in all strictness that Confucianism corresponds to the *sharīʿa* and Taoism to the *ḥaqīqa*.

[6] The words *sharīʿa* and *ṭarīqa* both contain the idea of "progressing," and thus of movement (and one should note the symbolism of circular movement for the first term, and linear movement for the second); there is in fact change and multiplicity in both cases, the first having to adapt itself to the diversity of exterior conditions, and the second to that of individual natures; but the being who has effectively attained *ḥaqīqa*, by that very fact participates in its unity and immutability.

[7] This convergence is represented by that of the *qibla* (ritual orientation) of all places toward the *Kaʿba*, which is the "House of God" (*Baytu ʾLlah*) and of which the form is a cube (the image of stability) occupying the center of a circumference that is the terrestrial (human) cross-section of universal existence.

fruit prevents one from seeing its inside; and this inside can be attained only by those capable of piercing through the casing, that is, of seeing the Principle through its manifestation, and even of seeing it alone in all things, for manifestation itself, taken all together, is no more than a totality of symbolic expressions. It is easy to apply this to exoterism and esoterism understood in their ordinary sense, that is, as aspects of a traditional doctrine; there also, the exterior forms hide profound truth from the eyes of the common man, whereas on the contrary they may be seen by the elite, for whom what seems an obstacle or a limitation to others becomes instead a support and a means of realization. One must clearly understand that this difference results directly and necessarily from the very nature of the beings, from the possibilities and aptitudes that each carries within itself, so much so that for each of them the exoteric side of the doctrine thus always plays exactly the role that it should, giving to those that cannot go further what it is possible for them to receive in their present state, and at the same time furnishing to those that can go further, "supports," which, without ever being a strict necessity, since they are contingent, can nonetheless greatly aid them to advance in the interior life, and without which the difficulties would be such that, in certain cases, they would amount to a veritable impossibility.

We should point out in this regard that for the majority of men, that is, for those who inevitably abide by exterior law, this takes on a character which is less a limitation than a guide; it is always a bond, but a bond that prevents them from going astray or from losing themselves; without this law, which obliges them to follow a well-defined path, not only would they never attain the center, but they would risk distancing themselves indefinitely from it, whereas the circular movement keeps them at a more or less constant distance.[8] In this way, those who cannot directly contemplate the light can receive at least a reflection of and a participation in it; and they remain thus bound in some way to the Principle, even though they do not and could not have an effective

[8] Let us add that this law ought to be regarded normally as an application or a human specification of the cosmic law itself, which similarly links all manifestation to the Principle, as we have explained elsewhere in reference to the significance of the "laws of Manu" in Hindu doctrine.

consciousness of it. Indeed, the circumference could not exist without the center, from which, in reality, it proceeds entirely, and even if the beings who are linked to the circumference do not see the center at all, or even the radii, each of them is nonetheless inevitably situated at the extremity of a radius of which the other extremity is the center itself. But it is here that the shell intervenes and hides whatever is found in the interior, whereas the one who has pierced this shell, by that very fact becoming conscious of the path or radius corresponding to his own position on the circumference, will be liberated from the indefinite rotation of the latter and will only have to follow the radius in order to move toward the center; this radius is the *ṭarīqa* by which, starting from the *sharīʿa*, he will arrive at *ḥaqīqa*. We must make clear, moreover, that once the shell has been penetrated, one finds oneself in the domain of esoterism, this penetration, by its relationship to the shell itself, being a kind of turning about, of which the passage from the exterior to the interior consists. In one sense the designation "esoterism" belongs even more properly to *ṭarīqa*, for in reality *ḥaqīqa* is beyond the distinction of exoterism and esoterism, as this implies comparison and correlation; the center, of course, appears as the most interior part of all, but when it has been attained there can no longer be a question of exterior or interior, as every contingent distinction then disappears, resolving itself in principial unity.

That is why Allah, just as He is "the First and the Last" (*al-Awwal wa al-Ākhir*),[9] is also "the Exterior and the Interior" (*aẓ-Ẓāhir wa al-Bāṭin*),[10] for nothing of that which is could be outside of Him, and in Him alone is contained all reality, because He is Himself absolute Reality, and total Truth: *Huwa 'l-Ḥaqq*.

[9] That is, the Principle and the End, as in the symbol of the *alpha* and the *omega*.

[10] One could also translate this as the "Evident" (in relationship to manifestation) and the "Hidden" (in Himself), which correspond again to the two points of view of the *sharīʿa* (the social and religious order) and *ḥaqīqa* (the purely intellectual and metaphysical order), although this latter may also be said to be beyond all points of view, as comprising them all synthetically within itself.

SUFI ANSWERS TO QUESTIONS ON ULTIMATE REALITY*

Martin Lings

In connection with the origins of Sufism, attitudes have changed very rapidly in the last decades. The change has not been unanimous; but there is an undeniably increasing tendency for opinions to shift away from the notion that Sufism has its roots in Hinduism or Buddhism or Neoplatonism or Christianity rather than in Islam, and towards agreement with the Sufis themselves in maintaining that Sufism is an integral part of Islam, or more precisely that it is and always has been "the heart of Islam." But Islam has stood the test of time; and to do so—or even, we might say, to survive—a way of worship must be capable of appealing to the wisest and deepest elements in the collectivity which practices it, capable of enlisting those souls which are most imbued with a sense of Ultimate Reality. For this it must have the dimension of mysticism; and if Sufism is not Islam's mystical dimension, what is? Without Sufism Islam would be a strange anomaly. It would not even be a religion in the fullest sense of the word. That is of course what many people liked to think in the past.

Let us quote in this connection a recent definition of religion which is rigorous enough not to omit any necessary element while being at the same time supple enough to enable us to include, in one and the same breath, such dissimilars as Judaism and Buddhism, or as Christianity and the religion of the Red Indians:

> For a religion to be considered as intrinsically orthodox—and extrinsic orthodoxy hangs upon particular formal elements which cannot apply literally outside their own perspective—it must rest upon a fully adequate doctrine of the Absolute; then it must extol and actu-

* This article was written by request for the new Canadian journal *Ultimate Reality and Meaning* (Vol. 3, University of Toronto Press). It is here republished with some modifications (Martin Lings).

> alize a spirituality that is equal to this doctrine and thereby include sanctity within its ambit both as concept and reality; this means that it must be of Divine, and not philosophical, origin and thus be charged with a sacramental or theurgic presence manifesting itself particularly in miracles and—though this may surprise some—in sacred art. Particular formal elements such as apostolic personalities and sacred events are subordinate, as forms, to the above principial elements; they may therefore differ in significance and value from one religion to another—for human diversity makes such fluctuation inevitable—without causing any contradiction as regards the essential criteria which concern both metaphysical truth and the power to save.[1]

The mutual inextricability of Islam and Sufism is here affirmed by an implication which cannot be gainsaid; for it is precisely Sufism which "actualizes a spirituality that is equal to the doctrine," that is, equal to the Islamic doctrine of the Absolute; and it is through Sufism that Islam is able to "include sanctity within its ambit both as concept and reality." Every Islamic region or country has, as its Patron Saint, a man who was head of a Sufi order, except for those few places presided over by an "apostolic personality" who lived before the term *Sufi* was used; and indeed, with the same exceptions, all the generally recognized Saints of Islam are known to have been Sufis.

The conclusion is the same if we approach the question from yet another angle—that of the Koran, which is the direct source of Islam. As early as 1922, a study of the Koran compelled Massignon to say: "Contrary to the Pharasaical opinion of many *fuqahā'*, an opinion which has been accepted for the last sixty years by many Arabists, I have had to admit, with Margoliouth, that the Koran contains real seeds of mysticism, seeds capable of an autonomous development without being impregnated from any foreign source."[2]

A much more explicit formulation in the same direction was made not long ago by Schuon. From the Sufi point of view, Massignon's

[1] Frithjof Schuon, *Islam and the Perennial Philosophy* (London: World of Islam Festival Trust, 1976), p. 14.

[2] Louis Massignon, *La passion d'al-Ḥallāj*, p. 480.

"admission" is a marked understatement. Schuon does not understate, while at the same time he goes half-way to meet the residue of the resistance referred to by Massignon:

> One reason why Western people have difficulty in appreciating the Koran and have even many times questioned whether this book does contain the premises of a spiritual life lies in the fact that they look in a text for a meaning that is fully expressed and immediately intelligible, whereas Semites, and Eastern peoples in general, are lovers of verbal symbolism and read "in depth". . . . But even without taking into consideration the sibylline structure of very many sacred sentences, we can say that the Oriental extracts much from a few words: when, for example, the Koran recalls that "the world beyond is better for you than this lower world" or that "earthly life is but a play" or affirms: "In your wives and your children ye have an enemy" or "Say: Allah! then leave them to their empty play," or, finally, when it promises Paradise to "him who has feared the station of his Lord and refused desire to his soul"—when the Koran speaks thus, there emerges for the Muslim—we do not say "for every Muslim"—a whole ascetic and mystical doctrine, as penetrating and complete as no matter what other form of spirituality worthy of the name.[3]

The question of the origin of Sufism is also important—hence the insistence on it here—because its efficacy depends on its origin. Ultimate Reality is the aim and the end of Sufism, and that Reality, being Absolute, is by definition altogether independent of the relative, and not subject to it in any way. One mode of being subject to something is to be accessible to it or attainable by it. The relative has, in itself, no means whatsoever of reaching the Absolute. In other words it would be in vain for man simply to decide, of himself, to approach Ultimate Reality with a view to attainment. The Absolute must first as it were hold out a hand, or throw out a life-line. It must offer a power from itself, for the means of approach, in order to prevail, must have something of the Absolute about it. It must be no less than a loan from the Absolute, and that loan is precisely what is meant by

[3] *Understanding Islam* (London: Allen & Unwin, 1976), pp. 59-60.

Revelation, whatever form it may take. The question may therefore be asked: If Sufism is non-Islamic yet effective, that is, endowed with a reintegrating power of ebb back to the Absolute, to what flow proceeding from the Absolute is that ebb a reaction, or in other words, on what Revelation does it depend? The answer should moreover be immediately and clearly forthcoming, for it is not conceivable that Providence should have acted surreptitiously in this matter. But if, as the Sufis have always maintained, Sufism results directly from the Islamic Revelation, there is no problem. And in fact what the Sufis *do* and have always *done* in order to approach the Ultimate incontestably derives from that Revelation just as the oral teaching they receive from their Shaykhs consists very largely of Koranic verses and sayings of the Prophet and comments on both.

Islam is the most recently established spirituality in the world. Its adherents have had correspondingly less time to dwindle in sensitivity to the tremendous impact of its Revelation, or to cause it to take on a "list" through over-emphasis of certain aspects at the expense of others, or to produce heresies from it—in a word, to diminish it; and what applies to the religion as a whole necessarily applies to the mysticism which is its heart. Moreover Sufism is something of a bridge between East and West, being more akin in many ways to Judaism and Christianity than Hinduism is, for example, not to speak of what lies further East.

It goes without saying however that the modern seeker is beset by dangers from those many groups of self-styled "Sufis" and others who, whatever their claims, have in fact nothing authentic to offer. And even an authentic order may prove not to correspond to the deepest aspirations of the seeker in question. It is generally said of the Sufis themselves that there are two kinds of orders. One of these is relatively "static," being under the direction of a Shaykh who has not in himself any mastership beyond such general guidance as he can transmit from the traditions of the order. The other is under a Shaykh who is a *murshid* ("spiritual guide"), one who has himself reached the end of the path and is capable of guiding others to the end if they are sufficiently qualified.

The difference between these two orders is factual but never "official," and the members of a "static" order are seldom conscious of not being *sālikūn* ("travelers"). Nor must the word "static" be taken in an absolute sense. But there are likely to be some seekers, if only a few, who are qualified for a *murshid* and who, without the guidance of a veritable master, could never do justice to their latent possibilities. What is the definition of the *murshid*, the *pīr*, the *guru*, in the fullest sense these terms can have?

This question is the theme of a chapter entitled "Nature and Function of the Spiritual Master" in Schuon's *Logic and Transcendence*.[4] Its opening passages are couched in Hindu terms,[5] but the truths it expresses are universal and apply just as much to the Sufi *murshid* as to the *guru*; and many of its illustrations are drawn from Sufism.

This domain is in fact spiritually too central for there to be any real divergence between the different traditional forms of mysticism. All are known to insist on the three conditions mentioned here as indispensable,[6] so that there is good reason to fear that if any one of the three is not fulfilled, the whole endeavor "can only end up as a psychological exploit without any relation to the development of our higher states." These conditions correspond to initiation, doctrine, and method. The first "results from the principle that it is impossible to approach the Absolute, or the Self, without the blessing and the aid of Heaven." The "blessing" in question is the sacrament of initiation which brings the recipient to a new "birth," for "the first condition of spirituality is to be virtually 'reborn.'" As regards the master, this first condition is extrinsic: unlike the others, it does not depend on his sanctity, but on his authority as duly mandated representative of a divinely instituted mystical tradition.

The master must also personify "a providential doctrine," that is, a doctrine which "depends on a Revelation in the direct and plenary sense." The essence of the doctrine is "truth which distinguishes

[4] Harper & Row, New York, 1974.

[5] This chapter was originally written for a volume presented to the Jagadguru Śrī Śaṅkarācārya Svāmigal of Kāñcī Kāmakōti Pītha in celebration of the 50th anniversary of his investiture.

[6] Apart from "very exceptional cases" of which Schuon gives some illuminating examples.

between the Real and the illusory." As an incarnation of this truth, the master is a living presence of discernment.

Finally he must be master of "the method which allows the initiated and consecrated contemplative to fix himself, at first mentally and later with the center of his being, on the Real."

It is clearly the first of these conditions which is the most frequently and easily fulfilled. The head of an authentic order which has become "static" is necessarily qualified to bestow initiation; but only a true *murshid* can be said to personify the doctrine of Ultimate Reality, and only he, as regards method, can enter into the Spiritual Path of his disciple to the point of enabling him "to fix himself . . . on the Real."

As to the seeker, the first condition presents no problems, since he can normally reassure himself, before taking any step, as to whether it has been fulfilled. He can also ascertain, to take the case of a Sufi brotherhood, whether it faithfully represents the Islamic mystical tradition as regards both doctrine and method. But there the criteria may be said to end, if by criteria we mean what can be made the object of an investigation in the ordinary sense of the word. It goes without saying that there is no infallible way for a would-be disciple to identify a true guide through purely mental processes. There is however a much repeated Sufi dictum—and its equivalent is to be found elsewhere[7]—that every aspirant (*murīd*) will find a true *murshid* if he deserves one. It is also said, again not only in Sufism, that in reality and despite appearances it is not the *murīd* who chooses the way but the way which chooses the *murīd*. In other words, since the *murshid* personifies the way, he has, mysteriously and providentially, an active function towards the *murīd* even before the master-disciple relationship is established by initiation. This helps to explain the following anecdote told by the Moroccan Shaykh al-ʿArabī ad-Darqāwī (d. 1823), one of the very greatest masters of Sufism in recent centuries. At the moment in question he was a younger man but already

[7] See Whitall Perry, *A Treasury of Traditional Wisdom* (London: Perennial Books, 1981), the section on "the Spiritual Master," pp. 288-295, for quotations from the mystics on this point and on others related to these paragraphs.

a representative of his own *murshid*, Shaykh ʿAlī al-Jamal, to whom he complained of having to go to a place where he feared there were no spiritual people. His Shaykh cut him short with the terse remark: "Beget the man you need." And later he reiterated plurally the same command: "Beget them!"[8] We have already seen that the initial step on the spiritual path is to be "reborn"; and all these considerations suggest that the seeker's "deserving" of a master must include a consciousness of "inexistence" or "emphasis," an anticipation of the spiritual poverty (*faqr*) from which the *faqīr* takes his name. The open door is an image of this state, and the Shaykh ad-Darqāwī mentions in general that one of the most powerful means of obtaining a solution to a spiritual problem is to hold open and beware of closing "the door of necessity."[9] It may thus be inferred that the "deserving" in question is to be measured by the degree of the acuteness of the *murīd*'s sense of the necessity for a *murshid*, and that it depends on whether his soul is sufficiently imperative, as a "vacuum," to precipitate the advent of what he needs. Nor is such passivity incompatible with the more active attitude enjoined in Christ's "Seek and ye shall find; knock and it shall be opened unto you," since the most powerful way of "knocking" is prayer,[10] and supplication is a display of emptiness and an avowal of neediness. In a word, not only the *murshid* but also the *murīd* has qualifications to fulfill.

Spiritual mastership means oneness with Ultimate Reality. In virtue of this the spiritual master may be said to be unsurpassed and unsurpassable. Yet although he personifies the Ultimate for his disciple, he is not its supreme manifestation in the universe. Schuon's chapter ends with the establishment of a hierarchy in which the spiritual master in the full and normal sense of the term occupies the lowest rank. Above him is the intermediary degree held by such persons as Christ's Apostles—Saint John, for example, and analogously by the

[8] *Letters of a Sufi Master* (London: Perennial Books, 1969), p. 19.

[9] Ibid., p. 11.

[10] This may be said to apply to every stage in the whole length of spiritual endeavor, and to prayer in all its degrees of inwardness—to petition, to litany, and to invocation.

Prophet's son-in-law ʿAlī; and finally there is the Divine Messenger himself, the founder of the religion.

It is also possible to consider a second intermediary degree:

> In comparing a Benedictine master—of the fifteenth century, for example—with Saint Benedict, and then comparing the latter with Saint John, we obtain a sufficiently clear picture of the principal degrees, not of spiritual mastership in itself, but of its manifestation in breadth, for it is important not to confuse an almost cosmic function with inward knowledge. . . . The less eminent does not necessarily represent a "lesser" as far as his inward reality is concerned. . . . It should not be too difficult to understand or to feel that, from the point of view of cosmic breadth, theurgic power, and the capacity to save, even a Shankara is not the equal of Krishna, and that from an analogous point of view no later master can be the equal of Shankara. . . . Nevertheless, every true master is altogether close, not only to the great instructors of "apostolic" rank but even to the founding *Avatāra.*

This brings us to another question. There is no difficulty in understanding that the end of the spiritual path is always one and the same, since it is no less than the One Absolute Infinite Eternal Truth. It is thus that the "inward reality" of the spiritual master, as regards the Ultimate, is unsurpassable. But how are we to understand the question of "cosmic breadth"?

Speaking with the voice of the Absolute, more than one great Sufi has declared himself to be without equal, and analogous claims are to be found in Hinduism and elsewhere. Some Western scholars have been thereby misled into supposing that the Sufis rank the Saints above the Prophets; and this opinion might in fact seem to be confirmed by the Koranic passage which tells of the strange and significant encounter between Moses and the mysterious al-Khiḍr,[11] who represent respectively exoterism and esoterism, or rather aspects of the one and the other. It is the Prophet here who implicitly recognizes the spiritual pre-eminence of the non-Prophet. But like the Sufi ejaculations, these verses from the *Sūrat al-Kahf* are something of a

[11] 18:60-82.

pitfall; for since the Prophet in question is also a Messenger, we are bound to conclude that the Koran is not portraying here the founder of Judaism in all his fullness, but has made as it were an abstract of the law-giving aspect of Moses to serve as a personification of exoterism; and as to the Sufi declarations, referred to above, these are made in virtue of their speakers' extinction in the Ultimate, and it is the incomparability of the Divine Self which they are affirming, not that of any particular Saint. Moreover, it was precisely one of the most explicitly self-affirming of the Saints who affirmed also, with regard to the founder of Islam: "If a single atom of the Prophet were to manifest itself to creation, naught that is beneath the Throne could endure it."[12] Similarly Ḥallāj, put to death for saying "I am the Truth," said of Muhammad that "he is the first in Union (with God)" and that "all sciences are as a drop from his ocean and all wisdoms as a sip from his river."[13] The Sufis certainly all agree with Ibn ʿArabī that although Sainthood is greater than Prophethood, the sainthood of a Prophet is greater than that of a non-Prophet. They are also unanimous in maintaining that among the Prophets it is the Divine Messengers (*rusūl*, pl. of *rasūl*) whose sainthood takes precedence. What constitutes this surpassing eminence—the highest greatness which can be said to "belong" to any differentiated being beneath the degree of the One Absolute Greatness of the Divinity? The inverted commas here are an admission that in reality all relative greatnesses are manifestations of the Absolute, but for which they would immediately vanish into nothing. But if the word "belong" had no point at all, then all Saints would be equal at every level, which is not the case. "And we have favored some of the Prophets above others, and unto David We gave the Psalms."[14]

On this phenomenon which, as we shall see, looms very large on the horizon of Sufism, Schuon throws further light in *Understanding*

[12] Abū Yazīd al-Bisṭāmī, quoted by Kalābādhī, *Taʿarruf*, chapter XXIV. See *The Doctrine of the Sufis* (Cambridge, UK: Cambridge University Press, 1935), p. 54.

[13] *Tā-Sīn as-Sirāj.*

[14] Koran, 17:55.

Islam. His concentrated chapter on the Prophet is more concerned with a particular example of cosmic greatness as compared with other examples than with what they all have in common, but he makes it convincingly clear that what Islam terms a *rasūl* ("Divine Messenger") is no less than what Hindus would consider to be a major *avatāra*; and he adds that from the Buddhist point of view neither Christ nor the Prophet could be assigned to any degree lower than that of a Buddha. The inverse of this is affirmed in his book on Buddhism; and it is here, in the chapter entitled "Mystery of the Bodhisattva," that he broaches the general question of "cosmic greatness" perhaps more directly than anywhere else:

> The Enlightenment which occurred in the lifetime of Śākyamuni beneath the Bodhi tree is none other than what in Western parlance would he called "Revelation," that is to say the reception of the Message or the assuming of the prophetic function. . . . Just as the soul descends suddenly on the embryo once it is sufficiently formed, so Enlightenment descends on the Bodhisattva who has acquired, side by side with his Knowledge and his *Nirvāṇa*, those specific cosmic perfections which the shining forth of a Revealer requires.[15]

Later, in speaking of this same perfection of the Bodhisattva which qualifies him to become Buddha, he refers to its "unimaginable cosmic development." In this context we may remember that the Koran mentions Jesus and his mother as being "a sign for the worlds." The Prophet of Islam is likewise sent as a Messenger "to the worlds"; and the Koran affirms of him: "Verily of an immense magnitude is thy nature."[16]

Let us dwell for a moment on the significance of the Sufi litanies of blessings upon the Prophet as the human norm. It has already been made clear—and the existence of great Saints who are not Messengers proves it—that a perfection of such cosmic proportions as is required for a Revealer must not be considered as a necessary milestone upon

[15] Frithjof Schuon, *In the Tracks of Buddhism* (London: Allen & Unwin, 1968), p. 139.

[16] 68:4.

the spiritual path, for the Ultimate can be reached from a less ample threshold. But though it would be both pointless and presumptuous to aspire to the extremity of existential amplitude as such, the imitation of the Messenger or of the *Avatāra* is always none the less a fundamental aspect of the way. Nor is it difficult to understand that it should be "alchemically" effective to imitate the inimitable and to set before oneself the vastest ideal of perfection, even while remaining conscious that its dimensions are unattainable. The Islamic Revelation has provided its mysticism with a remarkably lavish liturgical means of approaching this ideal. The perfection of the Messenger needs to be capacious above all as a receptacle of the glory of the blessings in which it is perpetually whelmed from every transcendent level. The Koran bids the believers join the celestial hierarchy in this act of glorification: "Verily God and His angels invoke blessings upon the Prophet. O ye who believe, invoke blessings upon him and greetings of peace."[17] And more than one canonical Tradition promises that such benedictions will be refracted ten-fold upon the invoker, who thus has a virtual share in the supreme aspect, that is, the receptive aspect, of the prophetic plenitude—virtual because, since the benedictions require a perfection for their object, they will have to be treasured as it were in suspense until the object is ready for them.

This fundamental practice of Sufism, rooted in a fundamental attitude, ranks only second to the invocation of the Divine Name. The practice and the attitude, which may be said to provide each other with mutual sustenance, have produced throughout the centuries a multitude of litanies in praise of the Messenger, some of them composed by Saints, and of great beauty.

The immense disparity between the human plenitude of the Messenger and other human perfections is merely a reduced image of the disparity it reflects from higher planes. The Koran says: "Behold how We have given precedence of favor unto some over others; and verily the Beyond is greater in degrees, and greater in hierarchic precedences."[18] But if the plenitude in question can never be acquired subjectively—except in that the path's Ultimate End, the Supreme

[17] 33:56.

[18] 17:21.

Self, may be said to include everything subjectively—it can none the less be acquired in a sense objectively: every religion promises, as one of the greatest blessings of Paradise, the presence there of these spiritual summits; and the sacred books give us to know that in the supra-formal freedom of the worlds of the Spirit, object and subject are not separated by the same barriers as they are in the rigid domain of forms.

The consideration of man's final ends brings us to our concluding question, and makes relevant a brief reference to the Koranic doctrine of the four Paradises. The *Sūrat ar-Raḥmān* (chapter 55) mentions these Paradises, not necessarily in an exclusive sense, but rather as affirming four main divisions in the hierarchy. According to a well-known Sufi commentary, often attributed to Ibn ʿArabī and published under his name, *Tafsīr ash-Shaykh al-Akbar*, though the author is almost certainly ʿAbd ar-Razzāq al-Qāshānī, these are, in ascending order, the Gardens of the Soul, of the Heart, of the Spirit, and of the Essence. The commentator differentiates between them[19] but he does not dwell on the starting point of this Koranic passage, which is the promise that every pious believer may expect for himself or herself not only one Paradise but two—that at least is the gist, though it is worded more elliptically. Let us consider this promise simply in relation to the two higher Paradises, for only here could the duality be in any sense a problem. The Garden of the Essence is no less than the Absolute and Infinite Oneness of God. From this point of view it might seem that all other Paradises cease to exist. How then can it be said that the supreme Saint, who is by definition in the highest Paradise, has "also" a second Paradise? This question can be parried with another: If it is possible for a supreme Saint to say, during his life on earth, in all sincerity of gnosis, "I am the Truth," why should it not be possible for such a statement to be made eventually, by the same Saint or by another, in the penultimate Paradise, the Garden of the Spirit?

This brings us once more to Schuon's *Islam and the Perennial Philosophy*, from which our second question is analogically borrowed.

[19] See Abū Bakr Sirāj ad-Dīn, *The Book of Certainty* (Cambridge, UK: Islamic Texts Society, 1992) which is partly based on this doctrine.

In its final chapter, "The Two Paradises," he reminds us "that there are in man two subjects—or two subjectivities—with no common measure and with opposite tendencies, even though there is also coincidence between them in a certain sense." The Divine and human natures of Jesus and their equivalent in Muhammad are ideal examples; and if it were not possible for the two subjectivities to co-exist, albeit at different levels of reality, in the next world, then the Prophets and the Messengers, once they had departed this life and been integrated into the Paradise of the Essence, would be altogether withdrawn from existence as differentiated persons, and the possibility of contact with them would be irretrievably lost. As Schuon says: "We should have to conclude that the *Avatāra* had totally disappeared from the cosmos, and this has never been admitted in traditional doctrine. Christ 'is God' but this in no way prevents him from saying: 'Today shalt thou be with me in Paradise,' or from predicting his own return at the end of the cycle."[20]

Schuon's chapter may be taken as a commentary not only on the above-mentioned Koranic verses but also on an utterance of the Prophet of Islam which immediately preceded, and in a sense heralded, his final illness: "I have been offered the keys of the treasuries of this world and immortality therein followed by Paradise, and I have been given the choice between that and the meeting with my Lord and Paradise." The man who was with him begged him to choose the former, but the Prophet said: "I have chosen the meeting with my Lord and Paradise."

The "meeting with my Lord" is the Garden of the Essence. The Paradise which accompanies it can be no less than that of the Spirit, and this is directly confirmed by the last words which the Prophet was heard to speak and which express a foretaste of his beatitude therein: "With the supreme communion in Paradise, 'with those upon whom God hath lavished His favor, the Prophets and the Saints and the Martyrs and the Righteous—most excellent for communion are they!'[21]"

The Sufi conception of our final ends certainly allows for the duality in question. Rābiʿa al-ʿAdawiyya's utterance of the adage "the

[20] Schuon, *Islam and the Perennial Philosophy*, p. 199.

[21] Koran, 4:69.

neighbor first, then the house" in the sense of "God before Paradise" is an echo—not necessarily a conscious one—of the Prophet's choice, and it likewise affirms not only a precedence but also a co-existence; and it may well be asked if there has ever been a Sufi who did not hope to see the Prophets in Paradise, despite such formulations—more methodical than doctrinal—as have misled some Western scholars into supposing that what the Sufis aim at as regards their individualities, is "blank infinite negation." Christ's "Seek ye first the Kingdom of Heaven, and all the rest shall be added unto you" expresses a universal principle which dominates every mysticism and which is often, as in Sufism, transposed to the highest possible level to mean, by "the Kingdom of Heaven," no less than the Garden of the Essence. If Sufi treatises tend to be silent about the second half, it is no doubt mainly because of the extreme urgency of the first half: but it is also because the mystic has absolutely no initiative with regard to "all the rest," as the very grammar of the wording makes clear. Silence is here a pious courtesy (*adab*) of trust (*tawakkul*) in Providence.

If it is true to say with Schuon that "the Absolute alone is absolutely real," which means that only the Garden of the Essence can be unreservedly termed Ultimate Reality, it is also true to say with him, of the three other gardens which together constitute Paradise in the ordinary sense of the word, "that Paradise, like the Prophet, is a theophany and that as such it cannot be spoken of as we speak of the created in respect of its non-divinity or separativity."

Let us also quote the parallel he offers us from Buddhism: "The idea of the 'heavenly homeland'—the 'Pure Land'—refers then to a certain mode of nirvanic or divine radiation and not to some 'creation' that is 'other than God'; the paradisal region appears as the emanation of the 'uncreated' Center."[22]

By way of conclusion, if a Sufi were asked "What is Ultimate Reality?", let us suppose that his answer, "the Divine Essence," calls forth the objection: "But I mean your Ultimate Reality." His answer to this might well be: "The beginning and the end of my subjectivity are in the very Self of the Divine Essence." And if it were still further

22 Schuon, *Islam and the Perennial Philosophy*, pp. 183-184.

objected: "But I mean you as distinct from anyone else," he could insist: "You cannot escape from the Divine Essence as answer, for Ultimate Reality is One. That which you ask of is there, among the immutable essences (*al-aʿyān ath-thābita*[23]) which are the supreme archetypes of all differentiation, mysteriously united in the Oneness of the Self." But a possible answer to the last question would be: "The Paradise of the Spirit." That is the summit of what is normally understood by Paradise; and though this answer is not so rigorously metaphysical as the first, it may none the less be also acceptable to Ultimate Reality Itself, which has ordained that Paradise shall be "not other" than the Ultimate.

[23] See Titus Burckhardt, *Introduction to Sufi Doctrine* (Wellingborough: Thorsons, 1976), part 2, chapter 3.

SUFISM IN MUSLIM SPAIN*

Angus Macnab

Spanish Sufism

The question of Islam's influence on Spain has often been discussed, but the question of Spain's influence on Islam is equally deserving of attention. The chief area in which a particularly Spanish contribution to Islam is to be found is that of Islamic mysticism, known as Sufism. There was a rich flowering of Sufism in Andalusia during the period of the Moors.

Mysticism or spirituality is generally regarded as the heart, or inward dimension, of a given religion, and as such it is often contrasted with the more formal or institutional side. This distinction is nowhere more pronounced than in Islam. Even the most casual observer can note the main elements of Islam's "outward" form, such as the five-times-daily prayer, the annual month of fasting, and the pilgrimage to Mecca. The "inward" side, on the other hand, is invisible by definition, but it nevertheless reveals itself in mystical treatises and mystical poetry, and above all in the lives of its saints.

Religions differ from one another in their precise disposition of these two realms. Islam possesses an exoteric domain—the *sharīʿa* or (outward) Law—which contains the basic elements necessary for salvation and is consequently incumbent upon all, and an esoteric domain—the *ḥaqīqa* or (inward) Truth or Reality—the aspiration to which is a matter of vocation. This latter domain—which comprises both doctrines and practices—is the affair of Sufism.

Christianity, from a certain Islamic point of view, is purely a *ḥaqīqa* or esoterism (a "mystery," in Christian terms), having come into the world without a complementary exoteric component. In the

* Editors' Note: This selection comes from two chapters of Macnab's excellent book *Spain Under the Crescent Moon* (Fons Vitae, 1999). These two chapters appear here in their entirety.

words of Christ: "My Kingdom is not of this world." In principle, Christianity (unlike Judaism and Islam), does not have a "Law": rather it is a matter of "worshiping God in spirit and in truth." Historically, however, merely in order to exist—and above all in view of the nature and needs of fallen man—this esoterism had, so to speak, to be made into a religion for all kinds and conditions of men (an exoterism), in an effort as it were to make good the exoteric element which was not part of the original revelation. It is important, however, to stress that this *de facto* application of the Christian revelation (in itself an esoterism or "mystery") to the communal or exoteric domain could not and did not in any way alter the original nature of the Christian dogmas and sacraments, which continued to be, *de jure* and in their essence, "esoteric" formulations and "initiatic" rites respectively.[1]

In practice, this essential difference between the Islamic and Christian spiritual economies means that, to the superficial Christian eye, exoteric Islam seems to have something of a "pharisaic" character—a reproach seen to be unjustified when one understands the providential purpose, and the salutary individual and communal effects, of a revealed "Law." Contrariwise, in Muslim eyes, Christianity seems to be a perpetual striving after a well-nigh unattainable "perfection"—something which it is unrealistic to demand of the majority of men, and which consequently leads to hypocrisy and so runs the risk of bringing religion into disrepute.

But there is also another important difference in principle between the two religions, and it is as follows: There are three fundamental degrees or levels of worship: "Fear of God," "Love of God," and "Knowledge of God." (The "Knowledge" referred to here is not ordinary mental knowledge, but "heart knowledge," which is not unrelated to the voice of conscience.)[2] All religions comprise the element "Fear": in the words of Solomon, "the Fear of God is the

[1] See "Mystères Christiques" by Frithjof Schuon in *Études Traditionnelles* (Paris), July-August 1948.

[2] The three Arabic terms are *makhāfa* ("Fear"), *maḥabba* ("Love"), and *maʿrifa* ("Heart Knowledge" or gnosis). These correspond to the three *mārgas* ("paths") of Hinduism: *karma* ("good works"), *bhakti* ("devotion"), and *jñāna* ("knowledge").

beginning of Wisdom." But from that starting-point, Christianity, as everyone knows, is pre-eminently the religion of Love. Islam, for its part (and not only Sufism, but also the general religion), comprises all three modes: "Fear," "Love," and "Knowledge." The presence of the last-mentioned element confers on Islam a certain "gnostic" or "jñanic" flavor—uncharacteristic of Christianity—which becomes particularly evident in "theosophic" Sufism.

The element "Knowledge" is by no means totally absent from Christianity, but it is unquestionably not the predominating mode. It appears in Meister Eckhart, Angelus Silesius, and others, but it is precisely this current in Christianity which is the first to fall under suspicion in the prevailing "bhaktic" climate.[3]

This, then, is the second great difference—and frequent source of incomprehension—between Christianity and Islam.

To return to the question of outward form and inward content—"letter" and "spirit", if one will—it has been said that exoterism may be compared to the circumference of a circle and esoterism to the circle's center. In this symbolism, the spiritual path is represented by the radius, which leads from the former to the latter. It follows that, since there are many radii, there are many spiritual paths.

To embark on a spiritual path (in Islam, *ṭarīqa*), a rite of initiation is necessary. Whereas in Islam, as in most religions, only some (i.e., those with a spiritual calling) receive this rite, in Christianity (which, as has already been explained, is an "esoterism" by definition) *all* adherents receive it, for Baptism (which is conferred on all) is in Christianity the rite of initiation. This is a particularly striking example of what is meant by the "exoteric application" of a rite which in itself carries an esoteric grace—a grace which in fact will never be fully exploited by the vast majority of those receiving it. This is indeed "folly to the Greeks," since it is a state of affairs—a "scandal"!—virtually unheard of elsewhere.

In view of the fact that a rite of initiation is indispensable for making a beginning on the spiritual path, the latter is sometimes referred to as the "initiatic" path.

[3] This in spite of Christ's words: "I am the Light of the world" (John 8:12) and "Ye shall know the Truth and the Truth shall make you free" (John 8:32).

In Islam, members of a *ṭarīqa* (a "spiritual path," and also a "spiritual brotherhood") are called Sufis, a word which derives from *ṣūf* ("wool")—a reference to the woolen robe worn by the earliest Sufis. Strictly speaking the term should apply only to those who have attained the goal, but in practice it is applied, not only to spiritual masters, but also to their initiated disciples. Upon initiation, an aspirant attaches himself to a *shaykh*, more or less in the same way as a Hindu devotee attaches himself to a *guru*.

Spain was for many centuries a nursery of Sufism, and the Islamic tradition is indebted to her for some of the greatest of the Muslim saints. One of the earliest Spanish Sufis about whom something is known—the founder of a school which still flourishes in the Islamic world today, and which produced one of the most renowned sages of all time—was Ibn Masarrā. He was born in Córdoba in 883 and died in his mountain hermitage there in 932, at the age of only forty-eight. In his lifetime he escaped the suspicion of heresy, and was favored by the great Caliph ʿAbd ar-Raḥmān III. Persecutions, exiles, and the burning of his books came later, under less enlightened rulers such as Almanzor (al-Manṣūr), but his school and his teaching survived. Its last representative in Spain was Ibn ʿAbbād of Ronda, who died in 1389 and whose sermons were still being read before the Sultan of Morocco in the seventeenth century. Ibn ʿAbbād has been described by the Spanish Arabist Asín Palacios (himself a Catholic priest) as a veritable precursor of St. John of the Cross; many of his teachings and sayings are almost word for word the same. This of course does not mean that St. John of the Cross copied him, or even necessarily knew of his existence; it merely illustrates the similarity of the language and conceptions of whoever follows the way of divine Love, whatever the denomination of the lover may be. Consequently, if one took a passage from, say, St. Bonaventure's *Incendium Amoris*, from Raymond Lull's *Book of the Lover and the Beloved*, from a treatise by a Sufi follower of the way of *maḥabba*, or, for that matter, from the writings of a Hindu practitioner of *bhakti*, one would find oneself, not only in the same devotional, but also in the same literary and stylistic climate.

Of all the spiritual posterity of Ibn Masarrā in Spain, the most illustrious was undoubtedly Muḥyi ʾd-Dīn ibn ʿArabī, who was born at Murcia in 1165 and died in Damascus in 1240. In spiritual circles throughout the Islamic world he is known as *ash-shaykh al-akbar*, "the greatest of spiritual masters," and his tomb at Damascus is a major place of pilgrimage. He was a prolific writer, and his metaphysical and "theosophical"[4] treatises are widely read and intensively studied to this day. We shall return to him in our next chapter.

Ibn Masarrā's doctrine had a cosmological starting point. The creation of the world is explained as a series of "emanations" from God, which constitute the multiple "levels" of reality, themselves manifestations of the Supreme Reality which Itself remains transcendent and unmanifested. The symbolical form in which this cosmogony is presented is attributed by Ibn Masarrā to the Greek philosopher Empedocles, a fifth century follower of the Pythagorean School. Other elements in his teaching appear to derive from the Neoplatonists and the Gnostics, and also from an earlier Sufi called Dhū'n-Nūn the Egyptian, who himself claimed to transmit the doctrines of Hermes Trismegistos (known to the ancient Egyptians as T-huti or Thoth)—in other words Hermeticism, a philosophy well-known to the medieval Christian schools of Western Europe.

(This profound understanding of Greek "emanationism" by certain gnostic or theosophic Sufis was in no sense to the detriment of their acceptance—and understanding—of the Semitic "creationism" of the general Islamic religion.)

In all of this, we do not attribute prime importance to the theory of "borrowing," as spiritual pioneers scouting out the same territory have the same landmarks to describe, whether they use their own or someone else's terminology. In our eyes, Ibn Masarrā and the other Spanish Sufis were simply expressing, in the forms most appropriate to their perspective and their religion, that "wisdom uncreate" (as St. Augustine called it), which is most commonly known as the *philosophia perennis*, and which reappears, in different clothing but in essence the same, in the Far East, among the Hindus, in ancient Ireland and Gaul, among the early Christian hermits of the Egyptian desert, and also in North America, in the form of the Religion of the Sun Dance and the Sacred Pipe. This is the wisdom which the Bible describes in

[4] We use this term in its etymological (and not sectarian) sense, that is to say, in the sense in which it is applied to Jakob Böhme.

the words: "From the beginning and before the world, was I created, and unto the world to come I shall not cease to be."[5]

Sultans and Sufis

Although the Saracen and Moorish emirs were "despotic," like all traditional rulers, it would be erroneous to suppose that freedom was non-existent in their domains. The idea that no government can provide any freedom of speech or action, unless it has been voted into power at an "election"—or unless there is a "free press"!—is unique to the twentieth century, and is a notion which nothing in history, either ancient or modern, can confirm.

Not only the legitimate Muslim rulers of Spain, but even many of the usurpers, tolerated liberties of which some modern "democratic" states would be quite unable to conceive. The reason is that the secular power did not claim omnipotence; above all men stood God and His Law. The following story is closely reminiscent of certain Biblical episodes in which kings like Saul or David meekly submit to the stern rebukes of a Samuel or a Nathan. It concerns a twelfth-century sultan and a celebrated Sufi shaykh called Abū Muḥammad ʿAbdullah al-Qaṭṭān, and is taken from "The Epistle on Sanctity" (*Risālat al-Quds*) by Muḥyi ʾd-Dīn ibn ʿArabī of Murcia.[6]

> All the revelations that God imparted to him, he received through the Koran. Spurred on by his zeal for the observance of God's law, he would openly and courageously condemn any prevarication he

[5] Ecclesiasticus 24:14. See also: Ecclesiasticus 1:1 and Proverbs 8:22 ff. The first and last of these passages are used in the Catholic liturgical offices of the Blessed Virgin Mary, who is herself a manifestation of the *sancta sophia* and who in her cosmic aspect has a role analogous to the "Preserved Tablet" (*al-lauḥ al-maḥfūẓ*) of Islamic esoterism.

[6] I have translated this passage from Asín Palacios' Spanish translation *Vidas de Santones andaluces* (Madrid, 1939). For an excellent English translation of the *Risālat al-Quds*, see Ralph Austin's *Sufis of Andalusia* (London: Allen & Unwin, 1971). This book, like few others, provides a fascinating insight into medieval Sufism in its Spanish setting.

knew of, regardless of censure from anyone. He dared to contradict sultans, and to rebuke them unceremoniously to their faces, and on these occasions he showed such ardent zeal that he would openly accuse anyone he thought guilty of injustice or sin, and he did so without restraint, though he knew that his invective might cost him dearly. On many occasions he had violent disputes with sultans in order to denounce them for their infringements of the divine law; but an account of all these cases in detail would take up more time than we can afford.

In his explanations he used no authorities but texts from the Koran, and he regarded no other book as worthy of study, nor did he ever possess any other. At a gathering in Córdoba, I once heard him say: "Alas for the writers of books! What a long account they will have to render on the coming day! The Book of God and the sayings (*aḥādīth*) of His Messenger are enough."

He watched over his disciples and observed them carefully. He never cared to enjoy the comforts of life, and never possessed two silver coins at one time.

The sultan once gave orders to fetch him, to be condemned to death, and the sultan's minions arrested him and brought him before the vizier, who made him sit down. ʿAbdullah then upbraided him as follows: "O tyrant, O enemy of God and of thine own soul! Why hast thou sent for me?" The vizier replied: "God has now placed thee in my hands, and I assure thee that thou shalt not live one day longer, after today." The shaykh told him: "Thou canst not hasten the time of my death, nor postpone the decree of God either. No such thing will come to pass, despite thy claims. I, on the contrary, swear by God that I shall attend thy funeral."

The vizier said to his henchmen: "Put him in prison until I consult with the sultan as to his death." That night they put him in prison, and as he went in he said: "This is nothing strange for the man of faith, for the believer knows that as long as he lives here below he is always in a prison. This dungeon, then, is merely one of the rooms of that prison which is the world."

Next day the vizier told the sultan of the shaykh and his words. The sultan had him brought in, and when he saw him he thought him a contemptible man, of whom no notice need be taken. That was what all worldly persons thought: none liked him, because he told them all the truth and showed up their vices and injustices. After asking his name and lineage, the sultan said: "Knowest thou, perchance, the creed of thy religion?" The master's sole reply was to start quoting passages from the Koran, with an analysis of their contents. The sultan marveled at this, and began to unbend, and they conversed on various topics, until the talk came round to the political administration of the kingdoms and its importance. Then he asked: "And what sayest thou about this kingdom of mine?" The shaykh's only answer was to burst out laughing.

"What art thou laughing at?" said the sultan. "At thee," said the master, "and at thy calling this folly in which thou livest a kingdom, and at people's calling thee thyself a king, whereas in reality thou art like him of whom God says: 'Behind them comes a king who steals all their ships' (Koran, 18:79). The true king is he alone who bakes his daily bread on his own fire, or earns it by himself. But thou art only a poor man whose bread is kneaded by others and then they tell thee, 'Go on, eat it up!'"

And so he went on heaping every kind of invective on the sultan, expressed in the harshest terms, and this in the presence of the royal council of ministers and doctors of the law. Yet the sultan was silent, dumb with confusion and shame.

Then he said: "This is a man whom God aids with his grace." He turned to the shaykh and added: "Abū ʿAbdullah, from today shalt thou attend our council!"

"Certainly not," replied the shaykh. "This chamber in which thou holdest thy council is the fruit of robbery, and thy palace thou didst seize unrightfully. Had I not been deprived of my freedom by force, I would never have entered this place. God preserve me from associating with thee and with persons like thee!"

The sultan then pardoned him and commanded that he be given a present. The shaykh refused the present, but accepted his release. So he left the palace, but the sultan ordered the present to be sent to his relatives. Not long afterwards, the vizier died. The shaykh went out to attend the funeral, and said to himself, "My oath was true!"

I was with this spiritual master as his disciple and he loved me much. Once I invited him to spend the evening in our house, and when he had already begun his discourse, my father (may God have pardoned him!) made his appearance; he was one of the sultan's courtiers. As soon as he entered, he saluted him. My father had a few grey hairs by that time. We recited the evening prayer, and then I offered supper to the shaykh and sat down with him to eat.

> My father joined us, with the intention of sharing in the spiritual merits of my master, but he turned to my father and exclaimed: "O unhappy old man! How canst thou not feel shame before God? How long wilt thou live in the company of tyrants? What effrontery thou hast! Thou livest as calmly as if thou wert certain that death will not come upon thee in that state of wickedness thou livest in! Yet hast thou not in this son [pointing to me] a living example that can serve as a moral exhortation to thee? Young as he is, with his bodily appetites in full bloom, he has already tamed them, has overcome the temptations of the devil, has been converted to God and seeks the company of the servants of God. But thou, old man, standest on the brink of an abyss!" My father wept and confessed his guilt, while I witnessed the scene dumbfounded.
>
> Many more are the deeds of this shaykh that I could relate. One day I heard him say: "How I marvel to see that some people seek a horse to ride, without first hastening to thank God for the food He gives them to eat and the clothing He gives them to wear." For his own part, he never used more food or clothing than was strictly necessary. Against the proud, he was terrible. He never failed to take part in the military campaigns against the Christians, and always as a foot soldier, without taking any provisions with him.

The last sentence in the above narrative may come as a surprise, particularly since the point of view adopted throughout this book is that of the *philosophia perennis.*

Saints, by definition, "break the shell to reach the kernel" (transcend the form to reach the essence); but the least that can be said is that this operation has many degrees and modes. All saints accomplish it to a certain extent and in a certain fashion. Many, even, are aware of the "relativity" of the forms of their own religion; but few indeed are those (outside the realm of *maʿrifa, jñāna,* or gnosis) who can recognize the validity of a *foreign* religious form. (Paradoxically the "philosophers" [i.e., *traditional*—Platonic or Arab—philosophers] can do so more readily than the "mystics.")

At the very moment that the formidable Abū Muḥammad ʿAbdullah al-Qaṭṭān was fulminating in Andalusia (and participating in battles against Christian forces), St. Bernard of Clairvaux was preaching the second crusade (which, by sheer strength of character, he brought about almost single-handedly). Nevertheless Providence ordained that Andalusia was to be reconquered by the Christians and that Jerusalem was to be held by the Muslims. "Nor all their piety nor wit" could cancel out the mysterious decrees of God Himself.

Outside the realm of "gnosis," these battles (crusades or "holy wars"), though much to be regretted, still have their symbolic significance and very real spiritual utility. Returning from a victory on the battlefield, the Prophet Muhammad said: "We are returning from the *lesser* holy war (against our outward enemies) to the *greater* holy war (against the enemy within ourselves)."

The "Way of Knowledge" (gnosis, *jñāna*, or *maʿrifa*) can dispense with the "lesser holy war." The "Way of Love" (*bhakti* or *maḥabba*) cannot. This does not mean that devotees or lovers have to go around fighting people. It means that they require an outward support for their inward spiritual endeavor.[7]

A very different case is that of Muḥyi ʾd-Dīn ibn ʿArabī. All Muslims venerate Jesus and Mary (these prophets are part of their religion), but Ibn ʿArabī's reverence for Jesus ran particularly deep. He called Jesus the "Seal of Sanctity" (*khatam al-wilāya*) and in his book "The Meccan Revelations" (*al-Futūḥāt al-Makkīyya*) [2, 64-65] he refers to him thus:

> The Seal of universal holiness, above which there is no other holy, is Our Lord Jesus (*Sayyidnā ʿĪsā*). We have met several contemplatives of the Heart of Jesus. . . . I myself have been united to him several times in my ecstasies, and by his ministry I returned to God at my conversion. . . . He has given me the name of friend and has prescribed austerity and nakedness of spirit.

But it was precisely with regard to the "universality" of all religious forms that Ibn ʿArabī wrote his most oft-quoted words:

[7] An example of this is the Christian military-monastic orders, such as Calatrava and Santiago, which participated in the reconquest of Spain; on this subject, see the evocative play *The Master of Santiago* by Henry de Montherlant. These Spanish military-monastic orders owed much to the prototype of the Muslim *al-murābiṭūn* (literally "the men of the *ribāṭ*," *ribāṭ* being a "castle" or "abode"). The name *al-murābiṭūn* became the name of a dynasty, and passed into Spanish as "Almorávids."

> My heart has opened unto every form: it is a pasture for gazelles, a cloister for Christian monks, a temple for idols, the Kaʿba of the pilgrim, the tablets of the Torah, and the book of the Koran.
>
> I practice the religion of Love; in whatsoever directions its caravans advance, the religion of Love shall be my religion and my faith.[8]

But to write such things as these, and for them to be sincere, the sage must have transcended forms himself. The perfect *ṣūfī* (or the *yogi* who has "realized *Brahman*"), needs forms no longer; he is no longer the mere individual, he has passed beyond individuality and transcended oppositions; he has reached the center of the "cosmic wheel," the "Invariable Middle" (*Ching-Ying*) of Taoism, the "Great Peace" (*as-Sakīna*) of Sufism, the *Pax Profunda* of the ancient Rose-Croix. But if that sage has reached the ultimate goal by one path or another, it follows that those separate paths were established by God for the members of this religion or that, and it is both a sin and worse than useless, to mix or confound the paths. Thus we see Ibn ʿArabī himself, in 1212, writing to the Sultan al-Ghālib bi-Amri ʾLlāh (also known as Kay-Kāʾūs [Caicaus I]), king of northern Asia Minor, urging him to maintain certain restrictions against the Christian communities in his realm, lest otherwise Islam be corrupted. Another wise Caliph speaks of "the pure and holy law of the Christians" and states that if he himself had been born a pagan, he would certainly become a Christian; yet this Caliph never dreamed of repealing the laws which kept the two communities distinct. Naturally the Christian rulers took just as stringent precautions to ensure that their sacred heritage, firstly as a divinely-given form and subsequently as a communal institution, should not suffer any "formal" erosion.

[8] Regarding Ibn ʿArabī's use of the expression "the religion of Love," Frithjof Schuon comments as follows: "Here it is not a question of *maḥabba* in the psychological or methodological sense, but of a truth that is lived [not merely theoretical], and of divine 'attraction.' Here 'love' is opposed to 'forms,' which are envisaged as 'cold' and 'dead.' St. Paul also says that 'the letter killeth, but the spirit maketh alive.' 'Spirit' and 'love' are here synonymous" (*Understanding Islam* [Bloomington, Indiana: World Wisdom Books, 1994]).

The modalities of this principle vary slightly in the case of the Aryan religions (such as Hinduism and Buddhism), and the Shamanistic religions (such as Confucianism, Taoism, Shinto, and the Red Indian religion), but even in these cases the principle remains the same.*

That the conduct of Abū Muḥammad ʿAbdullah al-Qaṭṭān towards the sultan was not altogether exceptional, is shown by an episode related by Ibn ʿArabī concerning his own uncle, related in his enormous work "The Meccan Revelations" (*al-Futūḥāt al-Makkīya*), 2, 23:

> One of my maternal uncles, called Yaḥya ibn Yogan, was king in the city of Tlemsen [near Oran]. In his time there lived retired from the world a lawyer and ascetic, named ʿAbdullah the Tunisian, who was famed as the most devout of his century. He dwelt in a village on the outskirts of Tlemsen called al-Obad, and spent his life in isolation from other men and dedicated to the service of God in the mosque. While this holy man was walking through the city of Tlemsen one day, he met my uncle the king, surrounded by his suite and guard. Someone told my uncle that the man was Abū ʿAbdullah the Tunisian, the most famous ascetic of his time. The king then drew rein and stopped, and greeted the holy man, who returned the greeting. The king, who was wearing magnificent attire, asked him: "O shaykh, will it be lawful for me to perform the ritual prayer while dressed thus?" Instead of answering the shaykh started to laugh. "What art thou laughing at?" inquired the king. "At the dimness of thine understanding," he replied, "at the ignorance thou livest in regarding the state of thy soul. In my judgment, there is nothing so like thee as the dog: it wallows amid the blood of rotting carcasses

* Editors' Note: This passage makes reference to the nature of shamanistic traditions, which are very different from the Semitic religions. The shamanistic traditions do not have the character of rigid "denominations." This allows many Chinese to be, for example, both Confucian and Taoist, or many Japanese to be both Shintoist and Buddhist, or many Red Indians to practice both Christianity and the Religion of the Sun Dance and Sacred Pipe. There is, in general, no similar mixing of Buddhist and Hindu practice; however, the case of Balinese religion remains an exception, probably because of the catalyst of an even more ancient shamanism that pre-dated the coming of the Aryan religions.

and eats them, despite their filthiness; yet later, when it goes to urinate, it lifts its leg so as not to soil itself. Thou art a vessel filled with uncleanness, thou art responsible for the injustices done to thy subjects, yet thou enquirest about thy dress."

The king burst into tears, dismounted from his horse, and then and there abdicated his throne and dedicated himself to the life of devotion in the shaykh's service. The shaykh kept him at his side for three days, and after that he took a cord and told him: "O king, the three days of hospitality are over: get up and go and cut wood." The king cut it, stacked it on his head and went into Tlemsen to sell it. People looked at him with tears in their eyes. He would sell the wood, keep such money as he needed for his maintenance, and give away the rest in charity. He did this for the rest of his life. When he died, he was buried in the outer part of his spiritual master's tomb. His burial place is much visited today. The shaykh, when people used to go and ask him to pray to God for them, would say: "Pray for what you want through the intercession of Yaḥya ibn Yogan, for he was a king and he renounced the world."

"WALKING UPON THE PATH OF GOD LIKE MEN"?
Women and the Feminine in the Islamic Mystical Tradition

Maria Massi Dakake

In recent years, numerous books have been published that attempt to correct the decidedly negative Orientalist view of the role of women in Islamic society. These works have made a point of stressing the essential spiritual equality and dignity that Islam gives to women, as well as the special importance many Islamic women had in the life of the Prophet Muhammad and the early establishment of the Islamic community. More specifically, within the last decade a number of works have been published which reveal the exceptionally strong presence of the feminine element in one of the most important aspects of Islamic civilization—the Islamic mystical tradition, or Sufism. In 1992, Sachiko Murata published *The Tao of Islam*, a masterful and thoroughly unique work which brought to light the feminine elements present in the Islamic mystical tradition (particularly in the works of Ibn ʿArabī) and analyzed them with reference to the mystical symbolism of the Taoist tradition. More recently, the renowned scholar of Islam, Annemarie Schimmel, published a small volume dealing with several aspects of women in Islamic tradition, which contains a considerable amount of material related to Sufism (*My Soul Is Woman*). Perhaps the most significant contribution to the study of this issue was Rkia Cornell's discovery of a manuscript containing the Sufi biographer, as-Sulamī's section on female Sufi devotees—previously considered to have been lost. She published an edited version and translation of the text in 1999 as *Early Sufi Women*. The present article, which attempts an analysis of the role of the feminine in the Sufi tradition, is deeply indebted to their scholarship.

There are two aspects to the presence of the feminine in the Sufi tradition that will be addressed in the present work. First, there is the metaphysical aspect—that is, the role that the feminine principle plays in symbolic and mystical interpretations of the nature of God and the world. The second aspect of the role of the feminine in the Sufi tradition has to do with the historical role that female practitioners of the mystical path have played in the development and history of Sufism. While allowed only limited participation in most other public activities, many women found the Sufi path to be a realm in which their participation and even original contributions were eventually validated, if not always immediately accepted.

These two aspects—the metaphysical and the practical—tend to be mentioned together in many cursory treatments of the subject of women and Sufism, as if they were part and parcel of the same basic phenomenon—namely a female presence of some sort in the Islamic mystical tradition. But I would like to make the point that these two things do not necessarily go hand in hand—that is, a more feminine, mystical view of God does not always entail an active role for human females in the worldly institution of a mystical tradition. What I want to do in this article, then, is first to distinguish these two aspects from one another, and secondly to show the relationship between the two as expressed in the particular formulations of Sufi truths attributed to women.

Metaphysical Symbolism of the Feminine

In Sufi symbolism, and indeed in Islam itself, man (and here I mean human beings in general) is surrounded by the feminine in his own existence. It is through the Divine *raḥma*, "Mercy, Compassion," that the world is made manifest—through the "breath of the Compassionate" (*nafas ar-Raḥmān*) all things come into being—and God's Mercy is said to "encompass all things." The word for mercy, *raḥma*, is grammatically feminine, and is etymologically related to the word *raḥam*, meaning "womb." God's Compassion and Mercy can thus be said to encompass and nurture everything in existence, just as the womb initially encompasses, nourishes, and protects every human being. Thus the mercy of existence itself is symbolized as a kind of "Divine womb" which embraces and sustains all being. While the experience of "being in the womb" is common to all humanity—male and female alike—the "womb" itself is, of course, a specifically feminine concept. Man's relation to the Divine perceived in this way is the relationship of the child to the mother, and so it is a relationship universally understood among human beings—male and female—while it is also one in which the Divine is considered from the feminine aspect of maternity.

If men, like all created beings, are surrounded by the feminine element of Divine Mercy, they are also from another perspective situated between two poles of femininity. For all men potentially, and for the Sufi mystic in particular, life is a constant struggle to overcome, conquer, and detach oneself from the *nafs*, that is, the "ego" or "soul" or "passionate self," on the one hand, and on the other, to draw ever nearer to the Divine, striving ultimately for knowledge of, or union with, the Divine Essence or *Dhāt*. Both the *nafs*, which man must dominate and subdue on the path to spiritual realization, and the Divine Essence, or *Dhāt*, to which man must strive to move ever closer, are grammatically feminine in the Arabic language and are designated by the feminine pronoun. The feminine aspect of these two "poles" of man's spiritual journey has been the source of richly symbolic mystical interpretation and poetic imagery.

The Sufi conquering his *nafs* (specifically here the *nafs al-ammārah bi'l-su'*, or the "soul that commands to evil") is often portrayed as man dominating and subjugating the "feminine" within himself, usually understood to mean his spiritual weakness, or his weakness for women and attachments in this world (and the world, in this negative sense, is referred to in Arabic as *dunyā*, also grammatically feminine). For a proper marital life, in traditional Islamic terms, the husband must rule over his wife ("Men are in charge of women") and the woman must submit to her husband's rational demands. When the roles are reversed, according to traditional interpretations, chaos ensues. Similarly, the Sufis made it clear that a proper spiritual life requires that the spirit or intellect (*'aql* or *rūḥ*—grammatically masculine terms) rule over the passions of the *nafs* or soul. Thus considered from this perspective, the feminine represents that which is deficient in man—his weakness and his desire for the world—with the world itself being symbolized as a feminine temptress.

At the same time, the hidden and eternally unmanifest Essence of God, the God Beyond-Being, the *Dhāt*, is also symbolically feminine. If the *nafs* may kindle man's baser desires, the *Dhāt*, or Essence, standing at the opposite end of the Sufi's mystical path, is on the contrary the source of his greatest and most ennobling desire. In the first relationship, the Sufi strives to dominate the *nafs*; while in his relationship with the Divine Essence, the Sufi must inculcate and then surrender himself to the desire for the Essence, and allow himself to be attracted by Its hidden beauties. That is, he must allow the Essence to dominate his every earthly desire and he must actively seek to be an increasingly perfect and worthy suitor for Its sublime beauty. The *nafs* attracts men to the world with a false and fleeting, if manifest, beauty; while the *Dhāt* attracts with Its perfect, eternal, and infinitely unmanifest beauty. If the *nafs*, like a prostitute, is bold and quick to reveal the ugliness that lies below her gilded surface, the *Dhāt* is silent and still, like a chaste woman, only revealing a glimpse of Its beauty to those who are patient and worthy. If the *nafs* hides its ugliness behind the veil of deceit, the *Dhāt* preserves its sacredness behind an existential veil.

The symbolism of the veil, in this regard then, is also crucial. Veiling is a potent symbol in Islamic culture. While both men and women are supposed to dress modestly and cover their private parts (*ʿawra*, lit., shame), the veil is particularly associated with women, who traditionally covered even their faces—that is, their very identities. Insofar as the veil is associated with women or the feminine, it also has a dual nature, for one veils both that which is shameful and that which is sublime—that which is too vile to show to strangers and that which is too beautiful to expose to them. The Divine Essence in Islamic mysticism is always portrayed as a veiled reality, chastely refusing to reveal "Her" beauty except in fleeting glimpses, and then only to the truly deserving. The *nafs*, on the other hand, veils itself only for deceit, and in fact, is often portrayed as the veil itself. It is man's passions and attachments to the world—or the world itself—which is the veil that covers the eyes of the intellect and prevents it from seeing Ultimate Truth. It may even be said that the veil covering the Essence in reality does not cover the Essence, but rather covers the eyes that strive to see It.

Given that both the passionate soul and the Divine Essence are connected with the feminine, human women could serve as symbols of both that which is lowest in man and that which is most sublime in God. In one passage from that most famous of all Sufi poets, Jalāl ad-Dīn Rūmī, we read:

> Know that your ego is indeed a woman—it is worse than a woman,
> for the woman is a part of evil, your ego the whole.[1]

Elsewhere:

> Woman is she whose way and goal are color and scent: She is the reality of the ego that commands to evil embodied in the physical constitution of humankind.[2]

But Rūmī also alludes to woman as a means of contemplating the Divine when he tells us that in the "coquetry and subtle movements" of women, man may recognize "God's theophany behind a gossamer veil."[3] He also tells us that the Prophet once said that women "totally dominate men of intellect" and only "ignorant men dominate women, for they are shackled by the ferocity of animals. They have no kindness, gentleness, or love, since animality dominates their nature. . . . She (meaning woman) is the radiance of God, she is not your beloved. She is the Creator—you could say that she is not created."[4] Thus from Rūmī's perspective, woman could symbolize, on one level, the more negative qualities of humankind, and on another level she could be seen as the "radiance of God," even as the "Creator"—perhaps alluding to the creative nature of the Divine *raḥma.*

The polarity between the two "feminines" is also manifest in other, related symbolic interpretations. For example, Ibn ʿArabī gives a mystical commentary on the Quranic verse: "We have created thee from a single soul, and from it We have created its mate."[5] Ibn ʿArabī

[1] William Chittick, *The Sufi Path of Love: The Spiritual Teachings of Rumi* (Albany: SUNY Press, 1983), p. 165.

[2] Ibid., p. 165.

[3] Ibid., p. 287.

[4] Ibid., p. 169.

[5] Quran, 4:1.

tells us that the meaning of this verse is that man stands between the perfect, "single soul" (grammatically feminine) from which he was created, and the woman, his mate, created from himself.[6] (Ibn ʿArabī reads this verse as alluding to the idea that Eve was created from Adam, an idea that is not found explicitly in the Quran, but which is found in Islamic *ḥadīth* and commentary on the Quran). Ibn ʿArabī also gives a long exposition on the famous Prophetic *ḥadīth* in which the Prophet said that three things had been made lovable to him—women, perfume, and prayer. Both the word "women" and the word "prayer" are grammatically feminine with the intermediate perfume being grammatically masculine, and so again we have the symbolic masculine situated between the two symbolic feminines of women and prayer. He explains why in this *ḥadīth* the Prophet begins with woman and ends with ritual prayer:

> The reason for this is that woman is a part of the man in the root of the manifestation of her entity. A human being's knowledge of his soul is prior to the knowledge of his Lord, since his knowledge of his Lord is the result of his knowledge of his soul. That is why the Prophet said: "He who knows his soul, knows his Lord."[7]

In this particular exposition, woman is again connected with the idea of the soul—but far from being the veil that veils the face of God, the soul is here the primary means of knowing God. Indeed, for Ibn ʿArabī, woman is the created being who offers the most perfect vehicle for the contemplation of the Divine—since man, in considering his physical power over woman, realizes the power of the Divine over all men; and in realizing her attracting power over him, he realizes the saving power of attraction in the Divine Itself.[8] It should also be noted that for Ibn ʿArabī, perhaps more so than for any other major Sufi thinker, women figure positively and prominently in both

[6] Sachiko Murata, *The Tao of Islam: A Sourcebook on Gender Relationships in Islamic Thought* (Albany: SUNY Press, 1992), p. 197.

[7] Ibid., p. 189.

[8] Ibid., p. 192.

his metaphysical expositions and his practical spiritual life—having himself been profoundly influenced by his female Sufi masters and companions, and having initiated a number of female disciples.[9]

One could go on and on, finding numerous ways and instances in which the idea of the dual nature of the feminine and of the *nafs-Dhāt* polarity is poetically and metaphorically expressed throughout Sufi writings. I have only had time to give a few examples of these ideas in Sufi literature, but they should suffice to make clear the powerful symbolism of the feminine in Sufi thought.

Woman as Symbol, Woman as *Sālik*

The symbolism of the feminine polarity I have just described in Islamic mysticism derives its power, in no small part, from the presumption that it is a man, a masculine being, who is torn between these two poles, seeking always to journey from one to the other. Man's authority over woman in traditional Islamic society serves as a symbol for the domination of the masculine intellect over the female passions; while his desire for woman on a physical and emotional level serves as a symbol of his yearning for his spiritual Beloved. But the question arises, what does this symbolism mean for a female mystic, for the female *sālik* or "traveler" journeying from her own soul to her Divine Beloved? How can she relate to this symbolism and what can it possibly mean for her?

A simple resolution of this issue might be to reverse the symbolic structure and say that if for man, his authority over the feminine symbolizes his dominance over his ego, then for a woman, her obedience to the masculine symbolizes or becomes a reflection of her ego's obedience to the intellect or the spirit. Logically, of course, this makes sense, but the power and dynamism of the original symbol does not carry into its adaptation. In this reversal of the symbolism, the female mystic is identified more directly with the ego, and only indirectly with the intellect that actively seeks to subdue the ego and attach itself to the Divine. Thus the idea of the *sālik*, as the middle element of intellect between two feminine polarities, actively moving

[9] See, e.g., Annemarie Schimmel, *My Soul Is Woman* (New York: Continuum, 1999), pp. 45-46.

between the two, is compromised. One female mystic, Umm Talq, gave her own "masculine" interpretation of the passionate soul or ego, saying that "the lower soul is a king (*mālik*) if you indulge it, but a slave (*mamlūk*) if you torment it."[10] This succeeds on one level, but does not convey the powerful male-female polarity of the original symbolism.

Another answer, and one that would solve, in a sense, the above problem, is the widely expressed Sufi idea that "every woman is a man on the path." That is, every woman actively journeying on the path is necessarily "a man" in a symbolic—perhaps even an existential—sense, since she is "active" (as opposed to passive) in her journeying, and insofar as journeying requires the intellect as its guiding force, every woman actively journeying on the mystical path is identified directly with the masculine element of the "intellect" or "spirit," having subdued her ego to a sufficient extent. Farīd ad-Dīn ʿAṭṭār notes in his biographical treatment of the famous female Sufi, Rābiʿa al-ʿAdawiyya, "When a woman becomes a man in the path of God, she is a man and one cannot any more call her a woman."[11] Rūmī poetically expresses a similar idea:

> An effeminate man is not suited to fight against the ego; incense and musk are not suited for the back parts of a donkey.
> Since women never go out to fight the holy war, how should they engage in the Greater Holy War? Except rarely, when a Rustam is hidden within a woman's body, as in the case of Mary.
> In the same way, women are hidden in the bodies of those men who are feminine from faintness of heart.[12]

The clear problem with this solution—that every woman on the path is, so to speak, inwardly a man—is that it denies any natural or normative understanding of the mystical path for women. Only

[10] Rkia Cornell, *Early Sufi Women: Dhikr an-Niswa al-Mutaʿabbidat as-Sufiyyat* (Louisville, KY: Fons Vitae, 1999), p. 118 (Cornell's translation).

[11] A.J. Arberry (trans.), *Muslim Saints and Mystics: Episodes from the Tadhkirat al-Auliyaʾ (Memorial of the Saints) by Farid ad-Din Attar*, p. 40.

[12] Chittick, *The Sufi Path of Love*, pp. 165-166.

women who are highly exceptional, who are in some sense "not really women" can have the vocation to "walk upon the path." Frithjof Schuon notes that to conceive of a saintly woman as somehow a man is "absurd in itself, but defensible"[13] from a certain perspective; however, he further states that "to allege that the woman who is holy has become a man by the fact of her sanctity, amounts to presenting her as a denatured being: in reality, a holy woman can only be such on the basis of her perfect femininity. . . ."[14]

The identification of spiritual realization with masculinity is furthered by the use among certain mystical writers, including Ibn ʿArabī, of the term *rajuliyya* or "manliness," to refer to those who have reached the highest spiritual station, the state of the "Perfect Man" or the *insān al-kāmil.*[15] While Ibn ʿArabī notes that he is not using the term in a gender specific sense, and that women as well as men might reach this state of spiritual "manliness," it is significant that the term itself employs the gender specific Arabic word for "man." Such usage would seem, in effect, to be a contradiction in terms. For the term *rajul*, meaning man in a purely masculine sense, is not the same as the term *insān* used in the phrase "perfect man." *Insān* is precisely not gender specific. It refers to man in the universal sense; thus every human being—male or female—by virtue of being human, has the potential to reach the state of the "perfect man." If the hierarchical relationship between intellect and the passionate soul are reflected in the physical and social hierarchy of men and women in the traditional Islamic view, then the gender neutrality of the *insān al-kāmil*, or the "perfect man" that all true seekers strive to become is an affirmation of the profound spiritual equality between men and women that is clearly indicated in the Quran. The prototype of the *insān al-kāmil*, or "perfect man," is not the masculine Adam as opposed to the feminine Eve, but the as-yet-undifferentiated Adam, the "single soul" from which both men and women were created. This

[13] Frithjof Schuon, *Esoterism as Principle and as Way* (Bedfont: Perennial Books, 1981), p. 142.

[14] Ibid., p. 143.

[15] Murata, *The Tao of Islam*, p. 268.

primordial Adam, this undifferentiated human soul, was made "in the image of God" and so reflected on a human plane the perfection of the Divine. As God contains both masculine and feminine qualities in Islam—possessing both names of "majesty," such as Judge, King, Lord, the Transcendent, the Strong, and names of "beauty," such as Merciful, Compassionate, Intimate Friend, the Gentle, the One Who Loves—so too did this primordial Adam contain both masculine and feminine qualities and virtues. Thus it stands to reason that in order to reach this state of original Adamic purity, man must attain all of the virtues, masculine and feminine alike. It is not enough that a man be brave, strong, chivalrous, and detached, but he must also be, at least inwardly, gentle, nurturing, merciful, and devoted.

To the extent that these virtues obtained more or less naturally in their respective gender affinities among human beings—and experience tells us that this is not always the case—then a man's spiritual struggle would be to perfect his masculine virtues outwardly, while acquiring the feminine virtues inwardly. Likewise, a woman may have to acquire certain masculine virtues not inherent to her nature—such as detachment and bravery. Viewed from this perspective, if "every woman on the path is a man," then every man on the path must also be, at least from one perspective, "a woman"—in the sense that he must acquire the positive feminine elements of his original self, lost in the initial separation of male and female "from a single soul." Perhaps it is for this reason that Rūmī, in the passage I just quoted, spoke about the virtues of "kindness and gentleness"—stereotypically feminine virtues—as "human attributes," while excessive "domination" and "ferocity"—particularly male vices—are described as signs of "animality." In other words, the human *sālikūn*, or mystical seekers, of whatever gender they may be, and regardless of their natural or inherent inclinations, must reintegrate in themselves all the positive human virtues—masculine and feminine.

Women Sufis—"Walking upon the Path of God like Men"?

Turning from the theoretical or symbolic level, I want to address in the remainder of my article some of the particular qualities of the Sufi life as practiced by historical Sufi women and the degree to which they reflect the theoretical or metaphysical issues regarding the masculine-feminine symbolism I have raised. The questions I will seek to answer here are: Can we identify a particularly feminine strain of Islamic mysticism? Are the struggles and the victories along the path to spiritual realization different for a female *sālik* than they are for their male counterparts? And do female Sufis express the sublime spiritual experiences of the Divine Beloved in ways that differ from men, reflecting a different understanding of the relationship between the lover and the Beloved when the lover is a woman?

If every woman on the path is striving toward becoming *al-insān al-kāmil*, then she must struggle to embody traditionally masculine virtues, on the one hand, and avoid certain exaggerations of her feminine nature which might be spiritually limiting. When we examine the words and actions of Sufi women as recorded in Sufi biographical dictionaries, we see that these women indeed seem to have attained to a certain level of "masculine" virtue. In the first place, following the Sufi path—if ultimately a private undertaking—was at least at some stages, a public one. Especially as Sufism developed, the attachment of the Sufi initiate to a recognized Sufi *shaykh* came to be seen as a necessity for journeying upon the path, and a Sufi's social connection with his fellow mystics in the Sufi brotherhood became increasingly customary. Women, it seems, were not altogether infrequently accepted as the initiates of male Sufi *shaykhs* and in some cases, also became attached in one way or another to the order.[16] While the public sphere was not one generally considered appropriate for women in the classical Islamic period, nonetheless, the many women whose lives and words are recorded in the Sufi biographical works were necessarily public figures, otherwise they would never have come to the attention of their male biographers. The insistence of at least one of these biographers, Farīd ad-Dīn ʿAṭṭār, that a woman who journeys like a man on the spiritual path cannot be called a woman was, of course, one way in which the presence of these women in the public sphere—their attachment to male Sufi *shaykhs* and their social inter-

[16] Note that Murata mentions in her book that Ibn ʿArabī dealt with the question of Platonic male-female interaction in the context of the Sufi life, indicating that the presence of women among these orders was an issue for discussion (cf. *The Tao of Islam*, p. 266).

action with their male counterparts—could be legitimized in the face of strict Islamic insistence upon the necessary separation of unrelated men and women.

In addition to their role as "public figures"—already a decidedly masculine position—Sufi women are also frequently portrayed as possessing the masculine virtues of detachment, fortitude, and a lack of crippling sentimentality—sometimes to a dazzling extent. There is a story of the famous Basran Sufi, Rābiʿa al-ʿAdawiyya, for example, in which she is said to have looked upon an executed man hanging on the gibbet. With cold objectivity, Rābiʿa addressed the dead man, saying: "With that tongue, you used to say 'There is no god but God'!"[17] A similar story is told regarding the Andalusian Sufi, Nūna Fāṭima bint al-Muthannā, who was one of the female masters of Ibn ʿArabī. In this case, Nūna Fāṭima, already an elderly woman, was visiting a mosque and was struck with a whip by the *muʾadhdhin* of the mosque (perhaps for excessive devotions). She was immediately angered by this, scowled at the *muʾadhdhin* and left. Later, when she heard the *muʾadhdhin*'s call to prayer, she regretted her ill-will toward him, and asked forgiveness for harboring negative feelings toward one who chanted the name of God so beautifully. Rābiʿa, looking at the dead man, feels no human or sentimental sympathy for him, but only regret at the loss of a tongue that once proclaimed the oneness of God. And Nūna Fāṭima relented toward the *muʾadhdhin*, not because of a kind of sympathetic forgiveness for his human failing, but only because of the service he rendered to God and those who worship Him. In other words, their attachment to creatures was strictly on account of the divine elements manifest in them, rather than a matter of human sentimentality.

If the feminine virtues of devotion, mercy, compassion, and nurturing were positive in themselves but negative in their tendency to attach one to worldly things (hence the female Sufi desire to purify these qualities and direct them inwardly and counter them with a healthy detachment), masculine virtues like strength and bravery—noble in themselves—could become corrupted and the source of spiritual ailment. In particular, masculine dominance, when not

[17] Cornell, *Early Sufi Women*, p. 80 (Cornell's translation).

set within proper limits, had the possibility of leading to particular masculine vices of pride and a hunger for domination and conquest. Murata defines this as "negative masculinity," and even associates it directly with the evil argument with which Satan is said to have opposed God's command that he prostrate himself before Adam.[18] Satan's moral error is the prototype of a particularly masculine vice, for it involves a perverted use of reason or intellect in the service of self-pride and a reluctance to submit to another. Thus men, perhaps more so than women, were prone to falling into the vices of pride and love of dominance. And women Sufis, according to the biographical and historical accounts of their lives, not only exhibited positive "masculine" virtues in their own persons, but also frequently took the liberty of publicly and privately rebuking the men around them when they displayed particularly masculine faults. In fact, some of the most prominent male spiritual authorities in Islamic history are recorded as being corrected by their female Sufi counterparts. In this literature, their correction takes two main forms: criticism of male sexuality or desire for marriage and criticism of public claims of spiritual authority.

Sexual Asceticism

One of the characteristics of some early female saints and pietists in Islam was a state of celibacy and the avoidance of sexuality, even in its licit forms. While this is something immediately noticed by Western scholars more familiar with the Christian spiritual tradition, this kind of celibacy or asceticism is not true of all or perhaps even most female Islamic mystics. Many, for example, chose to marry for spiritual reasons, often marrying male mystics who could serve as their spiritual guides. However, the rejection of offers of marriage and male sexual attention—particularly from prominent male spiritual authorities—is a significant theme in the Sufi literature pertaining to women. For example, there is the case of the Meccan devotee, Malīka bint al-Munkadir. On one particular occasion, two of her most important male spiritual contemporaries, Mālik ibn Dīnār and Ayūb as-Sakhtiyānī, encountered her on the pilgrimage to Mecca. Noticing

[18] Murata, *The Tao of Islam*, pp. 269-270.

her piety and devotion, they approached her to tell her that she could improve her [spiritual] state by marrying.[19] Malīka was not convinced, and responded by saying, "Even if Mālik ibn Dīnār himself were to ask me, I would not be interested!" Mālik, perhaps pleased by her backhanded compliment to his spiritual reputation and sure she was exaggerating, responded triumphantly: "I am Mālik! And this is Ayūb as-Sakhtiyānī!" Malīka, however, was unimpressed. She responded disdainfully: "I would have thought that the two of you [given your reputations] would have been too preoccupied with the invocation of God to concern yourself with women!"[20]

An interesting example of apparent female Sufi criticism of male sexuality is to be found in an encounter between Fāṭima of Nishapur and Abū Yazīd al-Bisṭāmī. This apparently outspoken Sufi woman had been conversing with the famous tenth century Sufi, Abū Yazīd al-Bisṭāmī in an intimate way, with her face veil removed, when he suddenly happened to notice that her hands had been ornamented with henna, presumably from her recently concluded wedding celebration. Abū Yazīd commented on her henna-adorned hands with surprise and perhaps some disdain for the feminine desire for worldly luxury that it seemed to indicate. Yet she immediately reversed the situation by criticizing the attention he paid to this aspect of her feminine nature. She immediately put her face veil back on and declared that so long as Abū Yazīd had been speaking to her without taking notice of her hands, their intimate conversation was lawful and appropriate and she did not feel the slightest bit of unease; but as soon as he noticed her hands, their intimacy had become *ḥarām*.[21]

[19] Marriage in Islam, unlike in Christianity, was seen as an important part of one's religious life. A famous *ḥadīth* of the Prophet declared that "marriage is half of your religion." For this reason, monasticism and celibacy are not generally celebrated virtues in the Islamic view, and might even be considered blameworthy, especially for a woman.

[20] Ibn al-Jawzī, *Sifat as-Safwā*, vol. 2, p. 135.

[21] Arberry, *Muslim Saints and Mystics*, p. 174.

Spiritual Pride and the Virtue of Silence

As already made abundantly clear, the goal of the Sufi path is the suppression of the ego. The ego, however, is a clever thing, which having been defeated on one front, stealthily moves to another. Thus the Sufi is told to always be on guard against the clever maneuvers of the ego to subvert his spiritual progress. One of the more subtle forms of egoism, and one which reportedly plagued even the greatest of Sufi masters, was the mistaken or arrogant belief that one had reached a high spiritual station—a kind of spiritual pride (again, not unlike that attributed to Satan in his refusal to prostrate himself before Adam). In Sufi biographical works, one Sufi after another falls victim to this moral failure. And in many cases, it is a woman who is given the task of pointing it out. While there are many such instances in the hagiographical literature, I will here mention only a few of the most revealing episodes.

Some of the most interesting such encounters take place between Rābiʿa al-ʿAdawiyya and the early, prominent pietist, Ḥasan al-Baṣrī. Historically speaking, Rābiʿa was only a rough contemporary of Ḥasan, and it is highly unlikely that the two ever met; yet she constantly served as a foil for Ḥasan in the hagiographical literature. In one particular instance, Ḥasan apparently challenged Rābiʿa to a battle of spiritual power or will, *himmah*. Ḥasan reportedly threw his prayer carpet on the river, where it remained afloat, and invited Rābiʿa to do the same and join him in prayer. Rābiʿa, seeming rather annoyed by his petty challenge, threw her own prayer carpet into the air, where it remained suspended. In the battle of spiritual *himmah*, Rābiʿa won because, as the narrator tells us, Ḥasan had not yet achieved the spiritual station that would allow him to perform such a feat. But this is not the primary point of the story. Rather, Rābiʿa demonstrated not only her superior spiritual *himmah*, but also her superior level of mystical understanding when she told Ḥasan that such feats, whether on water or air matter little. "That which you did," she noted, "a fish can do just the same, and that which I did, a fly can do. The real [spiritual] work . . . lies beyond both of these and it is necessary to occupy ourselves with real work."[22]

[22] Margaret Smith, *Rābiʿa: The Life and Work of Rābiʿa and Other Women Mystics in Islam*, pp. 56-57.

Besides the legendary encounters frequently related between Rābiʿa and Ḥasan al-Baṣrī, there are also many other similar instances in which male spiritual pride is cut down to size by female critics. For example, Sulamī's recently edited biographical compilation on early female devotees mentions a certain Fāṭima bint Aḥmad who came upon the spiritual teacher, Abu'l-ʿAbbās ad-Dīnāwārī lecturing on the nature of *uns*, or intimacy with God. She raised her voice to silence his own, saying: "How excellent is your description of that which you lack! Had you tasted anything of what you describe or witnessed anything about which you speak, you would remain silent!"[23] In another example, Fāṭima ad-Dimashqiyya is said to have silenced a religious scholar lecturing in the main mosque of Damascus saying to him: "You spoke very well, and you have perfected the art of rhetoric, have you perfected the art of silence?"[24] The report concludes by saying that this scholar never spoke again. As-Sulamī even reports an incident in which one of his own spiritual masters, Abu'l-Qāsim an-Naṣrābādhī, was heckled continuously by a woman named Qurashiyya an-Nasawiyya. As-Sulamī's short biographical entry on Qurashiyya informs us that she considered silence to be an important and useful spiritual virtue. This was the immediate backdrop for her criticisms of an-Naṣrābādhī's public teaching sessions. She contrasted his fine words with what she describes as his "ugly morals." When he tried to silence her, she responded: "I will be quiet when you are quiet!"[25] It should be noted, however, that while Naṣrābādhī responded with irritation to his female critic, most of the Sufi men reportedly chastised by women in similar instances, responded with humility and an honorable acceptance and validation of the criticism—if only through their lack of protest. Thus, in many cases, such incidents may have been recorded primarily for the purpose of demonstrating the virtues of humility and self-objectivity that characterized these male Sufi masters, who were able to accept valid criticism of their behavior without regard for the nature of its source.

[23] Cornell, *Early Sufi Women*, pp. 180-181. My translation is based on Cornell's own translation with minor modification.

[24] Ibid., p. 204 (Cornell's translation).

[25] See ibid., p. 224, n. 182.

In any case, all three of these examples portray women as using quick wit and sharp words to silence male spiritual authorities. These women enter the public realm to confront the spiritual shortcomings of some of the spiritual authorities they see around them. But in the expressed views of these women, the flaws of these men (almost all recognized spiritual authorities) would seem to stem from the desire for public recognition. If it was a keen feminine insight that allowed these women to discern the flaws to which men were particularly susceptible, the manner in which these women pointed out those flaws was hardly stereotypically feminine. The moral voice they exhibit in these sources is not a voice that is soft or gentle. Their words are pithy and pointed, witty and authoritative. Their method is direct and public confrontation, not subtle insinuation. They are opposing their own positive "masculinity" acquired on the path, to the vices of negative masculinity that they perceive in some of their male Sufi contemporaries.

In fact, these women's attainment to the masculine virtue of worldly detachment is often portrayed as being so complete as to blind to them all that was not God. Rābiʿa, for example, is recorded to have insisted that her love for God was so all-encompassing that it left no room for the love of His creatures or created things. On one occasion, Rābiʿa is said to have encountered a fellow mystic, Rabāḥ al-Qaysī, lovingly embracing a child. Rābiʿa chastised him for this, expressing amazement that a person of his spiritual station could have such love for a created being. Rabāḥ objected—and perhaps quite rightly so—that such love is a mercy from the Divine, implying that to ignore it would be ungrateful.[26] The text does not record Rābiʿa's response to his argument, but it is clear that it is a perspective to which she cannot relate. Not only did Rābiʿa insist that God alone is deserving of her love, she insisted that this love be a purely disinterested and selfless love. Hence the famous story of Rābiʿa running through the streets of Basra with a bucket of water in one hand and a flaming torch in the other, saying that she wanted to put out the fires of hell and burn up the Garden of Paradise so that God would be loved for nothing other

[26] Ibid., p. 78.

than Himself alone.[27] Ibn ʿArabī criticized Rābiʿa for this perspective, saying that to deny the virtues of the pleasures of Paradise was to be ungrateful for God's gifts. But again, for Rābiʿa, God's earthly gifts were nothing compared to the gift of His Presence. While for Rabāḥ al-Qaysi and Ibn ʿArabī, their love of God seemed to lead them to a new appreciation of His manifestation in earthly creatures, for Rābiʿa, her love of Him made her insensitive to all created reality.

Indeed one of the qualities attributed emphatically to nearly all female Sufis in the biographical tradition is an extreme asceticism—again, an asceticism for which they are often portrayed as having more fortitude than their male contemporaries, who express surprise at the ascetic abilities of their female counterparts and often suggest a merciful softening of their mortifications of the flesh. Many women on the Sufi path, as mentioned above, remained celibate and unmarried. Rābiʿa, for example, is said to have refused numerous offers of marriage, and others were said to have put limits on their marriages, refusing to let them interfere with their spiritual life. Rābiʿa's older namesake, Rābiʿa bint Ismāʿīl of Syria, for example, married a younger man who was a promising Sufi, so that she could render service to God by supporting his spiritual pursuits with her inherited financial wealth. After they were married, she told him that he was like a brother to her, and they remained married in a purely platonic manner, with Rābiʿa supporting her husband and his other wives, without desire for her own earthly marital fulfillment.[28] Fāṭima of Nishapur, mentioned above in her encounter with Abū Yazīd al-Bisṭāmī, is said to have proposed—indeed insisted upon—marriage to one of the great Sufi men of her age. But she married him primarily to support her own spiritual pursuits. When her future husband, Aḥmad, first refused her marital proposal, she chastised him for not being chivalrous enough to take on the responsibility of taking care of her materially and spiritually, and she eventually shamed him into marrying her. But she was determined that her new husband should be an aid and not a hindrance to her following the mystical path. Soon after their marriage

[27] Schimmel, *My Soul Is Woman*, p. 35. See also Arberry, *Muslim Saints and Mystics*, p. 51.

[28] Schimmel, *My Soul Is Woman*, p. 40; Cornell, *Early Sufi Women*, p. 138.

she journeyed with her husband to her above-mentioned encounter with Abū Yazīd al-Bisṭāmī, who both husband and wife recognized as their Sufi master. When she initially removed her face veil in Abū Yazīd's presence, her husband objected to her boldness toward the Sufi master. But she responded by telling him that while he, Aḥmad, is her worldly husband, and so fulfills her physical desires, Abū Yazīd is her spiritual master, and thus fulfills her spiritual needs, and that physical attraction does not enter into their relationship.[29]

However, it should be noted that while these women sometimes seem impervious to the sentiment of love in relation to earthly creatures, they are hardly so cold and restrained in their expressions of love for the Divine. In fact, the harshness with which they sometimes approach men contrasts sharply with the tenderness and longing found in their words addressed to God. For Rābiʿa, in particular, numerous loving addresses to God are recorded, and she is said to have considered these kinds of intimate conversations with her Beloved to be more valuable than canonical prayer for bringing one close to God. In beautiful verses attributed to both Ḥabība al-ʿAdawiyya and Fāṭima bint Muḥammad, we read:

> O my Lord, the stars are shining and the eyes of men are closed and kings have shut their doors and every lover is alone with his beloved; and here I am alone with Thee.[30]

Rābiʿa bint Ismāʿīl, married platonically to her Sufi husband, and devoted inwardly only to God, says:

> I have made Thee the Intimate of my inmost heart, but my body is made permissible for those who desire to sit with me;
> And my body is friendly toward guests; but the Beloved of my heart is the guest of my inmost self (*fuʾād*).[31]

[29] Arberry, *Muslim Saints and Mystics*, pp. 173-174.

[30] For its attribution to Ḥabība al-ʿAdawiyya, see Cornell, *Early Sufi Women*, p. 202; for the attribution to Fāṭima bint Muḥammad al-Munkadir, see Ibn al-Jawzī, *Sifat as-Safwā*, vol. 2, p. 137.

[31] Cornell, *Early Sufi Women*, p. 317 (my translation).

Elsewhere, Rābiʿa is quoted as saying of God:

> A beloved no other beloved can rival
> No one but He has a share of my heart
> A Beloved who, though absent from my sight and my person
> Is never absent from my inmost self.[32]

The asceticism of these women, so extreme outwardly, gave way to a flood of loving tenderness directed toward the true aim of their affections. If only a single spouse was decreed for women in Islam, while polygamy was permitted for men, these women perhaps felt the importance of not compromising their devotion to God with devotion to any other thing. Thus the Jerusalemite devotee, Lubāba, declares that she is ashamed for God to see her preoccupied with anything other than Him.[33] And Rayḥāna of Basra says to God: "Thou art my Intimate Companion, my Hope and my Joy; and my heart refuses to love anything but Thee."[34] Indeed, there is a case where a Sufi woman lamented the fact that her friend's husband had decided to take a second wife, not for her friend's loss, but because the husband would then be distracted by two wives from his spiritual devotion to God.[35] The asceticism of these Sufi women, then, was not an asceticism of fear, as was the case, for example, with Ḥasan al-Baṣrī, who was always weeping and denying himself out of a deep-seated dread of hell-fire. Rābiʿa rarely complained of a fear of hell, and when she once had a passing doubt about being put in hell, a divine inspiration reassured her that God would never do something so cruel to her. Rather, female Sufi asceticism is more often than not an asceticism of love. For these Sufi women, it was not a question of denying themselves certain worldly pleasures, but of their complete disinterest in any pleasure other than Him. The Damascene mystic Muʾmina declares: "O most Beloved. This world and the next are not pleasurable except

[32] Ibid., p. 316 (Cornell's translation with slight modification).

[33] Ibid., p. 82.

[34] Ibid., p. 95 (my translation).

[35] Ibid., p. 126.

through Thee. So do not overwhelm me with the loss of Thee and the punishment that results from it!"[36] The punishment is not hell, only separation from their true "spouse."

Thus far from making these Sufi women hardened and embittered, their asceticism and detachment from worldly love allowed them to direct all their feminine qualities of devotion and tenderness inwardly, toward the Divine Essence. In other words, their harshness and detachment toward earthly creatures and human men was not necessarily a denial or rejection of their feminine virtue or even of the important Islamic institution of marriage (as much as it may have seemed so on the outside), but rather a determination to direct all of their feminine devotion and love toward the only "Spouse" worthy of it—the Divine, Himself.

[36] Cornell, *Early Sufi Women*, p. 86 (Cornell's translation with slight modification).

SACRED MUSIC AND DANCE IN ISLAM*

Jean-Louis Michon

A Controversial Question

"O Lord! Make us see things as they are!" asked the Prophet when addressing himself to his Lord.[1] The same prayer was to be repeated later over and over by devout Muslims desiring to judge objectively a more or less ambiguous situation. These words are therefore well placed at the beginning of an essay on the art of music such as it was and such as it is still practiced in the countries of *dār al-islām*. Few subjects have been debated or have raised as many contradictory emotions and opinions as the statute (*ḥukm*) of music vis-à-vis religious law and at the heart of Islamic society. In fact, the debate is not yet over and, no doubt, never will be because it concerns a domain in which it seems that Providence wanted to give Muslims the greatest possible freedom of choice and of appreciation. No Quranic prescription explicitly aims at music. The *Sunna*, the "customs" of the Prophet, cites only anecdotal elements, none of which constitutes a peremptory argument either for or against musical practice. The third source of Islamic Law, the opinion of doctors of the Law, spokesmen recognized by social consensus, varies extremely ranging from a categorical condemnation of music to its panegyric while passing through various degrees of acceptance and reservation.

* Editors' Note: This essay has been shortened from its full length in *Islamic Spirituality: Manifestations* (The Crossroad Publishing Co., 1997) to focus specifically on Sufism, along with some requisite background.

[1] *Arinā'l-ashyā' kamā hiya*; *ḥadīth* cited by Fakhr ad-Dīn ar-Rāzī in his *Great Commentary* on the Quran (*Mafātiḥ al-Ghayb*) with respect to the verse 17:85: "They will question thee concerning the Spirit . . ."(*Al-Tafsīr al-Kabīr* [2nd ed.; Tehran, n.d.) vols. 21-22, p. 37. Also cited by Hujwīrī in his *Kashf al-Maḥjūb* (see n. 5 below) with respect specifically to the contradictory opinions concerning the spiritual concert (*as-samā'*).

To understand how such divergent positions could have arisen and been expressed in the same context on the subject of Islamic thought and ethics, it is useful to refer to their interpreters who knew how to take into consideration ideas at once metaphysical, philosophical, or theosophical as well as the imperative of the Muslim ethic, both individual and social. To this category belong the Ikhwān aṣ-Ṣafā', the Brethren of Purity, whose vast encyclopedia of philosophy, science, and art, compiled in the fourth/tenth century, contains a precious epistle on music.[2]

Like the Greek philosophers, the Ikhwān recognized in terrestrial music the echo of the music of the spheres, "inhabited by the angels of God and by the elite of his servants." Thus, "the rhythm produced by the motion of the musician evokes for certain souls residing in the world of generation and corruption the felicity of the world of the spheres, in the same way that the rhythms produced by the motion of the spheres and the stars evoke for souls who are there the beatitude of the world of the spirit." By reason of the law of harmony, which reigns over all the levels of existence, linking them according to an order at once hierarchical and analogical, "the beings produced by secondary reactions imitate in their modalities the first beings which are their causes . . . from which it must be deduced that the notes of terrestrial music necessarily imitate those of celestial music." Like Pythagoras, who "heard, thanks to the purity of the substance of his soul and the wisdom of his heart, the music produced by the rotation of the spheres and the stars" and who "was the first to have spoken of this science," other philosophers such as Nichomacus, Ptolemy, and Euclid, had "the habit of singing accompanied by percussive instruments which produced chords from words and measured verses that were composed for exhortation to the spiritual life and described the delights of the world of the spirit, the pleasure and the happiness of its inhabitants." Later came the Muslim conquerors, who, when given the signal to attack, recited certain verses of the Quran or declaimed

[2] The complete work includes fifty-one (or fifty-two) "Epistles" (*rasā'il*), of which the one treating music is the fifth. See "L'épître sur la musique des Ikhwān al-ṣafā'," translation and annotation by A. Shiloah, *Revue des études islamiques* 31 (1964), pp. 125-162; 33 (1966), pp. 159-193. The passages cited hereafter are found on pp. 155-158 (1964).

Arabic or Persian poems describing the paradisal delights reserved for those who died while fighting on the path of God. Returning to music, in inventing the principles of its melodies and the constitution of its rhythms, the sages had no goal except "to soften hardened hearts, to wake the negligent souls from their sleep of forgetfulness and the misguided spirits from their slumber of ignorance, to make them desire their spiritual world, their luminous place and their journey of life, to make them leave the world of generation and corruption, to save them from submersion in the ocean of the material world and to deliver them from the prison of nature."

How, under these circumstances, can it be explained that music could become an object of reprobation? Because, explain the Ikhwān, even if it is good in itself, music can be turned aside from its natural and legitimate ends. "As for the reason for the interdiction of music in certain laws of the prophets . . . it relates to the fact that people do not use music for the purpose assigned it by the philosophers, but for the purpose of diversion, for sport, for the incitation to enjoy the pleasures of this lower world." Thus, that which can become reprehensible is not music itself but the use to which certain people put it. "Be watchful while listening to music, that the appetites of the animal soul do not push you toward the splendor of nature. Nature will lead you astray from the paths of salvation and prevent you from discourse with the superior soul."[3] The warning issued by the Ikhwān goes along with the teaching given a century earlier by the Sufi Dhū 'n-Nūn the Egyptian (d. 246/861): "Listening (*as-samā*ʿ) is a divine influence which stirs the heart to see Allāh; those who listen to it spiritually attain to Allāh, and those who listen to it sensually fall into heresy."[4] In the same way, Hujwīrī wrote in his *Kashf al-Maḥjūb* (*The Unveiling of the Veiled*), the first treatise on Sufism written in Persian, "Listening

[3] Shiloah, *Revue des études islamiques* 33 (1966), p. 185. In the same way, F. Schuon writes, "while listening to beautiful music, the guilty will feel innocent. But the contemplative, on the contrary, while listening to the same music, will forget himself while fathoming the essences" (*Sur les traces de la religion pérenne* [Paris: Le Courier du Livre, 1982], pp. 66-67).

[4] Cited by H. G. Farmer, *A History of Arabian Music* (London: Luzac, 1929; repr. 1973), p. 36.

to sweet sounds produces an effervescence of the substance molded in man; true, if the substance be true, false, if the substance be false."[5]

Such was, generally speaking, the attitude of the philosophers and theoreticians of music, as well as that of the majority of Sufis and a good number of canonists. Aware of the benefits of the art of music, they did not show themselves less circumspect about its utilization, distinguishing between noble and vulgar genres, between sensual melodies, "useful" melodies, etc.[6]

However, numerous jurists went much further and, seeing the evil usage that could be made of the practice of music, concluded that music itself was evil or, at least, that it involved more disadvantages than advantages and had, therefore, to be banned from society. Poetry that was sung and the use of instruments gave rise, they said, to corrupting excitations of the soul, which turned one aside from religious duties, encouraged one to seek out sensual satisfactions and bad company, pushed one into drunkenness and debauchery. Such jurists went so far as to say that the public singer, even if he sings the Quran to arouse pleasure in his listeners, could not be heard as a legal witness. They also maintained that it was lawful to break musical instruments.[7]

For the Jurist and moralist Ibn Abī 'l-Dunyā (d. 281/894), who wrote a short treatise entitled *Dhamm al-Malāhī* (*Censure of Instruments of Diversion*),[8] singing and music were condemnable dis-

[5] This work dates to the second half of the fifth/eleventh century, according to R. A. Nicholson, who gave an English translation of it in the E. J. W. Gibb Memorial Series, vol. 17 (London: Luzac, 1911; repr. 1959).

[6] As by Ibn ʿAlī al-Kātib, who cites al-Fārābī. See A. Shiloah, *La Perfection des connaissances musicales* (Paris: Geuthner, 1972), pp. 65-68.

[7] On this see especially Farmer, *History*, chap. 2 ("Islam and Music"); J. Robson (see n. 8 below); and M. Molé (see n. 9 below).

[8] A translation was made of this by J. Robson, *Tracts on Listening to Music*, Oriental Translation Fund n.s. 34, R.A.S. (London: Royal Asiatic Society, 1938). It is followed by the translation of the treatise entitled *Bawāriq al-Ilmāʿ*, attributed to the Sufi Aḥmad al-Ghazzālī surnamed Majd ad-Dīn (d. 520/1126), brother of the celebrated Abū Ḥāmid al-Ghazzālī (Algazel), author of the *Iḥyāʾ*. In contrast to Ibn Abīʾl-Dunyā, the author supports the

tractions of the same type as the games of chess and backgammon. Later, the Ḥanbalite jurist Ibn al-Jawzī (d. 597/1200) was to show himself to be just as severe vis-à-vis music, which the evil human nature, "the soul which incites to evil" (*an-nafs al-ammāra bi'l-sū'* according to the Quran 12:53) has a tendency to seize upon in order to anchor man in sensuality. "The spiritual concert (*as-samā'*) includes two things," he wrote in his *Talbīs Iblīs* (*The Dissimulation of the Devil*). "In the first place, it leads the heart away from reflection upon the power of God and from assiduity in His service. In the second place, it encourages enjoyment of the pleasures of this world. . . ." Furthermore:

> Music makes man forget moderation and it troubles his mind. This implies that man, when he is excited, commits things which he judges reprehensible in others when he is in his normal state. He makes movements with his head, claps his hands, strikes the ground with his feet, and commits acts similar to those of the insane. Music leads one to this; its action appears to be like that of wine, because it clouds the mind. This is why it is necessary to prohibit it.[9]

Ibn al-Jawzī admits, however, that there are certain musical genres in which the emotional element does not enter and which, therefore, are legal, such as songs of pilgrims to Mecca, songs of fighters for the faith, and songs of camel drivers. He recognized also that in the epoch in which Ibn Ḥanbal lived (third/ninth century), poems were sung that exalted only religious feeling, which consequently escaped interdiction. But such times, according to him, are over and the innovations introduced since then in music and poetry are such that these arts can only have a deleterious influence.

legality of music and exalts the virtues of the spiritual concert. In his introduction to these two treatises (pp. 1-13), J. Robson summarizes well the arguments employed by the defenders of these antithetical positions.

[9] Cited by M. Molé, in *Les Danses sacrées* (Paris: Seuil, 1963), p. 164 ("La Danse extatique en Islam"). This study contains abundant documentation, drawn from original and often little-known sources, on the arguments for and against the use of music and dance in the mystical path.

The Philosopher-Musicologists

Although arguments of this nature must be regarded as admissible on the part of the jurists, who are concerned above all with the moral health of the man of the community and the collectivity, these arguments did not apply to seekers of Truth, to those who had sufficiently refined themselves so as not to fall into the trap of sensuality. For them music occupied an important place in the hierarchy of the arts and the sciences, and they practiced it as a discipline capable of elevating man above the gross world, of making him participate in the universal harmony. Such seekers were numerous and with abundant talent in the Islamic world, which, thanks to them, can pride itself on an extremely fecund tradition on the level of theory as well as that of the practice of vocal and instrumental music.

Among the theoreticians who thought and wrote about music, two clearly distinguishable schools can be recognized which sometimes converged but, more often, went along their separate paths, drawing on their own sources and applying different methods of investigation. They are, on one side, the philosophers, *falāsifa*, *ḥukamā'* (pl. of *ḥakīm*, "sage") and, on the other side, the mystics, *ṣūfiyya* (pl. of *ṣūfī*), *'ārifūn*, *'urafa'* (pl. of *'ārif*, "gnostic").

To the first group are linked the great thinkers whose names are forever inseparable from the history of Islamic philosophy, names such as Ya'qūb al-Kindī, Abū Bakr ar-Rāzī (Rhazes), Abū Naṣr al-Fārābī, whose *Kitāb al-Mūsiqa'l-kabīr* (*Grand Book of Music*) achieved considerable fame, Ibn Sīnā (Avicenna), Ibn Bājja (Avempace), and Ṣafī ad-Dīn (d. 629/1293).[10] If they inherited the legacy of ancient Greece and renewed the Pythagorean, Aristotelian, Platonic, and Neoplatonic discourse, they imprinted upon it a unique and profoundly original mark, enriching it not only with numerous scientific developments but with the whole school of thought based on the Quranic revelation.[11] The Ikhwān aṣ-Ṣafā', previously mentioned, also belonged to this group. Their "Epistle on Music" opens as follows:

[10] For more information on all these philosophers who wrote extensively on musical theory, consult the first or second edition of *The Encyclopaedia of Islam* (Leiden: Brill) under their respective names.

[11] For a better understanding of the Greco-Islamic affinities and their influ-

> After having completed the study of the theoretical spiritual arts which are of a scientific genre, and the study of the corporeal, practical arts which are of an artistic genre, . . . we propose in the present epistle entitled "Music" to study the art which is made up of both the corporeal and the spiritual. It is the art of harmony (*ta'līf*) which can be defined by the function of proportions.[12]

Two ideas occur at the onset, the first being that music is composed of corporeal and spiritual elements, the second that it is based on proportions. Because of its dual composition, the art of music possesses the special power of freeing matter in order to spiritualize it, and of materializing the spiritual in order to render it perceptible. This power comes also from the fact that music is a science of proportions, as the Ikhwān explain in another epistle (the sixth) in which, after having shown by examples how number, proportion, and numerical relationship are applied to all phenomena they add, "All these examples demonstrate the nobility of the science of proportion which is music. This science is necessary for all the arts. Nevertheless, if it is connected with the name of music, it is because music offers the best illustration of harmony."[13]

That which, according to the Ikhwān, characterizes music and distinguishes it from other arts is that the substance upon which it works—the soul of the listeners—like the elements it employs—notes

ence on musical science, see the works of H. G. Farmer, especially *The Sources of Arabian Music* (Glasgow: Glasgow Bibliographical Society, 1939), which includes the writings of Arabic authors. See also P. Kraus, *Jābir ibn Ḥayyān: Contribution à l'histoire des idées scientifiques dans Islam, Jābir et la science grecque* (Paris: Les Belles Lettres, 1986); Y. Marquet, "Imāmat, résurrection et hiérarchie selon les Ikhwān aṣ-Ṣafā'," in *Revue des études islamiques* 29 (1962), pp. 49-142; E. Werner and J. Sonne, "The Philosophy and Theory of Music in Judeo-Arabic Literature," in *Hebrew Union College Annual* 16 (1941), pp. 251-319; 17 (1942-43), pp. 511-572, wherein the three chapters concerning music are translated from the *Kitāb Ādāb al-Falāsifah* of Ḥunayn ibn Isḥāq.

[12] *Revue des études islamiques* 31 (1964), pp. 126-127 (see n. 2 above).

[13] Ibid.

and rhythms—are of a subtle nature and not corporeal. "Music leaves in the souls of those who listen to it diverse impressions similar to those left by the work of the artisan in the matter which is the substratum of his art." The Ikhwān cite many examples of emotional states which melodies are capable of inspiring in man, such as regret and repentance for past mistakes, courage in battle, relief from suffering, and joyful excitation. Animals themselves are roused by hearing music; the camel quickens its step upon hearing the song of the camel driver; the horse drinks more willingly when its master whistles a tune; the gazelle allows itself to be approached at night by the hunter who hums a melody.

"Music (*ghinā'*)," exclaimed also Ibn Khurdādhbih (d. ca. 300/912), who was raised in Baghdad by the inspired Isḥāq al-Mawṣilī,[14] when beginning a speech delivered at the court of the caliph al-Mu'tamid, his protector and friend, "sharpens the intellect, softens the disposition, and agitates the soul. It gives cheer and courage to the heart, and high-mindedness to the debased. . . . It is to be preferred to speech, as health would be to sickness. . . ."[15]

Not only does music stir the soul and the emotions, it "descends" into the body and from there comes its power to move the body and make it dance. From there also come the therapeutic applications to which the classical treatises refer, notably those of al-Kindī and Ibn Sīnā. Besides this, it "rises" as far as the spirit because it is itself a vibration of supernatural origin like the *kun*, the primordial *fiat lux* from which, from nothingness, from silence, from darkness, existence was brought forth. Thus the remark of Ibn Zayla (d. 440/1048), a disciple of Ibn Sīnā: "Sound produces an influence on the soul in two directions. One is on account of its special composition (i.e., its physical

[14] Singer/composer, theoretician and historian as well as jurist (150/767-236/850), Isḥāq al-Mawṣilī played a considerable role in the transmission of an Arabo-Persian musical art that was highly refined under the Abbasid caliphate. His father, Ibrāhīm (124/742-188/804) was himself a consummate musician. A regular guest of Hārūn al-Rashīd, he owned the most richly endowed music school of Baghdad (see Farmer, *History*, pp. 124-126).

[15] Cited by Farmer, *History*, p. 156.

content); the other on account of its being similar to the soul (i.e., its spiritual content)."[16]

> Know, my brethren, that the effects imprinted by the rhythms and melodies (*naghamāt*) of the musician in the souls of listeners are of different types. In the same way, the pleasure which souls draw from these rhythms and melodies and the manner in which they enjoy them are variable and diverse. All that depends on the degree which each soul occupies in the domain of gnosis (*al-maʿārif*) and on the nature of the good actions which make up the permanent object of his love. Therefore, each soul, while listening to descriptions which correspond to the object of his desires and to melodies which are in accord with the object of his delight, rejoices, is exalted and delights in the image that music makes of his beloved. . . .[17]

The Ikhwān conclude their epistle with a justification of the most beautiful and the most perfect music, which is none other than the psalmody of sacred texts:

> Tradition teaches that the sweetest melody which the inhabitants of paradise have at their disposal and the most beautiful song they hear is the discourse of God—great be His praise. It is thus that the Word of God Most High states, "The greeting which [will welcome them] there will be peace!" (Quran 10:10-11). And the end of their invocation will be: "Praise to Allāh, Lord of the worlds." It is said that Moses—peace be upon him—upon hearing the words of his Lord, was overcome with joy, with happiness, and with rapture to the point of being unable to contain himself. He was overwhelmed by emotion, transported while listening to this serene melody and

[16] Cited by G. H. Farmer, "The Religious Music of Islam," *Journal of the Royal Asiatic Society* (1952), pp. 60-65. See also in M. M. Sharif, ed., *A History of Muslim Philosophy* (Wiesbaden: Harrassowitz, 1963), 2:1126 (chap. 57, "Music"). Chapter 58 in this last work contains a good summary of musical theories that were expressed at different epochs and in different regions of the Islamic world, such as the influence exercised by Islamic music in other cultural domains.

[17] Shiloah, *Revue des études islamiques* 33 (1966), pp. 192-193.

from that point on regarded all rhythms, all melodies, and all songs as insignificant.[18]

Sufis and the Spiritual Concert (*as-samāʿ*)

To listen to music is therefore, in the final analysis, to open oneself to an influence, to a vibration of suprahuman origin "made sound" in order to awaken in us the echoes of a primordial state and to arouse in the heart a longing for union with its own Essence. Abū Ḥāmid al-Ghazzālī (d. 505/1111) writes at the beginning of the long chapter of *Iḥyāʾ ʿUlūm ad-Dīn* (*The Revival of the Sciences of Religion*), which he consecrates to the laws governing the spiritual concert (*as-samāʿ*):

> Hearts and inmost thoughts, song and ecstasy, are treasuries of secrets and mines of jewels. Infolded in them are their jewels like as fire is infolded in iron and stone, and concealed like as water is concealed under dust and loam. There is no way to the extracting of their hidden things save by the flint and steel of listening to music and singing, and there is no entrance to the heart save by the antechamber of the ears. So musical tones, measured and pleasing, bring forth what is in it and make evident its beauties and defects. For when the heart is moved there is made evident that only which it contains like as a vessel drips only what is in it. And listening to music and singing is for the heart a true touchstone and a speaking standard; whenever the soul of the music and singing reaches the heart, then there stirs in the heart that which in it preponderates.[19]

For the man in whom the desire for the good and the beautiful predominates, him who has an ear made for listening to music, it becomes a privileged tool for self-knowledge and interior improvement. Manifesting the latent possibilities of an individual, it permits

[18] Ibid.

[19] It is the eighth book of the "quarter" of the *Iḥyāʾ* dealing with the "social customs" (*ʿādāt*). It has been translated into English by E. B. Macdonald, *Journal of the Royal Asiatic Society* (1901). pp. 195-252, 705-746; (1902), pp. 1-28, where the passage cited appears on p. 199.

him to observe, by their movements and their reciprocal interactions, the potentialities of which he was not aware until that moment. A discrimination operates in him, which makes him perceive in his inmost heart, with an acuity in proportion to the quality of the music and to his own receptive capacity, clear and obscure zones of aspirations toward the absolute light, in alternation often with emotional attractions. That this age-old doctrine, already taught by the sages of antiquity and raised up by generations of Sufis to the rank of a veritable alchemy of the soul, has been transmitted and maintained through to the present time, I have only a very simple, but significant fact as proof. It is a sentence in Turkish that the father of a contemporary musician who specialized in the songs of Sufi brotherhoods[20] inscribed on the tambourine with which his son accompanied himself. It says: *Aşikin aşkini fasikin fiskini arttirir bir alettir* ("this instrument augments the love of the lover, the hypocrisy of the hypocrite").

The use of the spiritual concert (*as-samāʿ*) as a technique for spiritual realization must necessarily surround itself with conditions and precautions that will guarantee its efficacy and avoid the strayings and the misguidings of the *nafs*. These conditions are generally the same as those demanded of the candidates of the initiatic path (*ṭarīqa*): moral and spiritual qualifications of the disciple and the acceptance of him by the master (*shaykh, pīr*), obedience to the *shaykh*, service to the *fuqarāʾ* (practitioners of Sufism), strict observance of ritual practices particular to the order, as well as those of the *Sharīʿa* (religious law). More especially, at the time of participation in sessions of spiritual concert (*samāʿ*), dervishes are enjoined to remain as sober as possible and to exteriorize their emotion only when it becomes an ecstatic rapture of an intensity so great that it exceeds all control. Referring to the example of the Prophet, who, at the time of the first appearances of the archangel of the Revelation, did not succeed in mastering his emotion, Hujwīrī excused the beginners who show excitement in *samāʿ*. He insisted that the states provoked by listening be spontaneous:

[20] This concerns Nezih Uzel, who has given several recitals in Europe and made recordings of Sufi music together with Kudsi Erguner, a player of the *nay*, the reed flute precious to the Mawlawīs.

> As long as *samā‘* does not reveal its strength, it is essential not to force it, but the moment it becomes powerful, it must not be resisted. It is necessary to follow the "moment" in whatever it indicates: if it excites you, excite yourself; if it keeps you tranquil, keep yourself tranquil. . . . It is necessary that he who participates in *samā‘* have sufficient discernment to be capable of receiving the divine influence and to recognize in it its true value so that, when this influence takes hold of his heart, he does not endeavor to chase it out and, when its power has abated, he does not endeavor to recapture it.[21]

Abū Ḥāmid al-Ghazzālī, in the *Iḥyā'*, expressed a similar opinion:

> That the participant remain seated, his head lowered as if he were deep in meditation, avoiding clapping his hands, dancing, and making any other movement designed to artificially induce ecstasy or to make a display of it. . . . But when ecstasy takes hold of him and causes him to make movements independent of his will, he is to be excused and must not be blamed.

However, the same master admits that it is certainly not blameworthy to imitate the attitudes and movements of an ecstatic if the intention is not to make a display of a state that one has not attained, but rather to put oneself into a frame of mind receptive to grace.

> Know that ecstasy (*wajd*) is divided into that which itself attacks and that which is forced, and that is called affecting ecstasy (*tawājud*). Of this forced affecting of ecstasy there is that which is blameworthy, and it is what aims at hypocrisy and at the manifesting of the Glorious States in spite of being destitute of them. And of it there is that which is praiseworthy, and it leads to the invoking of the Glorious States and the gaining of them for oneself and bringing them to oneself by device. And therefore the Apostle of God commanded him who did not weep at the reading of the Qur'an that he should force weeping and mourning; for the beginning of these States is sometimes forced while their ends thereafter are true.[22]

[21] *Kashf al-Maḥjūb*; cited by Molé in *Danses sacrées*, p. 192.

[22] Trans. E. B. Macdonald, *Journal of the Royal Asiatic Society* (1901), pp.

Summarizing the teachings of numerous masters of Sufism in his glossary of technical terms, Ibn ʿAjība describes four successive degrees of approach toward ecstasy.[23] First, the "seeking out of ecstasy" (*tawājud*):

> One affects the appearances of ecstatic emotion (*wajd*) and one uses them methodically; thus one employs dance (*raqṣ*), rhythmic movements, etc. This seeking out is only admissible among the *fuqarāʾ* who have made vows of total renunciation. For them, there is nothing wrong in simulating ecstasy and in repeating its gestures in order to respond to an inner call (*ḥāl*). . . . It is, certainly, the station of the weak but the strong practice it nevertheless, either in order to sustain and encourage the weaker ones, or because they find a sweetness in it. . . . Myself, when I participated in a session of spiritual concert with our Shaykh al-Būzīdī, I saw him sway from right to left. One of the disciples of Mawlāy al-ʿArabī ad-Darqāwī told me that his master would not stop dancing until the end of the concert. . . .

In the second place comes "ecstatic emotion" (*wajd*) through which must be heard "that which befalls the heart and takes hold of it unexpectedly, without the man having any part in it. It can be an ardent and anxious desire or a troubling fear. . . ."

Third, "one speaks of 'ecstatic meeting' (*wijdān*) when the sweetness of the presence is prolonged, accompanied most frequently by intoxication and stupor."

730-731. The *ḥadīth* to which Ghazzālī alluded states: "If ye weep not, try to weep," and it is often cited to justify certain Sufi practices, such as the sacred dance (see M. Lings, *A Sufi Saint of the Twentieth Century, Shaykh Aḥmad Al-ʿAlawī* [Berkeley: University of California Press, 1971], pp. 92-93).

[23] Aḥmad ibn ʿAjība (1160/1747-1224/1809), his master Muḥammad al-Būzīdī (d. 1229/1814), and the latter's master, Mawlāy al-ʿArabī ad-Darqāwī (d. 1238/1823) belong to the great initiatic line of the Shādhilīyya, who, in Morocco, gave rise to numerous ramifications such as the Darqāwī Order, founded by the last named of these three masters.

Finally:

> If the meeting lasts until the stupor and hindrances dissipate and the faculties of meditation and insight are purified, it becomes ecstasy (*wujūd*), the station to which Junayd[24] alluded in this verse: "My ecstasy is that I remove myself from existence, by the grace of Him who shows to me the Presence" (*wujūdī an aghība ʿan al-wujūd bimā yabdū ʿalayya minaʾl-shuhūd*).[25]

The Elements of the Spiritual Concert

The animating power of music comes, we have seen, from that which it is in essence, a manifestation of the Divine Word, a language that reminds man of the state in which, before creation, he was still united with the Universal Soul, radiated from the original light, which reminds him of that instant in pre-eternity when, according to a Quranic saying frequently cited by the Sufis (7:172) the Lord asked souls: "Am I not your Lord?" They answered: "Yea!" It is the memory of this primordial covenant (*al-mīthāq al-awwal*) and the nostalgia for it that music evokes in hearts entrapped in earthly attachments.

There is in music an interpenetration of two aspects inherent in the Supreme Being, Allāh. One is the aspect of Majesty (*al-jalāl*), which is translated by rhythm, and the other the aspect of Beauty (*al-jamāl*), which is rendered by melody. The drum announces the arrival and the presence of the all-powerful King. It is the sign of transcendence, of the discontinuity which separates us, the impoverished, the dependent, from Him, the Highest, subsisting in Himself, while the human voice and the flute sing of the Immanence, the inexhaustible Wealth (*al-ghanāʾ*) that no human imagination will ever be able to comprehend but whose every manifestation, mode, or station (*maqām*) is capable of becoming a grace and a blessing for the believer.

[24] The "master of the circle" of the Sufis, who taught and died in Baghdad in 298/911.

[25] J.-L. Michon, *Le Soufi marocain Aḥmad Ibn ʿAjība et son Miʿrāj, Glossaire de la mystique musulmane* (Paris: J. Vrin, 1973 and 1990), pp. 241-242.

Instruments

Each of the elements of the spiritual concert is invested with a symbolic value and becomes an aid in recollection, in remembrance (*dhikr*) for those who are attentive to the language of signs. Aḥmad Ghazzālī (d. 520/1126), who taught Sufism approximately a century and a half before Rūmī, states:

> The saints of Allāh apply the forms to the realities (*ma'ānī*) on account of their abandoning the ranks of the forms and their moving in the ranks of the branches of gnosis. So among them the drum is a reference to the circle of existing things (*dā'irat al-akwān*); the skin which is fitted onto it is a reference to the Absolute Being; the striking which takes place on the drum is a reference to the descent of the divine visitations from the innermost arcana within the Absolute Being to bring forth the things pertaining to the essence from the interior to the exterior. . . . And the breath of the musician is the form of the degree of the Real (Exalted and Holy is He!), since it is He who sets it [i.e. the breath] in motion, brings it into existence, and causes it to vanish. And the voice of the singer is a reference to the divine life which comes down from the innermost arcana to the levels of the spirits, the hearts, and the consciences (*asrār*). The flute (*qaṣab*) is a reference to the human essence, and the nine holes are a reference to the openings in the outer frame (*ẓāhir*), which are nine, viz. the ears, the nostrils, the eyes, the mouth, and the private parts. And the breath which penetrates the flute is a reference to the light of Allāh penetrating the reed of man's essence. And the dancing is a reference to the circling of the spirit round the cycle of existing things in order to receive the effects of the unveilings and revelations; and this is the state of the gnostic. The whirling is a reference to the spirit's standing with Allāh in its inner nature (*sirr*) and being (*wujūd*), the circling of its look and thought, and its penetrating the ranks of existing things; and this is the state of the seeker of Truth. And his leaping up is a reference to his being drawn from the human station to the unitive station and to existing things acquiring from him spiritual effects and illuminative aids.[26]

[26] *Bawāriq* (see n. 8 above). Cited by Molé, *Les Danses sacrées*, pp. 205-206; and Robson, *Tracts*, pp. 98-99.

In this passage, Aḥmad Ghazzālī makes no mention of stringed instruments. That is because he, like his brother, considered them to be forbidden "by general consensus" by reason of the frequent use that was made of them in the first centuries of Islam by effeminates (*mukhannathūn*) for evenings of entertainment hardly compatible with the concerns of men of God. This ostracism, however, was not universal and only reflected the uncertainties which, even in mystical circles, existed in the matter of musical practice. It did not prevent the lute, the *tanbūr* (pandore), the *rabāb* (rebec), and the *qānūn* (zither) from finding their place next to the drums and the reed flute (*nay*) in the oratorios of several Sufi orders such as the Mawlawīs ("whirling dervishes") and the Bektāshīs of Turkey, the Chishtīs of India, and, much later (mid-thirteenth/nineteenth century), the Shādhilīs-Ḥarrāqīs of Morocco, who adopted for their sessions of remembrance the instruments of *nawba*, the classical music of Andalusia.

In fact, these instruments have always been held in the highest esteem by musicologists, who have based scholarly studies concerning the groupings and divisions of notes on them. It must be remembered that al-Fārābī, among others, was himself such a marvelous lutist that he was able, according to his contemporaries, to hold his listeners in rapt attention or to put them to sleep, to make them laugh or cry and to inspire in them feeling in concordance with his own "moments." Such performances are, moreover, consistent with the theory of the tuning of the lute, formulated by al-Kindī among others, according to which the four strings of the instrument correspond to other micro- and macrocosmic quaternaries such as the "animal tendencies" (gentleness, cowardice, intelligence, courage), the "faculties of the soul" (memorative, attentive, imaginative, cognitive), the elements (water, earth, air, fire), the seasons, and the signs of the zodiac.[27]

[27] On the subject of these correspondences, which the Arabs systematized starting with Greek sources but which also had roots in the ancient Semites, see H. G. Farmer, *Sa'adyah Gaon on the Influence of Music* (London: A. Probsthain, 1943), p. 9.

Melodic Modes

The effect that Islamic music, whether vocal or instrumental, has on the soul is directly connected with its modal structure, which, technically speaking, is without doubt its fundamental characteristic. In contrast to Western music, which has only two modes, the major and the minor, Oriental modes are quite numerous: the contemporary Arab, Turkish, and Persian musicians list them most often as numbering either thirty-two or twenty-four, twelve of which are very common, whereas during the classical epoch, a hundred were used.[28]

A mode (Arabic *maqām*;[29] Turkish *makām*; Persian *dastgāh* or *āwāz*) is a type of melody that is expressed by a series of well-defined sounds. It is a series (*sullam*) corresponding approximately to a Western scale, which does not have to use the same notes for ascending and descending to the octave. Each mode carries a specific name, which denotes, for example, its geographic origin such as *ḥijāz*, *nahāwand*, *ʿirāqī* or the position of its dominant note on the lute: *dugāh* (second position, or A), *sigāh* (third position, or B), or suggests the state of the soul or the cosmic phenomenon that the mode is supposed to translate into music: *faraḥfazā*, "the joyous"; *nesīm*, "the breeze"; *ṣabā*, "the morning wind," bringer of longing; *zemzeme*, "the murmur." It is said that the musicians in former times had a precise knowledge of the virtues of the *maqāms* and performed them in accordance with this knowledge, exactly as still occurs in Pakistan and northern India, where the system of *rāgas* obeys rules very similar to those of Persian, Turkish, and Arabic modes. It is thus that they played certain melodies only during certain seasons or at certain hours of the day or on special occasions in conjunction with the places and the ceremonies for which one wished to create a propitious ambience,

[28] On the theory of *maqām*, see in particular R. Erlanger, *La Musique arabe* (Paris: P. Geuthner, 1949) vol. 5; on its current practice in the diverse areas of the Arabo-Muslim world, see S. Jargy, *La Musique arabe* (Paris: Que sais-je?, 1971), pp. 49-69.

[29] The most anciently used term was *ṣawt*, literally, "the voice," which clearly marks the principally vocal character of the Arabo-Islamic music during its first period. Later, authors spoke of *ṭarīqa*, "way," "manner of acting," a term that has also fallen into disuse.

a spiritual or emotional aura. In the opinion of specialists of Turkish music, "The emancipation of music, its detachment from a complex background of human activities, has certainly taken from *makām* much of its original character, but a portion remains alive, even if it is unconscious. Musicians recognize a *makām* right from the first notes. . . . Therefore the *makām* always exerts an influence, but only long practice permits one to feel it."[30]

In the mystical perspective, the exploration of a *maqām* by a performer who, on the one hand, humbly adapts himself to the model or pre-existing pattern which makes up the mode and, on the other hand, improvises a series of melodic passages, of grace notes, and of vocalizations around the essential notes constitutes a true spiritual discipline. It demands as its basic condition *faqr*, detachment or interior emptiness, and in compensation brings the unveiling of a state (*ḥāl*) or rather a contemplative station, that is, in Sufi terminology, a *maqām*, a term which rejoins—and this is not an accident—that of the musicians. Lifted up on the wings of the melody, the musician is able to progress from *maqām* to *maqām*, up to the extreme limits of joy and plenitude, carrying along in his wake those listeners whose hearts are open.

Rhythm

The rhythmic structures—*uṣūl* (from *aṣl*, "root") or *īqāʿāt* (sing. *īqāʿ*)—serve the function of sustaining the melody while providing it with divisions, a temporal framework, and sometimes also a profound and majestic sonorous base. They produce periods of equal duration which, like the meters of prosody, are composed of beats now regular, now uneven, broken, and precipitous. The blows themselves are of two kinds, muffled and clear, and their infinitely varied combinations evoke the game of complementary principles such as heat and cold, dry and humid, active and passive, in the sustenance and renewal of cosmic harmony.

The effect of rhythm on the human soul is thus described by a contemporary scholar of the sciences and sacred art of Islam:

30 K. Reinhard and U. Reinhard, *Les Traditions musicales-Turquie* (Paris: Buchet-Chastel, 1969), pp. 69-70.

> The rhythm, the meter of the music changes the relation of man with ordinary time—which is the most important characteristic of the life of this world. Persian music possesses extremely fast and regular rhythms in which there are no beats or any form of temporal determination. In the first instance man is united with the pulsation of cosmic life, which in the human individual is always present in the form of the beating of the heart. Man's life and the life of the cosmos become one, the microcosm is united to the macrocosm. . . . In the second case, which transcends all rhythm and temporal distinction, man is suddenly cut off from the world of time; he feels himself situated face to face with eternity and for a moment benefits from the joy of extinction (*fanā*) and permanence (*baqā*).[31]

The Human Voice

Among the Arabs as among the ancient Semites, music was an exclusively vocal art, designated by the word *ghinā*, "song," which for a long time served to signify it, before being supplanted by the term *mūsīqā*, derived from Greek.[32] In pre-Islamic Arabia, it was in sung verses that the soothsayers and magicians rendered their oracles and uttered their incantations. Even if bards and professional singers (*qāinat*) played several instruments, these served above all to introduce or to accompany the sung poems.

The advent of Islam did not change at all the attraction exercised by vocal music, and song and poetry stayed in honor during the lifetime of the Prophet as well as after it. It is told, for example, how the Prophet admitted the presence of singers among his wives or how, while traveling, he asked some of his Companions to sing the *ḥudā*, poems that punctuate the march of the caravans.[33] When the chronicler al-Iṣfahānī reports, in the twenty volumes of his *Kitāb al-Aghānī* (*Book of Songs*), composed in the third/tenth century, the acts and gestures of the successive generations of musicians up to the Abbasid

[31] S. H. Nasr, "The Influence of Sufism on Traditional Persian Music," in *Islamic Art and Spirituality*, pp. 163-174.

[32] *Encyclopaedia of Islam*, under "Mūsīkī."

[33] Farmer, *History*, 25.

caliphate, it is all the cultural life of Arabia and the Near East, before and after Islamization, which he brings to life before our eyes.

For the philosopher and musicologist al-Fārābī, only the human voice is capable of attaining to perfect music, that is, to that which reunites the three virtues of the art of music: the ability to bring pleasure and calm, that of provoking certain emotions and certain sentiments, and that of speaking to the imagination and of inspiring ideas.[34] "Instrumental music sometimes possesses certain of these qualities," concludes al-Fārābī, implying by this that it never possesses them all; and he expresses thus a consensus that has always generally prevailed in the world of Islam. When, in a rare exception an instrument such as the *nay*, the reed flute of the Mawlawī dervishes, itself also attains by all evidence to the "perfect music," the initiated will explain that this is because it is itself a voice, a breath, that of the human soul which traverses the body, the microcosm purified by love.

Praises upon the Prophet (*amdāḥ nabawiyya*)

The second great source of knowledge after the Quran is the Prophet Muhammad, whose teachings, transmitted in the collections of *Ḥadīth*, and whose deeds, related in the *Sīra*, make up the prophetic "custom," the *Sunna*. If Quranic psalmody was able to give birth to different forms of modulated recitation, the person of the Prophet, for its part, has given rise to a great wealth of literary compositions and devotional songs. The importance of these litanies is linked in Islamic mysticism to the doctrine of the Perfect Man, *al-insān al-kāmil*, for Muhammad, if he is a man, is not a man like others. He is, according to a Sufi saying, "like a diamond among stones." He is also called "the best of created beings" or "the evident prototype," meaning by this that he is the summation of the entire creation, a universal model. To offer a prayer upon the Prophet is thus to pray for the salvation of all beings and is also to pray for the rediscovery of one's own primordial nature, to pray for one's own deliverance. Moreover, mystical gatherings almost always begin with praises upon the Prophet. In the Syrian *zāwiyas* of the Qādirī or Shādhilī orders for example, the gatherings

34 Erlanger, *La musique arabe*, 1:14-16.

open with a song, performed as a solo, of the *Mawlidiyya* of Shaykh Barzanjī (d. 1190/1766). The words are notably the following:

> Our Lord Muhammad was always smiling, affable; he never showed the least brutality, the least violence in his words or in his criticisms; he never made a show of his desires and he abstained from judging others and speaking ill of them. When he spoke, his companions kept silent as if a bird had perched on their heads; never did they raise their voices in argument, and when they spoke, it was he who was silent.

Another poem also very popular among the Sufis of North Africa and the Middle East is the *Burda*, the "Cloak," composed in Egypt by Muḥammad al-Būṣīrī (d. 694/1296), a work whose title recalls a miraculous healing. Being stricken by paralysis and moribund, in a dream Shaykh al-Būṣīrī saw the Prophet, who enveloped him in his cloak. Upon awakening, he found himself cured and able to move, and he carried the poem within him. It needed only to be transcribed. For seven centuries, it has been taken up in chorus by generations of *fuqarā*ʾ. Rhyming in *mī*, including 162 verses, it lends itself admirably to quick rhythmic variations and, always sung in unison, possesses a great emotional charge.

In Turkey, the meetings of the whirling dervishes, the Mawlawīs, also open with a song in praise of the Prophet, the *naat-i sherīf* by the composer Itrī (1050/1640-1123/1711), whose solemnity, reminiscent of Byzantine psalmody, plunges those attending into a state of recollection which prepares them to perform the whirling dance. It says:

> O Beloved of God, incomparable Envoy. . . .
> preferred among all the creatures. Light of our eyes. . . .
> Thou knowest the weakness of nations,
> Thou art the guide for the infirm,
> the guardian of the garden of prophecy,
> the springtime of gnosis,
> Thou art the rose garden of religious law and
> its most beautiful flower.

These examples, which could be multiplied, illustrate the way that Islam, while keeping itself from anything appearing as a divinization of the intermediary, recognized Muhammad as an ever-present spiritual guide, able to help the seeker through his influence and his intercession to approach the Lord of the Worlds. This manner of recognition, moreover, was not reserved solely for the Prophet, but includes, in Sufism, several categories of saints living or dead and, in Shiʿite Islam, the Imams and certain of their representatives.

Ecstatic Dance

Numerous Sufi orders practice various forms of "dance" accompanied by instrumental, vocal, or simply rhythmic background music. It is thus, at least in Western languages, that these corporeal exercises are named, although the Sufis themselves, cautious to avoid any confusion with the forms of entertainment that accompany popular or worldly merrymaking, generally avoid using the Arabic word *raqṣ*, which properly signifies "dance," and substitute other conventional expressions. In the classical treatises of Sufism,[35] dance is commonly designated by the term *samāʿ*, which, of course, applies to the totality of the spiritual concert but, taken in this limited sense, makes felt once again the central importance certain orders of dervishes accord to physical movements in the context of their mystical gatherings. In addition, the Sufis often speak of *ḥaḍra*, "presence," to designate ecstatic dance, suggesting by this, on the one hand, that the Prophet himself, together with the angels, attends the assembly of the *fuqarāʾ* and, on the other hand, that the rhythmic movement that animates the participants is made by a suprahuman power lent to man, so that it is not man who dances but God who makes him dance. They speak also, especially in the Maghrib, of *ʿimāra*, "plenitude," since he who, by the honesty of his intention and the strength of the collective dance

[35] Such as the *Risāla* (*Epistle*) of al-Qushayrī (d. 465/1072) and, by the same author, a short treatise on the conditions and the modalities of *samāʿ* (*aḥkām al-samāʿ*). See *al-Risāʾil al-Qushayriyya*, ed. F. Muḥammad Ḥasan (Beirut, n.d.); reprinted by the same editor (Karachi, 1964), pp. 50-63. See also the *ʿAwārif al-Maʿārif* of ʿUmar as-Suhrawardī, which contains a very interesting chapter on the *ādāb al-samāʿ*, a French translation of which was made by E. Blochet, *Études sur l'ésotérisme musulman* (Louvain, 1910).

empties himself of selfish thoughts and desires, receives in compensation an abundance of blessings.

The dance of the Sufis has nothing in common with either that which the word "dance" signifies in the West, or even with the traditional forms of Oriental and Far Eastern sacred dance, such as that of the Brahmanic temples or the Shinto sanctuaries, for example, where the protagonists mime and play the parts of supernatural powers. Nor is it a representation, because in principle only the participants take part in it; spectators are not admitted to gatherings except in exceptional cases, such as those of relatives or sympathizers wishing to benefit from the blessed ambience which issues from the gathering.

The movements that make up a *ḥaḍra* differ according to the brotherhood but can be reduced to a few fairly simple motions. According to the explanations given by the Sufis, in the beginning of the dance there is usually a spontaneous movement, of the same nature as that elicited by the arrival of good news. It is thus that the words of the Prophet addressed to certain of his Companions would have caused physical expressions of overflowing joy, which, imitated by other Companions and repeated from generation to generation, would be at the base of the *ḥaḍra*. An ecstasy of Abū Bakr was to give birth to the whirling dance practiced by the first group of Sufis before becoming the preferred rite of the Mawlawīs. Another, from Jaʿfar ibn Abī Ṭālib, was to be carried on in the leaps into the air to which numerous brotherhoods of *fuqarāʾ* give themselves over, particularly the Qādirī or Shādhilī orders.[36] Other movements such as the rapid lowering of the upper part of the body passing from a vertical position to a horizontal one and then returning quickly to the vertical in an increasingly rapid rhythm, or the rotation of the head alternatively to the right and to the left derive without doubt from the motions of the canonical prayer and appear linked to the punctuations of Semitic speech, which provoke a spontaneous rocking of the body during Quranic psalmody or Judaic prayer.

[36] We have already seen the explanation of the symbolism of these gestures given by Aḥmad Ghazzālī in his *Bawāriq*. The two great "styles" of the mystical gathering which they incorporate are described in greater detail in our chapter "The Spiritual Practices of Sufism" in *Islamic Spirituality: Foundations*, pp. 265-293.

Sacred dance, like music itself, grafted certain ethnic elements that the Sufis adopted onto the ancient Arabo-Semitic base, already enriched by the coming of Islam. These elements responded to the Sufis' own concerns. Rhythms of African singers (*griots*) entered into the Moroccan brotherhoods—the ʿIsawiyya, for example—by way of converted black slaves;[37] fragments of shamanistic ritual were integrated, it is said, into the *samāʿ* of the whirling dervishes;[38] breathing techniques were taken from Christian or Hindu monks, etc. The mystic path, by the same definition, has no borders, and the identical end sought by the seekers of God justifies the sharing of their means.

Whatever their methods, the dances of the dervishes all concur in the same goal, which identifies itself with other Sufi practices and is summed up in the single word *dhikr* (recollection, remembrance of the Divine), ending in the effacement of the creature and in his being taken over by the Being who knows no limits. Sometimes this "state of being" or "ecstasy" (*wijdān, wujūd*) already exists at the beginning of the dance, and this dance then is only the incoercible, spontaneous, and exterior manifestation of an interior state. Sometimes the dance appears like an "effort of seeking" (*tawājud*), which, according to the predisposition of the dancer, may or may not lead to a veritable ecstatic experience.[39] In all the cases, the ideas of spontaneity, simplicity, and absence of affectation reappear constantly in the teaching of the masters, who stress their importance in the validity of the *samāʿ* and its efficacy. Wishing to exculpate themselves and their disciples from the accusation of hypocrisy hurled by the exoteric scholars who accuse them of feigning ecstasy, certain masters went so far as to say that the dance should begin only when one or more dervishes had already entered into a state of rapture and become incapable of con-

[37] See J.-L. Michon, "ʿĪsawiyya," in *The Encyclopaedia of Islam*, 2nd ed.

[38] See M. Köprülüzade, "Influence du chamanisme turcomongol sur les ordres mystiques musulmans," *Mémoire Institut de Turcologie Université Stamboul*, N.S.I., 1929.

[39] The question of the relationships between *dhikr* and *samāʿ* and the primacy which, depending on the period and the school, was given to one or the other of these two is examined by F. Meier, "Der Derwischtanz," *Études Asiatiques* 8/1-4 (1954), pp. 107-136.

trolling themselves. At this moment their "brothers" had the duty of rising and joining them in the ecstatic dance. Most often, however, it is the enthusiasm of the dervish, his desire to give himself to God that is taken as the criterion of sincerity and, for the dervish, constitutes the authorization to throw body and soul into the *samā*ʿ and with the help of Grace to reach the desired goal, the extinction of self, the inner illumination.

THE SPIRITUAL NEEDS OF WESTERN MAN AND THE MESSAGE OF SUFISM

Seyyed Hossein Nasr

The need to recover a vision of the Center becomes ever more urgent for Western man as the illusory world he has created around himself in order to forget the loss of the transcendent dimension in his life begins to reveal ever more fully its true character. In such a situation, the response cannot, of course, come from anywhere but sacred tradition in all its authentic forms. But inasmuch as we are concerned here with Islam, the last of these traditions to manifest itself on the scene of human history, it is to this tradition that we shall confine ourselves, although much of what we have to say here would apply to other traditions as well. Moreover, since in viewing a mountain from far away it is first of all the peak that is seen and then sought after, it is Sufism, the peak as well as the spiritual essence and esoteric dimension of Islam, which attracts most of those from the outside who feel the need to recover the Center by submitting themselves to the message from the Center in its Islamic form. The amazing increase of interest in the West in recent years in the study of Sufism, much of which is unfortunately diverted by counterfeit presentations of Sufi teachings, is a result of both the growing spiritual need felt by many men and women today and the particular characteristics which Sufism possesses as the esoteric dimension of the Islamic tradition. A perspicacious application of the comparative method, taking into account the structure of the Islamic and the Occidental traditions, would reveal that nearly every aspect of the Islamic tradition, from the procedures of law at *Sharīʿite* courts to the description of Divine Beauty in poetry, can be of immense benefit in solving the problems of modern man. But it would also show that it is most of all the purely metaphysical and gnostic teachings of Islam, contained primarily in Sufism,[1] that

[1] We say "primarily in Sufism" because as far as Islamic esoteric doctrines are concerned Shiʿite gnosis in both its Twelve-Imam and Ismāʿīlī forms is

can provide the answers to the most pressing intellectual needs of men today, and that it is the spiritual presence contained within Sufism that can quench more readily the thirst of aspirants in search of God.

Today the need to benefit from the teachings of sacred tradition leads naturally, because of the anomalous situation of the modern world where the usual channels of transmission no longer exist, to the heart or to the most universal aspect of various sacred traditions, to the *Bhagavad-Gītā* and the *Tao Te Ching*, rather than to their more outward expressions. Islam is no exception to this general tendency, and as more Westerners seek outside the confines of their own religion for ways of escaping from the labyrinth within which they have become imprisoned, and turn in the direction of Islam, the interest in Sufism and in its amazingly rich message grows, a message which on the doctrinal level contains so wide a range, from the simple aphorisms of Abu Madyan to the vast metaphysical compendia of Ibn ʿArabī, from the gnostic prayers of Abu'l-Ḥasan ash-Shādhilī to the ocean of mystical poetry of Rūmī.

Before turning specifically to Sufism, it is necessary to make a few general remarks about the meaning of sacred tradition and its relation to the present spiritual and intellectual needs of Western man. In order to understand sacred tradition and to discuss the truth in its metaphysical sense, there must be (besides interest and the sense of need) the aid of Heaven and the presence of a discerning intelligence. It is, therefore, necessary first of all to concern ourselves with the meaning of "sacred tradition," of which Islam is an eminent example and also to the real nature of man's present-day spiritual needs. So much confusion has been cast upon these subjects as a result of the recent "pseudo-spiritual" explosion in the West that there is no way of understanding what kind of contribution Sufism can make to the task of saving man from his current plight without clearing the ground of prevalent errors and misconceptions.

Today many people speak of tradition in ways very different from the usage we employ here and throughout our writings. It is therefore necessary to clarify the meaning of this key term once again. Those who are acquainted with the majestic works of the traditional authors in the West such as F. Schuon, R. Guénon, and A. K. Coomaraswamy already have an understanding of the meaning of this term. It is the definition of tradition contained in the writings of these authors to which we adhere fully in all of our works. Therefore, by "tradition" we do not mean habit or custom or the automatic transmission of ideas and motifs from one generation to another, but rather a set of principles which have descended from Heaven and which are identified at their origin with a particular manifestation of the Divine, along with the application and deployment of these principles at different moments of time and in different conditions for a particular humanity. Tradition is therefore already sacred in itself and the term "sacred tradition" is, in a sense, a pleonasm which we have used only for the sake of emphasis. Moreover, tradition is both immutable and a living continuity, containing within itself the science of Ultimate Reality and the means for the actualization and realization of this knowledge at different moments of time and space. To quote Schuon, "Tradition is not a childish and outmoded mythology but a science that is terribly real."[2] Tradition is ultimately a sacred science, a *scientia sacra*,[3] rooted in the nature of Reality, and itself the only integral means of access to this Reality, which at once surrounds man and shines at the innermost

also of great importance. Moreover, the theosophy of Suhrawardī and Mullā Ṣadrā, which developed mostly in Persia and within the bosom of Shīʿism, is of particular importance for solving the present *impasse* of Western thought because of its innate metaphysical richness, and because it has a more systematic character than the metaphysical expositions of the school of Ibn ʿArabī, to which it is, in fact, related. The comparative method could very profitably be applied to this theosophy to juxtapose its teachings to such subjects as structuralism, evolution, the relation between logic and intuition, etc., with which modern Western thought, in both its religious and its non-religious form, occupies itself. This would be a separate program to which, without doubt, Muslim intellectuals as well as those in quest of revivifying true intellectual activity in the West will no doubt turn in the future as this theosophy (*al-ḥikmat al-ilāhiyya*) becomes better known.

2 F. Schuon, *Understanding Islam* (Bloomington, IN: World Wisdom Books, 1994), Foreword, p. ii.

3 For further elaboration of the meaning of *scientia sacra* see S. H. Nasr, *Knowledge and the Sacred* (Albany, NY: SUNY Press, 1989), chapter 4, pp. 130 ff.

center of his being. It is the call from the Center which alone can allow man to return from the rim to the Center.

As far as Sufism is concerned, strictly speaking it should not be classified along with other integral traditions such as Hinduism and Buddhism, because Sufism is itself a part of Islam and not an independent tradition. Islam can be spoken of as a tradition in the same way as one speaks of Christianity or Buddhism, whereas Sufism must be understood as a dimension of the Islamic tradition. This rather obvious point needs to be labored because often today in certain circles Sufism is taken out of its Islamic context with particular motives in mind and then discussed along with other Oriental or Occidental traditions.

Sufism is actually like the flower of the tree of Islam, and in another sense the sap of that tree. Or it can be called the jewel in the crown of the Islamic tradition. But whatever image is used, there remains the undeniable fact that, taken out of the context of Islam, Sufism cannot be fully understood, and its methods, of course, can never be practiced efficaciously, to say the least. Nor can one do justice to the wholeness of the Islamic tradition and its immensely rich spiritual possibilities by putting aside its inner dimension.[4] In speaking about Sufism, therefore, in reality we shall be speaking about the Islamic tradition itself in its most inward and universal aspect.

As for the question of the present needs of Western man which the message of sacred tradition in general and Sufism in particular can fulfill, it is essential to analyze fully its content and meaning, considering the cloud of illusion which surrounds modern man and makes the clear discernment of his environment and "living space," both external and internal, well-nigh impossible. There has been so much talk during the past century about change, becoming, and evolution that the permanent and abiding inner nature of man has been nearly forgotten, along with the most profound needs of this inner man. In fact the pseudo-dogma of evolution, as generally understood, which

[4] For the relationship between Sufism and the rest of the Islamic tradition, see F. Schuon, *Understanding Islam*, chapter 5; F. Schuon, *The Transcendent Unity of Religions*, trans. P. Townsend (Wheaton, IL: The Theosophical Publishing House, 1993); S. H. Nasr, *Ideals and Realities of Islam* (London: George Allen & Unwin, 1966), chapter 5.

continues to dominate the horizon of much of modern anthropology and philosophy in the teeth of rapidly accumulating evidence concerning the essentially unchanged nature of man during the many millennia that have passed since his entering upon the stage of terrestrial history, has made it impossible for those who adhere to it to understand who man is.[5] Moreover, the permanent nature of man having been forgotten, the needs of man are reduced to the sphere of accidental changes which affect only the outer layer and crust of man's being. When people speak of human needs today, most often they mean the man who is confined to the rim and cut off from the Center, the man who is only accidentally human and essentially animal, the man who no longer fulfills his primordial mandate as God's vicegerent (*khalīfa*) on earth.

In reality, the needs of man, as far as the total nature of man is concerned, remain forever the same, precisely because of man's unchanging nature. "Man is what he is, or he is nothing."[6] The situation of man in the universal hierarchy of being, his standing between the two unknowns which comprise his state before terrestrial life and his state after death, his need for a "shelter" in the vast stretches of cosmic existence, and his deep need for certainty (*yaqīn* in the vocabulary of Sufism) remain unchanged. This latter element, the need to gain certainty, is in fact so fundamental that the Sufis have described the stages of gaining spiritual perfection as so many steps in the attainment of certainty.[7]

[5] See S. H. Nasr, *Man and Nature, the Spiritual Crisis of Modern Man* (London: George Allen & Unwin, 1976), pp. 124-129; S. H. Nasr, "Man in the Universe," in *Eternità e storia. I valori permanenti nel divenire storico* (Florence, 1970), pp. 182-193; also in S. H. Nasr, *Sufi Essays* (Chicago, IL: ABC International Group, 1999), chapter 6.

[6] F. Schuon, *Logic and Transcendence*, trans. P. Townsend (London: Perennial Books, 1984), "The Contradiction of Relativism," pp. 7-18.

[7] Usually, three stages of certainty are distinguished, based upon the language of the Quran: "the science of certainty" (*'ilm al-yaqīn*), "the eye of certainty" (*'ayn al-yaqīn*), and the "truth of certainty" (*ḥaqq al-yaqīn*). These stages have been compared to "hearing a description of fire," "seeing fire," and "being burned by fire." See Abū Bakr Sirāj ad-Dīn, *The Book of Certainty* (Cambridge, UK: The Islamic Texts Society, 1992).

The very fact that in the West there is so much interest today in Oriental metaphysics and spirituality, the fact that so many people in Europe and even more in America search avidly for books of instruction or poetry and music associated with Sufism, is itself indirect proof of the fact that there is a profounder nature in man which does not "evolve," a nature whose needs remain unchanged. This more permanent nature may be temporarily eclipsed but it cannot be permanently obliterated. The rationalistic philosophers of the eighteenth and nineteenth centuries never dreamt that a century or two after them so many people in the Western world would again become interested in religion, in metaphysics and cosmology, and even in the occult sciences, which in their unadulterated form are branches of the traditional cosmological sciences. These men would be surprised to discover that, a century or two after them, the works of Taoist sages or the rishis of India or Sufi masters would be read more avidly than much of their own writings. The rationalistic philosophers of the past two centuries along with their anti-rationalist but still profane opponents regarded only the outer crust or rim of man's being, and they saw in its condensation and consolidation, its gradual separation from the world of the Spirit or the Center, a progress and an evolution which they thought would be a continuous process. They did not realize that the crust would break of its own accord as a result of the advancement of the very process of its solidification, and that the needs of the inner man would manifest themselves once again on the scale we see before us today.

It was once asked of ʿAlī what existed before Adam. Echoing the teachings of the Prophet, he answered, "Adam." The question was repeated. He again answered, "Adam," and added that if he were to answer this question to the end of time he would repeat, "Adam." The profound meaning of this saying is that man in his essential reality has not undergone evolution and that there is no "before man" in the sense of a temporal predecessor or a state from which man developed "in time." A million years ago men already buried their dead and believed in the Invisible World.[8] Over ten thousand years

[8] See J. Servier, *L'Homme et l'invisible* (Paris: R. Laffont, 1964).

ago, man not only produced masterpieces of art but even described the motion of the heavens in a most remarkable manner in myths and stories which reveal a power of "abstraction" that could match any of the feats of men of later periods of history.[9]

It is this man—obliterated temporarily by the progressive and evolutionary theories of the past two centuries in the West—to whom tradition addresses itself and it is this inner man whom tradition seeks to liberate from the imprisonment of the ego and the suffocating influence of the purely externalized and forgetful aspect of the outer man. Moreover, it is tradition alone which possesses the means for his liberation, and not the pseudo-religions so prevalent today, which, seeing the resurgence of the needs of the inner man, try to entice those with a less discerning eye by means of parodies of the teachings of the sacred traditions, to which they almost invariably add something of the evolutionary pseudo-philosophy to make sure that men do not discover who they really are. But that inner man continues to abide within all men and to make its demands upon man no matter how far he seeks to escape from his own Center and no matter what means he uses to obliterate the traces of the inner man upon what he calls "himself."

Of course when all is said concerning the permanent needs of man—needs which in fact must be emphasized in the strongest terms possible because they have been so forgotten in the modern world—it must be remembered that these needs concern only one pole of man's being, namely the essential pole. As far as the other pole is concerned, the pole which involves man's temporality and the historico-cultural conditions that color the outer crust of his being, it can be said that man's needs have changed. They have changed not in their essence but in their mode and external form. Even in traditional societies, all of which have been based on immutable transcendent principles, the forms in which the spiritual needs of a Japanese have been fulfilled has not been the same as that of an Arab nor have these forms been externally the same over the centuries. So much more is this true in

[9] See G. Di Santillana and E. von Dechend, *Hamlet's Mill* (Ipswich: Gambit, 1969). These examples could be multiplied tenfold in many fields, not the least amazing of which are the remarkable alphabets developed by some of the indigenous nations of Africa.

the modern world, where men live in a desacralized *milieu* divorced from principles, where the psyche is separated from the Spirit which is its own source of life, where the experience of time and space, not to speak of all kinds of human relations, have altered completely and where the sense of authority has gradually disappeared. In such conditions there naturally appear new modes through which even the deepest human needs must be fulfilled.

The very fact of the advancement of the process of the consolidation of the world has introduced cracks in the closed world of materialism which permit not only the dark forces from below but also light from above to enter into this world.[10] This process causes at the same time a reawakening of man to his real needs, which leads naturally to a desperate attempt to find means of fulfilling these needs. But precisely because of the changed external circumstances, many modern men do not understand the conditions or are not willing to undergo the necessary sacrifices to become worthy of receiving the message of Heaven, which in its unadulterated form is contained only within the living orthodox and sacred traditions of the world. Also, many authorities from these traditions—leaving aside the pretenders who have recently flooded the Western scene—have become habituated to the traditional world from which they have issued and therefore are not aware of the differences existing between the psyche of Western man and that of men of traditional societies, nor of the different forms that Western man's spiritual needs take because of the particular world in which he has been nurtured.

In speaking of present needs, it is essential to keep in mind both these poles, namely the permanent nature of man's needs, which makes all the traditional teachings about man and his final end pertinent and in fact vital, and the changed external modes of man's needs due to the particular experiences of modern man, which necessitate the application of these teachings to existing conditions. It must be remembered that traditional authority and authenticity must be preserved, that Truth cannot evolve, that it is man who must make himself worthy of becoming the recipient of the message of Heaven, not

[10] See R. Guénon, *The Reign of Quantity and the Signs of the Times*, trans. Lord Northbourne (Ghent, NY: Sophia Perennis et Universalis, 1995).

vice versa, that Truth cannot be distorted to suit the passing whims and fashions of a particular period, and that there is an objective Reality that determines the value of man and his thoughts and actions and finally judges them and determines the mode of his existence in the world to come. At the same time, it must be recalled that this sacred tradition must be applied to the particular problems of modern man with a consideration of the anomalous conditions in which he lives, without this process distorting or destroying the authenticity of the tradition. The modern world is witness to an array of men and women and organizations which attempt to cater to the spiritual needs of modern man, ranging from authentic masters and organizations from the East often unaware of the particular nature of the audience they are addressing,[11] to the rare few who have succeeded in applying traditional teachings to the particular conditions of modern man,[12] to the vast number of pseudo-masters and dubious organizations, ranging from the innocuous to the veritably satanic, which remind one of the saying of Christ about false prophets arising at the end of time.

[11] We have in mind many spiritual masters and their spiritual organizations who have come to the West in the past few decades and sought to increase their following by disseminating exactly the same techniques and methods to Westerners as they were applying in the East, with the result that many people unqualified for initiation have been allowed to practice methods that have been either fruitless or harmful to them and in certain cases have led to insanity. Many authentic *bhakti* masters from India have spread their message to Western disciples as if they were addressing a traditional Hindu audience. The results of such efforts are clear for all to see. In any case, the tree is judged by the fruit it bears. Such cases must, however, be clearly distinguished from the self-proclaimed masters who do not issue from any orthodox traditional background but have the audacity to place themselves "above" traditional teachings and the perennial truths expounded by saints and sages throughout the centuries.

[12] The whole group of traditional writers in the Western world, consisting of such men as R. Guénon, A. K. Coomaraswamy, M. Pallis, T. Burckhardt, and especially F. Schuon, who occupies a special position among them, belong to this category and for this reason play a role of outstanding importance in the spiritual and religious life of the modern world even if their works have, until recently, been neglected in many circles.

To draw from the resources of sacred tradition to fulfill present needs necessitates remaining totally within the matrix of sacred tradition and at the same time applying its methods and teachings to a world in which men have needs that are at once perennial and yet conditioned by the particular experiences of modern man.

An important condition which has colored deeply the mental processes of modern man and today lies at the heart of the new religious movement in the West, albeit usually unconsciously, is Cartesian dualism and the reaction which has set in against materialism in the West within the context of this dualism. Cartesian dualism divided reality into the material and the mental, positing a non-material substance which somehow is able to gain knowledge of the levels of existence which it reduces to a single quantitative reality. The excessive materialism of the past centuries has now led many people to reject this materialism itself. But just as in physics a reaction is opposed to an existing action identified with matter on the same level of physical reality, so also has this philosophical and religious reaction set in within the already existing framework of classical Cartesian dualism. For a large number of people, the reaction against materialism means, almost unconsciously, attraction towards the other pole of Cartesian dualism, namely the non-material, but without there being any discrimination within the non-material domain between the Spirit and the psyche, the *rūḥ* and the *nafs* of Sufism. Hence, for many people who are unaware of this fundamental distinction, the psychic and mental realm has come to replace the spiritual and the religious.

Islam teaches that the rebellion against God takes place on the level of the psyche, not on that of the body. The flesh is only an instrument for the tendencies originating within the psyche. It is the psyche that must be trained and disciplined so as to become prepared for its wedding to the Spirit. Both the angelic and the demonic forces manifest themselves in this intermediate psychic plane, which is neither purely material nor purely spiritual. The paradisal and the infernal states of the soul refer to the macrocosmic counterparts of the various levels of this intermediate substance as it becomes molded and transformed by the Spirit and angelic or demonic influences. This substance, moreover, within the microcosm, or man, stretches from the corporeal to the Divine Center within the heart of man. Therefore, to identify all that is non-material with the sacred or spiritual is sheer folly and a most dangerous error, which has come into being as a result of the optical illusion lingering from the delimitation of reality into two domains by Cartesian dualism. But it is an error that is very prevalent in the new religious movements in the West and especially in America today, an error which in certain cases can open the soul of man to the most infernal and dissipating influences, throwing the personality of those who fall prey to them into disequilibrium. To identify simply the non-material with the spiritual is to misunderstand the nature of Reality, the complexity of the human soul, the source and reality of evil, and the spiritual work necessary to reach the Fountain of Life which alone can satisfy in a permanent and not an illusory and transient manner the spiritual thirst of man.

This mistaking of the psychic for the spiritual, so characteristic of our times, is reinforced by another powerful tendency issuing from man's need to break the boundaries of his limited world of external experience. The Sufis have always taught that man is in quest of the Infinite and that even his endless effort toward the gaining of material possessions and his dissatisfaction with what he has is an echo of this thirst, which cannot be quenched by the finite. That is why the Sufis consider the station of contentment (*riḍāʾ*)[13] to be an exalted spiritual condition attainable only by those who have reached the "proximity" of the Infinite and have shed the bonds of finite existence. This need to seek the Infinite and overcome the limits of whatever is finite is clearly discernible in the new religious ferment in the West today. Many modern men are tired of the finite psychological and physical experiences of everyday life no matter how materially comfortable that life may be. Having no access to the authentic spiritual experience which in traditional societies provides the natural means of breaking the limits of finite existence, they turn to new psychic experiences of all kinds which open for them new worlds and horizons, even if they be infernal. The great concern with psychic phenomena, "trips," extraordinary "experiences," and the like, is deeply related to this inner urge to break the suffocating and limited world of everyday life in a civilization which has no purpose beyond moving with acceler-

[13] Concerning this spiritual station, see S. H. Nasr, *Sufi Essays*, chapter 5.

ated speed toward an illusory ideal state of material well-being that is always just round the corner.

This tendency, added to the one which unconsciously identifies the non-corporeal with the spiritual, has succeeded in bringing about a most dangerous confusion in the religious life of modern man in the West and particularly in America, where the need for a rediscovery of the world of the Spirit is keenly felt. From the Sufi point of view, which has always distinguished clearly between the psychic and the spiritual, so many of those who claim to speak in the name of the Spirit today are really speaking in the name of the psyche, and are taking advantage of the thirst of modern man for something beyond the range of experiences that modern industrial civilization has made possible for him. It is precisely this confusion that lies at the heart of the profound disorder one observes in the religious field in the West today, and which enables elements that are as far removed as possible from the sacred to absorb the energies of men of good intention and to dissipate rather than to integrate their psychic forces.

The sacred, as already stated, is related to the world of the Spirit and not of the psyche. It is whole and holy; it illuminates and integrates rather than causing men to wander aimlessly through the labyrinth that characterizes the psychic and mental worlds whenever these worlds are deprived of the light of the Spirit. The sacred, precisely because it comes from God, asks of us all that we are. To sacralize life and to reach the sacred we must become ourselves sacred, like a sacred work of art. We must chisel the substance of our soul into an icon which will reveal us as we really are in the Divine Presence, as we were when we were created, the *imago Dei*; for as the Prophet of Islam has said, "God created man upon His image." In order for man to become this work of art, to become himself again, he must surrender and dedicate himself fully to the commands of the Spirit, to the sacred. It is only the sacred that can enable man to remove the veil which hides his true nature from himself and makes him forget his own primordial, theomorphic nature (the *fiṭra* mentioned in the Quran). And it is only the sacred, which comes from the Spirit and not the psyche, that can be the source of ethics, of aesthetics in its traditional sense, of metaphysical doctrine, and of methods of realization. The psyche may appear fascinating or absorbing. But in itself it is always no more than amorphous, full of impressions that are transitory and partial. It is only the spiritual or the sacred that is permanent and total and that, precisely because of its totality, embraces the psychic and even the corporeal aspects of man and transforms and illuminates them.

The application of sacred tradition—whether it be Sufism or some other Way—to the actual needs of man cannot begin at a more critical point than this present juncture of human history, where it can provide the means of discerning between the spiritual and the psychic and, by extension, between those whose teachings are of a truly spiritual nature and those whose message is rooted only in the psychic and supported solely by psychic phenomena, related to experiences which without the protective matrix of sacred tradition can lead to the most infernal depths of cosmic existence and to states that are much more dangerous to the soul of man than various forms of crass materialism.

Turning to the Sufi tradition itself, it must be said that the understanding of it, as of many other traditions, is made difficult in the modern West because of the presence of another optical illusion which mistakes the mental understanding of metaphysics for the full realization of its truths. This illusion, which is the result of the separation between the mental activity of certain men and the rest of their being, and which is directly related to a lack of spiritual virtues, is a major hindrance in the application of the sacred teachings of various traditions to the present needs of Western men. There are those who possess intellectual intuition, itself a gift of Heaven, and who can understand the doctrines of Sufism or other forms of Oriental metaphysics, but who are not willing to live their lives in accordance with the teachings of the sacred tradition whose flower they are able to scent from far away.[14] Such people confuse their vision of the mountain peak, *theôria* in its original sense, with actually being on

[14] "Metaphysical knowledge is one thing; its actualization in the mind quite another. All the knowledge which the brain can hold, even if it is immeasurably rich from a human point of view, is as nothing in the sight of Truth. As for metaphysical knowledge it is like a divine seed in the heart; thoughts are only very faint glimmers from It" (F. Schuon, *Spiritual Perspectives and Human Facts* [Bedfont: Perennial Books, 1987], p. 9).

top of the mountain. They therefore tend to belittle all the practical, moral, and operative teachings of tradition as being below their level of concern. Most of all they mistake the emphasis upon the attainment of spiritual virtues (*faḍāʾil* in Sufism) for sentimentality, and faith (*īmān*) for "common religion" belonging only to the exoteric level,[15] forgetting the fact that the greatest saints and sages have spoken most of all of spiritual virtues and that one of the most widely used names for Sufism is "Muhammadan poverty" (*al-faqr al-muḥammadī*).[16] Without this poverty or *faqr*, the cup of man's existence has no empty space into which the nectar of Divine Wisdom can be poured. Without it no spiritual attainment is possible, no matter how keen the intelligence may be.

This prevalent error of identifying the theoretical understanding of metaphysics with spiritual realization is related to the anomalous situation of our times in which the purest metaphysical teachings of various traditions are easily available in translation for just a few dollars at every bookshop, works ranging from the *Song of Solomon*

[15] For the role of "faith" in the realization of the highest metaphysical truths, see F. Schuon, "The Nature and Arguments of Faith," in *Stations of Wisdom* (Bloomington, IN: World Wisdom Books, 1995), pp. 43ff.

[16] The great Algerian saint of the twentieth century, Shaykh Aḥmad al-ʿAlawī, often repeated the Sufi saying, "He whose soul melteth not away like snow in the hand of religion, in his hand religion like snow away doth melt" (trans. M. Lings in his *A Sufi Saint of the Twentieth Century* [Berkeley: University of California Press, 1973]). This dictum is a direct allusion to the need for man's separate existence to melt away in the Truth through the attainment of the virtues, which are the only way in which the Truth can become actualized in the being of man. Despite the emphasis upon this basic feature of all authentic spirituality by masters of old as well as by the leading present-day exponents of traditional doctrines such as F. Schuon and T. Burckhardt, there has now formed a whole group of "traditionalists" in the West who accept the teachings of tradition mentally but who do not find it necessary to practice the disciplines of an authentic Way and to discipline their souls in order to become themselves embodiments of the Truth. It is in their case that the second part of the saying of Shaykh al-ʿAlawī applies, for religion or Truth simply melts away in their hands instead of becoming actualized in their being.

to the *Tao Te Ching*. Obviously, such was not the case in the normal historical situation. In a traditional society, most of those drawn to the metaphysical and gnostic aspects of their tradition are made to undergo gradual instruction which prepares them for the reception of gnostic doctrines only after long training. Moreover, their knowledge of tradition is through personal contact. They live the exoteric form of the tradition—which is absolutely necessary and indispensable—in their everyday lives, and they contact esoterism most often by encountering a master or his disciples, or by visiting the tomb of a saint, or by having a dream which incites them to seek a particular master or go to a particular place. Even when their contact with esoterism is through reading, it is most often through literature and parables that their interest in the Way is gradually aroused. For every thousand people in the Islamic world who read the poetry of Ḥāfiẓ or Rūmī, only one or two read the purely doctrinal treatises of Sufism.

Today in the West there is a truly anomalous situation in which the contact of most men with tradition must of necessity begin from the top and through the channel of the written word or books, which play a special role in an age when the usual channels of oral transmission have become blocked in so many parts of the world. As a matter of fact, the very availability of the highest metaphysical teachings of not one but most of the sacred traditions today—not to speak of the remarkable expositions of the authentic contemporary traditional writers in the West—is a result of the Divine Mercy, which has made possible this compensation during an age of spiritual eclipse, inasmuch as one irregularity deserves another. But the danger present in this situation is precisely the mistaking of the mental understanding of some sacred text for the living of a tradition, which involves not only the mind but the whole of man's being.

With this reserve in mind, it must nevertheless be added that even on the plane of the mind the presence of expositions of traditional doctrines, whether they be of a metaphysical or a cosmological order, can fulfill one of the deepest needs of modern man, who can be characterized as a being who thinks too much and often wrongly, and who is over-cerebral. Even a mental understanding of traditional doctrines can therefore be like a blanket of snow which brings with it peace and calm and quiets the agitation of the skeptical and questioning mind. It can bestow upon man an intellectual certitude which corresponds to what in traditional Sufi terminology is called "the science of certainty" (*'ilm al-yaqīn*)[17] and therefore make the person who has attained such a degree of knowledge aware of the fact that the ultimate aim of knowledge is not to collect an ever-increasing number of facts and to chart areas beyond the present "frontiers" of knowledge, but to reach the Center within and to gain a vision of or even become the knowledge which has always been and will always be. This calming of the agitated mind by providing answers to questions posed by reason, answers which are the fruit of revelation, illumination, or intellection, then provides the necessary background and condition for the actual illumination of the mind and, in fact, of the whole being of him whose reason has been nourished by traditional knowledge rather than having been left to its own machinations.[18]

[17] As already mentioned (note 7), the Sufis usually distinguish between three degrees of certainty, which cover the major steps of the initiatic process, from the mental knowledge of the sacred, to its vision, and finally to its realization in one's being. In one of his famous aphorisms, Ibn 'Aṭā'illāh al-Iskandarī, using a somewhat different terminology, refers to these fundamental stages in these words:

> The ray of light of spiritual vision (*shu'a' al-baṣīra*, corresponding to *'ilm al-yaqīn*) makes you witness His nearness to you. The eye of spiritual vision (*'ayn al-baṣīra*, corresponding to *'ayn al-yaqīn*) makes you witness your non-being as due to His Being. The truth of spiritual vision (*ḥaqq al-baṣīra*, corresponding to *ḥaqq al-yaqīn*) makes you witness His Being, not your non-being or your being.

See V. Danner, Ibn 'Aṭā' Allāh's *Sufi Aphorisms* (Leiden: Brill, 1973), p. 30, no. 36, containing the English translation of the aphorisms which we have here slightly modified. See also P. Nwyia, *Ibn'Aṭā' Allāh et la naissance de la confrérie šādilite* (Beirut: Dar-el-Machreq, 1972), pp. 102-103, no. 33, where both the Arabic original and the French translation are given.

[18] "In knowledge, reasoning can play no part other than that of being the occasional cause of intellection: intellection will come into play suddenly—not continuously or progressively as soon as the mental operation, which was in its turn conditioned by an intellectual intuition, has the quality which makes of it a pure symbol" (Schuon, *Spiritual Perspectives and Human Facts*, p. 13).

Considering the importance of doctrinal works in this process of calming the mind and preparing the person of a contemplative bent for true intellection, it is unfortunate that, as far as Islamic metaphysics is concerned, few of its riches in this domain have been translated into English in comparison with what one finds from Hindu, Buddhist, and Taoist sources. A few of the greatest masterpieces of Islamic metaphysics, such as the *Fuṣūṣ al-Ḥikam* of Ibn ʿArabī and *al-Insān al-Kāmil* of al-Jīlī are now known and partially translated,[19] but a vast treasury of works by both Sufis and Islamic theosophers such as Suhrawardī, Ṣadr ad-Dīn al-Qūnyawī, Ibn Turkah al-Iṣfahānī, Mīr Dāmād, and Mullā Ṣadrā, who have composed major doctrinal and metaphysical treatises, remain almost completely inaccessible to a Westerner without a mastery of Arabic or Persian.[20] In this way, the

[19] Thanks to the efforts of T. Burckhardt, there are excellent summaries with precious notes of both these works in French as *La Sagesse des prophètes* (Paris: Albin Michel, 1955), translated into English by A. Culme-Seymour as *The Wisdom of the Prophets* (Gloucestershire: Beshara Publications, 1975) and *De l'homme universel* (Paris: Dervy-Livres, 1976), translated by A. Culme-Seymour as *Universal Man* (Gloucestershire: Beshara Publications, 1983). Burckhardt has also summarized the doctrinal teachings of the school of Ibn ʿArabī in his *An Introduction to Sufism*, trans. D. M. Matheson (Northamptonshire: The Aquarian Press, 1990). In English also there are several partial translations of Sufi doctrinal works, including *Studies in Islamic Mysticism*, by R. A. Nicholson (Cambridge: The University Press, 1978), which contains a translation of parts of al-Jīlī's *al-Insān al-Kāmil*, and several translations by A. J. Arberry of al-Kalābādhī, Ibn al-Fāriḍ, and others. What are needed, however, are complete translations into English of these and the many other works of those Sufi masters who have given an open exposition of Sufi doctrine.

The case of Ibn ʿArabī is exceptional for the last few years have witnessed the appearance of many fine translations of his works into French and English. See J. Morris, "Ibn ʿArabī and His Interpreters," *Journal of the American Oriental Society*, vol. 106, 1986, pp. 539-51, 733-56; and vol. 107, 1987, pp. 101-19. See also the two major works of W. Chittick containing a great deal of translation of the master's texts: *The Sufi Path of Knowledge* (Albany, NY: State University of New York Press, 1989); and his *The Self-Disclosure of God* (Albany, NY: State University of New York Press, 1998).

[20] As far as this school of theosophy (*al-ḥikmat al-ilāhiyya*), to which we

application of the teachings of Islam in its esoteric and metaphysical aspects to the present-day needs of Western man is handicapped by a lack of well-translated material which would make the vast treasures of this tradition accessible to those capable of reaping their fruit. Also, the true appreciation of all that the Islamic tradition can offer to contemporary man has become difficult, since in the case of other traditions their most universal teachings are relatively well-known, but in the case of Islam most studies in Western languages have been devoted to its legalistic and formal aspects, while its most universal aspects have not received the attention they deserve, at least not in an unadulterated form. To this obstacle must be added the negative image of Islam propagated by so much of the media in the West.

Some who wish to follow a tradition today are in fact deceived by this situation into thinking that Islam is at best concerned only with law, Divine justice and punishment, rigor, etc., while it is possible to follow other traditions by simply reading their gnostic treatises or even by taking some of their particular initiatic practices out of context and practicing it, without having to be burdened with moral considerations or questions of Divine justice and punishment. Actually, this is a most unfortunate modern delusion arising from the fact that, as a result of a reaction against an unintelligible moralism within certain forms of modern Christianity, many people today belittle the importance of morality, and as a result of the rebellion of modern man against Heaven and of the loss of the meaning of authority, the importance of the fear of God in religious life has been well-nigh forgotten by most Western men today. The prophetic utterance, "Fear of God is the beginning of Wisdom" (*ra's al-ḥikma makhāfat Allāh*),

have already alluded above, and its importance for an understanding of Islamic metaphysics are concerned, see S. H. Nasr, *Three Muslim Sages* (Carefree, Arizona: Caravan Books, 1976), chapter 2; Nasr, "The School of Isfahan" and "Ṣadr al-Dīn Shīrāzī" in *The Islamic Intellectual Tradition in Persia* (London: Curzon, 1996), and the many works of H. Corbin, who has devoted a lifetime to making this as yet little studied aspect of Islamic intellectual and spiritual life better known in the West. See especially his *En Islam iranien*, particularly vols. 2 and 4. He has also translated one of the major treatises of Mullā Ṣadrā, the *Kitāb al-mashā'ir*, into French as *Le Livre des pénétrations métaphysiques*.

which echoes the well-known Pauline dictum, holds true not only for Islam or Christianity but for all traditions. In Islam there is a Divine Law (*Sharīʿa*) which concerns man's actions and which all Muslims, Sufis or non-Sufis, must follow.[21] There is also emphasis upon the fear of God, and an eschatology which is related to God's judgment of human action on earth. But then these elements are also present, in other forms, in Hinduism and other Oriental traditions. Hinduism has not only produced the *Gītā* and the *Vedānta* but also elaborate treatises on *pralaya*, the Last Judgment, and on *karma* and the serious consequences of human action on earth for man's posthumous states. It would be the worst illusion to imagine that one can practice, let us say, Yoga and forget all about morality or the consequences of human acts in the eyes of God simply because one has moved from one tradition to another. In every integral tradition one can find the fear, the love, and the knowledge of God in one form or another. As al-Ghazzālī has said, he who fears the Creator runs towards Him and loves Him, and he who loves Him knows Him.

The historic manifestations of Sufism reveal the phases of fear (*makhāfa*), love (*maḥabba*), and knowledge (*maʿrifa*), and the cycle repeats itself within the soul of every man who is able to attain spiritual realization. If one can complain from one point of view that the gnostic and metaphysical works of Islam have not been translated widely enough, one can be thankful from another point of view that the integral teachings of Islam, including the *Sharīʿa*, are there to test the seriousness of those who would aspire to reach its inner chamber, by requiring them to become first of all aware of the justice and majesty of God. Such an awareness creates in man an awe and fear that is absolutely positive and that melts away from the substance of the soul all that is alien to its primordial nature.

In fact, it is in order to evade this test and this protecting criterion that recently pretenders have appeared in the West who wish to divorce Sufism from Islam and present it as if it had nothing to do with the teachings of Islam and its *Sharīʿa*, which provides the Divine matrix for human action and protects the man who follows it from the wrath of God. This effort is no more than sheer delusion. In

[21] See S. H. Nasr, *Ideals and Realities of Islam*, chapter 4.

all authentic manifestations of Sufism, the fear of God, described so majestically in the Quran and incorporated in the attitudes promulgated by the *Sharīʿa*, prepares the ground for the love of God, and the love of God in turn leads to gnosis, the knowledge of God, which cannot sink its roots into the being of man unless the soil of this being has been prepared for such a Divine plant by the fear of God and His love, a love which in Islamic spirituality always accompanies knowledge.

So far, most of what has been said concerns all traditions, but it is now appropriate to ask what is unique about Sufism itself as it concerns the present needs of man. There is an Arabic saying which states that "the doctrine of Unity is unique" (*at-tawḥīd wāḥid*). This means that at the highest level there is only one truth, in which all traditions are unified. But as the Divine Truth descends from the one peak downwards towards men, it takes on the characteristics which distinguish one tradition from another.

Sufism, being the inner dimension of Islam, shares, in its formal aspect, in the particular features of this tradition. Since Islam is based on Unity (*at-tawḥīd*), all of its manifestations reflect unity in one way or another; this is especially true of Sufism, in which the principles of the revelation are most directly reflected. The presence of the principle of unity in Sufism means, among other things, that its methods and practices unify what in other traditions are usually separate and distinct. To use the terminology of Hinduism—which is a miracle on the religious plane because of the different spiritual forms that have existed within it—the way of *karma* Yoga, *bhakti* Yoga, and *jñāna* Yoga are combined in Sufism into a single way, one might say into an "integral Yoga." It is especially important to note that whereas in Hinduism the *jñāna* and *bhakti* types are quite distinct,[22] Sufi spirituality is essentially a *jñāna* one which, however, is never divorced from the *bhaktic* element. Some Sufis may emphasize one aspect more than another. Some, like Ibn ʿArabī, Ibn ʿAṭaʾillāh al-Iskandarī, and Shabistarī, may speak more of gnosis (*maʿrifa*) and some like ʿAṭṭār

[22] Even in Hinduism, however, there is the *parabhakti* form of spirituality which is gnostic but colored by *bhaktic* elements. Therefore, by referring to the clear separation between these two forms of spirituality in Hinduism, we did not mean to exclude their synthesis within the Hindu climate.

and Ḥāfiẓ more of love. But in no instance does one find in Sufism a path of knowledge completely separated from love or a path of love without the element of gnosis, such as the kind of love mysticism found in Christianity and also in mediaeval Hinduism. Moreover, this combination of knowledge and love in Sufism is always based on the support of the *Sharīʿa*, or, in a sense, on a way of work or action.

Also because of the unitary nature of the Islamic revelation, the contemplative and active ways have never been totally separated either outwardly or inwardly in Sufism. There is no outward monasticism in Islam, and the most intense contemplative life in Islam is carried out within the matrix of life within society. The Sufi has died to the world inwardly while outwardly he still participates in the life of society and bears the responsibilities of the station of life in which destiny has placed him. In fact he performs the most perfect action, because his acts emanate from an integrated will and an illuminated intelligence. Rather than being in any way contradictory, the contemplative and active lives complement each other in all Islamic spirituality,[23] and the methods and techniques of the contemplative life are such that they can be performed in whatever outward circumstances a person may find himself and in whichever form of active life he may have to participate.

This unitive character of Sufism, both in its own methods and in its relation to man's outward life in society, offers obvious advantages for men living in the modern world, where inner withdrawal is usually more of a possibility than is outward separation from the world. Also the unitive nature of Sufism is a powerful remedy for the disintegrated life from which so many people in the modern world suffer. The total integration of the personality achieved in Sufi training is the goal

[23] This does not mean to imply that there have never been any hermits or wandering dervishes among Muslims. They can still be found in various parts of the Islamic world today. It means that Islamic spirituality in its main current combines these two modes. Some Sufi orders such as the Shādhiliyya and the Niʿmatullāhiyya in fact insist on their adepts having a definite profession and practicing the contemplative life within active life in society. They prefer the life of the contemplative who lives in society (*mutasabbib*) to the contemplative who is withdrawn from society (*mutajarrid*).

sought by much of psychotherapy and psychoanalysis, which, however, can never achieve this goal, for their methods as practiced today are cut off from the grace of the Spirit which alone can integrate the psyche. As a result, they usually lead to its disintegration rather than to its integration. God has placed religion in the world to enable man to overcome his complexes, in addition to performing numerous other functions for him. Any caricature and parody of religion and especially of initiatic techniques cannot but result in a caricature and parody of the effect religion has had over the ages in removing man's complexes and integrating his personality.

The pertinent question that will undoubtedly be asked is: granted that Sufism does contain these characteristics, what are the possibilities of practicing it? Of course one cannot gauge the mercy of Heaven, for the "spirit bloweth where it listeth," but as far as the traditional teachings of Sufism are concerned, it is always emphasized that there is no practice of Sufism possible except through a master who is referred to traditionally as *shaykh*, *murshid*, or *pīr*. The only exception is that of special individuals (*afrād*) who are disciples of the ever-living but hidden prophet Khaḍir[24] and who are in any case chosen for the Way by Heaven. Therefore this possibility is not an option for man to choose. As far as the aspirant is concerned, the only way open to him is to find an authentic master. The question of the practical possibility of living according to the disciplines of Sufism, therefore, comes down essentially to the possibility of finding an authentic master who can instruct the disciple as to how and what he should practice. As far as the Western world and especially America are concerned, it is neces-

[24] Khaḍir, who corresponds to Elias, symbolizes the esoteric function in the story of Khaḍir and Moses in the Quran, and is represented usually as the "green prophet." See A. K. Coomaraswamy, "Khwaja Khadir and the Fountain of Life, in the Tradition of Persian and Mughal Art," *Studies in Comparative Religion*, vol. 4, Autumn 1970, pp. 221-230. In Shi'ite Islam, the Twelfth Imam fulfills a similar function, and in Sufism in general the Uwaysīs are a particular order who are said to receive initiation from the "invisible master." See also the numerous studies of L. Massignon on the spiritual significance of Khaḍir, for example, "Elie et son role transhistorique, Khadiriya en Islam," *Etudes carmélitaines: Elie le prophète*, Paris, 1956, vol. 2, pp. 269-290.

sary to mention the danger of false masters, of those who pretend to be guides without possessing the necessary qualifications, which are given by God alone. Even in classical times, when the danger of "false prophets" mentioned by Christ was much less than in these late hours of human history, authentic masters took care to warn against the perils of submitting oneself to an unqualified "master." In his incomparable *Mathnawī*, Jalāl ad-Dīn Rūmī says:

> Since there is many a devil who hath the face of Adam, it is not well to give your hand to every hand.[25]
> The vile man will steal the language of dervishes, that he may thereby chant a spell over (fascinate and deceive) one who is simple,
> The work of (holy) men is (as) light and heat, the work of vile men is trickery and shamelessness. They make a woolen garb for the purpose of begging.
> They give the title of Aḥmad (Muhammad) to Bā-Musaylim. . . .
> The wine of God, its seal (last result) is pure musk, (but) as for (the other) wine, its seal is stench and torment.[26]

There is a mystery in the way man chooses a master and a spiritual path, to which allusion is made by Rūmī himself and which cannot be solved by rational analysis alone. The problem is this: how can a candidate for initiation who does not as yet possess spiritual vision distinguish a true master from a false one when there must already be a true master to actualize the possibilities within the disciple and to enable him to distinguish the wheat from the chaff? Herein lies that mysterious relationship between the Spirit and its earthly embodiments which escapes being understood discursively. Man believes that he chooses the Way but in reality he is chosen by the Way. What

[25] This is a direct reference to the act of initiation through which a disciple becomes attached to a particular master and order.

[26] R. A. Nicholson, *The Mathnawī of Jalālu'ddin Rūmī* (London: Luzac & Co., 1926), vol. 2, pp. 20-21, with a small alteration in the verse "They make a woolen garb," which Nicholson has translated as "They make a woolen lion," basing himself on another version of the original Persian verse. See also S. H. Nasr, *Sufi Essays*, pp. 61 ff.

man can do is to pray to find a true master and have reliance upon God while searching. He can, moreover, apply the universal criteria of authenticity and orthodoxy at a time when there are many more pretenders than when Rūmī wrote about them, at a time to which Christ referred in his initiatic saying, "Many are called but few are chosen."

The Truth has a way of protecting itself from profanation, but the soul of man can be destroyed if molded in the hands of someone who does not possess the right qualifications and who is no more than a pretender. Better to remain an agnostic or a materialist than to become a follower of some pseudo-spiritual movement which cannot but do harm to what is most precious within man. The Sufis compare man to an egg that must be placed under a hen for a specific period in order to hatch. If, however, it is placed underneath a hen which leaves the egg early or does not take the necessary care of it, then the egg will never hatch and cannot even be eaten.[27] It will become useless and can only be thrown away. This parable depicts the danger of placing oneself in the hands of a pretender, in the care of those who brush aside centuries of tradition for a supposedly higher and more "evolved" form of spirituality, or who want to crash the gates of Heaven by means of Sufism without the grace and aid of the Prophet of Islam, whose spiritual presence (*baraka*) alone can enable the initiate to rise upon the ladder of perfection extending to Heaven. We live in dangerous times when the possibilities of error are many, but also by compensation the paths towards God are opened before men in ways never dreamt of before. It remains for each individual to practice discernment and to distinguish between the true and the false, between the way of God and the way of Satan, who is traditionally known as the "ape of God."

Despite all the false masters and forms of pseudo-spirituality, there are still authentic Sufi masters, and the possibility of practicing Sufism in the West is certainly present. But we believe that such a possibility will not involve all the people interested in Sufism today. Most likely in the near future Sufism will exercise its influence in the West not on one but on three different levels. First of all, there is the possibility of practicing Sufism in an active way. Such a path is naturally meant

[27] We have dealt more extensively with this theme in *Sufi Essays*, p. 63.

for the few. It demands of man complete surrender to the discipline of the Way. To practice it one must follow the famous saying of the Prophet, "Die before you die." One must die to oneself and be reborn spiritually here and now. One must devote oneself to meditation and invocation, to inner purification, to the examining of one's conscience and many other practices prevalent among those who actually walk upon the Path (*sālikūn*). There are already some who practice Sufism seriously in the West, and, besides the pseudo-Sufi movements of little import, certain branches of traditional and orthodox Sufism have already sunk their roots in the West and have established authentic branches there. This group is surely bound to grow, although it cannot embrace all of those who are attracted to Sufism in the West today.

The second level on which Sufism is likely to influence the West is by presenting Islam in a more appealing form to many who would find in general Islamic practices what they are seeking today in the name of Sufism. Because of a long historical background of conflict with the West, Islam has, until quite recently, been treated in the Occident in the most adverse manner possible. Many who would find exactly what they are looking for in the daily prayers and the fasting of Islam, in its integration of the secular into the sacred, in its dissemination of the sacerdotal function among all men, in its arts and sciences and many other features, are driven away from it because of the way in which it is usually presented to them. Sufism could help to explain Islam by elucidating its most universal and hence, in a sense, most comprehensible aspect, and therefore making it more approachable to outsiders. Usually when people want to study Hinduism they begin with the *Bhagavad-Gītā* and not the *Laws of Manu*, whereas in the case of Islam, as already stated, the legalistic aspects are usually taught first and the most universal teachings, if touched upon at all, follow afterwards in a disjointed manner. As it becomes more fully realized that Sufism is an integral part and in fact the heart of Islam and the flower of this tree of revelation, the possibility of the practice of Islam for many who are now attracted to Sufism but who cannot undertake the difficult disciplines of the Path itself will become more evident.

There is no question here of proselytizing, as far as we are concerned, but the fact remains that many in the West are seeking Oriental religious forms to practice and follow in their everyday lives, but put

Islam aside because they do not identify it with its spiritual aspect, of which Sufism is the essence. Once this identification is clearly made, Sufism may play a role (and in fact is doing so to some extent already) in the West similar to the role it played in India, Indonesia, and West Africa in spreading Islam itself. Of course in the West its method and the extent of its activity will certainly be different from what we find in the above instances, but its function will be similar. It will open a possibility within Islam for many earnest Western seekers attracted to Sufism today, and it can also make available to them that intermediate region between esoterism and exoterism which is known to those who have studied the structure of Islam carefully.

Finally, there is a third level upon which Sufism can play an important role in the West: that is, as an aid to recollection and reawakening. Because Sufism is a living tradition with a vast treasury of metaphysical and cosmological doctrines, a sacred psychology and psychotherapy rarely studied in the West, a doctrine of sacred art and traditional sciences, it can bring back to life many aspects of the Western tradition forgotten today. Until recently, the usual historical works in Western languages on Islam relegated Sufism, along with other aspects of Islamic intellectuality, back to the thirteenth century, and described it as if it had died out long ago. Now, as more people in the West discover that it is a living tradition, contact with its riches can certainly play the role of reawakening Western man to many of his own forgotten treasures. The trends of the past few decades have not been that hopeful, but the possibility is nevertheless present.

Moreover, Sufism possesses teachings concerning the nature of man and the world about him which contain keys to the solutions of the most acute problems of the modern world, such as the ecological crisis.[28] Its teachings, if conveyed in contemporary language, could aid in solving many present-day problems which have come into being in the first place because of the forgetting of first principles. Its very presence could create, through a kind of "sympathetic vibration," the revival of a more authentic intellectual activity and the revivification of precious aspects of the Western tradition which were covered by

[28] See S. H. Nasr, *Man and Nature, the Spiritual Crisis of Modern Man*, chapter 3.

the dust created by the storm which shook the West during the period that has paradoxically come to be known as the Renaissance.

If, however, Sufism is to provide for some of the present-day needs of the West, it must be able to preserve its own integrity and purity. It must be able to resist the powerful forces of deviation, distortion, and dilution visible everywhere today. It must serve the world about it like a crystal which gathers the light and disseminates it to its surroundings. At the same time it must be able to address the world around it in a language which that world understands. Sufism cannot leave unanswered the appeal of those who call upon it. Nor can it in any way compromise its principles in order to become more fashionable or more widely heard, to become a fad which would disappear from the scene with the same rapidity with which it had become popular. In order to present Sufism in a serious manner above and beyond transient fads and fancies, it is therefore necessary to remain strictly traditional and orthodox from the point of view of the Sufi tradition and at the same time intelligible to Western man with the particular mental habits he has acquired and the reactions towards things he has developed within himself. Also, in order really to accept and practice the teachings of Sufism, it is necessary for the modern aspirant to realize that, in fact, he is drowning, that sacred tradition is a rope thrown towards him by the Divine Mercy, and that with its aid alone can he save himself. In the present situation, those who are rooted in the Sufi tradition and who can also expound it in a manner that is comprehensible to modern men and that addresses their real needs bear a great responsibility upon their shoulders. It is for them to preserve the purity and integrity of the message, yet to be able to transmit it to men conditioned by the factors that characterize the modern world. But in performing this task, such men fulfill their highest duty and accomplish the most worthy act of charity, for there is no higher form of charity than the expression of the Truth, which alone can provide for man's deepest and most abiding needs.

ON THE NAME *ALLĀH*

Leo Schaya

The Name "*Allāh*"—which is written as *A-L-L-H* or, with all its vowels, *A-L-L-ā-H-u*[1]—results etymologically from a combination of the Arabic definite article *al-* ("the") with the noun *ilāhun* ("divinity"), which then becomes *al-ilāhu* through its linkage with the article. One translates this name as "the Divinity" which, in the meaning intended by the language of the Koran, excludes any other "god" (*ilāhun*). In Sufism, the Name *Allāh* is synonymous with "the Pure Reality": this can exclude or include, according to the point of view one takes on the relativeness of reality.

We are going to consider the Name *Allāh* in the light of Sufi doctrine. According to this doctrine, the Name indicates both the pure and supreme "Essence" (*adh-dhāt*) and Its "Quality of Divinity" (*al-ulūhiya*) or Its Universality. In the *Book of the Name of Majesty—Allāh* by Muḥyi 'd-Dīn ibn ʿArabī, we read that this Name, although it designates the supreme Essence alone, also appears within the various degrees of All-Reality. The Essence contains, indeed, all realities, and Its Name contains all the truths of the Divine Names; this is why Its Name is often used when a more particular name of God might be used to designate one of His specific aspects. In such cases, the name *Allāh*, which is beyond any limiting definition, "replaces" any such particular designation of the divine Reality.

Ibn ʿArabī also says: "The Name *Allāh* is, in relation to the other Divine Names, as the supreme Essence is in relation to the Qualities that are included in It. All the Divine Names are contained in this Name. They issue forth from it, and toward it they re-ascend." Finally, ʿAbd al-Karīm al-Jīlī says in *The Universal Man*:

> Know that the Divine Nature which encompasses all the Realities of Being and maintains them in their respective degrees is called the

[1] The word *Allāhu* is pronounced *Allāh* when it is in the nominative case and is not immediately followed by another word in a spoken phrase.

> "Quality of Divinity" (*al-ulūhiya*). And I mean by *Realities* of Being (*ḥaqā'iq al-wujūd*) both the principles (*aḥkam*) which condition the different states of manifestation, and that which is manifested therein, that is to say God (*al-Ḥaqq*) and the creature (*al-khalq*) at the same time. The "Quality of Divinity" signifies, then, that which totalizes the Divine Dignities (i.e. Divine Aspects), at the same time as all the degrees of existence, and which assigns to every thing that which returns to it from Being. The name *Allāh* designates the Master of this supreme dignity which can only belong to the Absolute Essence. The supreme affirmation of the Essence is, then, that of the "Quality of Divinity" which "Itself" encompasses and synthesizes all the affirmations and governs every Quality and every Name.[2]

He also says:

> [Since] there is access to the knowledge of God . . . only through the intermediary of His Names (which reveal the "Being of His Aspects") and His Qualities (which reveal the "mode of Being" or the "mode of manifestation" of His Aspects), and each Name and each (Divine) Quality being contained in the Name *Allāh*, it follows that there is no access to the knowledge of God except by way of this Name. In truth, it is this Name which in reality communicates (supreme and universal) Being and which leads toward Him.[3]

Thus, the Name *Allāh* is not merely the verbal expression that indicates the Divine Essence and Its All-Reality or Universality, but it actually "gives" what it designates. It thereby becomes in Sufism the means of spiritual assimilation of the one Real and of complete identification with It. This is also true for the other Divine Names, inasmuch as they represent aspects of the "Supreme Name" (*al-ism al-a'ẓam*) and represent access to It. This is true whether they are "Names of the Essence," "Names of the Qualities," or "Names of the

[2] *Universal Man* (*al-Insān al-Kāmil*) by 'Abd al-Karīm al-Jīlī, translated with commentary by Titus Burckhardt, English translation by Angela Culme-Seymour (Roberton: Beshara Publications, 1983), p. 16.

[3] Ibid, p. 8.

Activities" of God.[4] But when one considers each of these Names within its own function, it conveys "only that which corresponds to its condition," while from the name *Allāh* "one can reap all the fruits (of spiritual realization, namely All-Reality)," because it is "without any conditioning particularity."*

The mystery common to all the Divine Names is therefore that they "are" and that they actually "transmit" what they designate; thus, they allow the one who pronounces them to identify spiritually with the Named. This is not in any way the same with names of created beings, which are only analogical terms intended for the symbolic and mnemonic assimilation into thought of that which is named. This "non-total" assimilation or identification also occurs in the pronunciation of the Divine Names when a person stops at their verbal forms and doesn't fulfill the traditional conditions of "invocation" (*adh-dhikr*). These conditions vary according to the religion in question and to the levels of application, and they alone can elevate that person beyond himself.

From the sensorial or formal point of view, the Divine Name is only a simple word and a vestige of mental activity, like the designation of any thing, but from the spiritual point of view it is a sacred

[4] "One may distinguish . . . between 'Names of the Essence' (*asmā' dhātiya*) and 'Names of the Qualities' (*asmā' ṣifātiya*); it is that the former, such as the One (*al-aḥad*), the Most Holy (*al-quddūs*), the Independent (*aṣ-ṣamad*), express the Divine Transcendence and refer then more exclusively to the Essence, whereas the Names of the Qualities, like the Clement (*ar-raḥmān*), the Generous (*al-karīm*), the Peaceful (*as-salām*), etc., express at once the transcendence and the immanence of God. The latter Names include, moreover, also those of the Divine Activities (*al-af'āl*) like He-who-gives-life (*al-muḥyī*), He-who-gives-death (*al-mumīt*), etc." (Titus Burckhardt, introduction to *Universal Man*, pp. xvii-xviii).

* Editors' Note: The phrase "conditioning particularity" might best be understood by considering that all individual Divine Names are limited in the scope of what they refer to and thus what they convey, while the Name *Allāh* is not "individual" in this same sense (thus It is not "particular") and it is not possible that there could be any action of limiting or "conditioning" upon It. If something is "particular," it necessarily has limits or conditions imposed upon it, and this cannot be the case for the Name that subsumes all: *Allāh*.

word, a revealed ideogram that not only symbolizes but also contains, like a chalice ready to be emptied, the "real Presence" (*al-ḥuḍūr*) of the Named. The infinite Content of the "chalice" flows into the "heart" (*al-qalb*), the spiritual organ of "the invoker" (*adh-dhākir*), to the extent that he thirsts for It. When this "influx" occurs, the container, the Name, reveals Its identity with the Content or the Named; then the *dhākir* knows, according to the expression of Ibn ʿArabī, that "the Name is He"; and reaching the ultimate expression of the invocation, he realizes that the invoker, the Name, and the Invoked are but one.

The Divine Name is the mediator between the one who invokes and the One who is invoked. It is the non-human "Messenger" of God, just as the human "Messenger," because of his total and permanent realization of the Name, is called the "invocation of God" (*dhikru 'Llāh*). In truth, there is but one "Messenger," who is manifested within the formal world in one connection in human form and in another connection as an expression of language. These two forms unite spiritually in that invocation which actualizes their shared and supra-formal content: *Allāh*. Anyone who invokes the Name of God, conforming to His Will, is integrated by the same into His "Messenger," who alone is suited to lead the way to the Supreme. In the same way that the Prophet is both man and God, the Name is simultaneously speech and God. That which the Prophet accomplished in his time, namely the "direct mediation" between humanity and the Divinity, the Name achieves from generation to generation: It is the "Messenger" that is present in every era; It is the synthesis of all divine and created Names, of the entire Koranic revelation (which itself sums up all previous revelations), of all prayer and all ritual gesture, as well as of all deiform aspirations, virtuous acts, and wise thoughts; It is God Himself dwelling within and supporting the whole of creation and fully gratifying with His revelatory and saving Presence those who call to Him with sincerity. This is in accordance with God's word transmitted by the Prophet: "I keep company with the one who invokes Me."

The Name *Allāh* is the Divine Essence that knows Itself in Itself. This occurs even through the illusory appearances of Its manifestation of created beings. This illusion perpetually fades away into the Non-

Manifestation that is real only to the Name. Muḥyi ʾd-Dīn declares in his *Book of the Name of Majesty—Allāh*: "The Name *Allāh* is entirely non-manifestation. From within the domain of manifestation it offers, at the most, but an exhalation";* and: "*Allāh* is a negative term (denying everything that is not He, the only Real) that secludes Itself within the (infinite and absolute) higher-order World, and he who would interpret It vanishes along with It"; or, as has already been said: "The proper signification of this Name is that It designates the supreme Essence and nothing else." And here, in substance, is how Muḥyi ʾd-Dīn explains the symbolism of the constituent letters of the name *Allāhu*:*

* Editors' Note: This passage, taken from Vâlsan's translation of Ibn ʿArabī, goes on to explain that this "exhalation" comes about when someone actually pronounces the Divine Name. Ibn ʿArabī points out that when the final vowel "-u" appears (as in *Allāhu*), the last syllable is then "*Hu*," which refers to the most profound "exhalation" possible—"the *Huwa*, He, the Universal and Absolute Self." Indeed, many Sufis use "*Huwa*" or "*Hu*" as their primary invocation. Ibn ʿArabī also states that unlike the special case of when the Name is pronounced, when the Name is written "there is nothing outside of a pure non-manifestation." This is presumably because in the latter case the sacred syllables remain unvoiced, and thus unmanifested.

* Editors' Note: It may be useful for those unfamiliar with Arabic to see the letters. Here is a diagram of the Arabic letters that make up the Name. Note that they are read from right to left:

و ه ا ل ل ا

(6) (5) (4) (3) (2) (1)

(1) The first letter, *alif*. In the Name, it is pronounced like the vowel in "up."
(2) The second letter, *lām*. In the Name, it has a unique sound, somewhat heavier than the "l" in "love."
(3) The third letter, another *lām*. This doubled *lām* causes the "l" sound to be held longer.
(4) The fourth letter, *alif*. In pronunciation, this second *alif* is held longer than the first.
(5) The fifth letter, *hā*. This is pronounced as a voiced consonant, far back in the throat, like the "h" in "he."

- The first *A*(*lif*) signifies: the one Real;
- the first *L*(*ām*): His pure Knowledge of Himself;
- the second *L*(*ām*): His Knowledge of Himself through His "All-encompassing Possession," which penetrates the illusory aspects of all that is "other than Him";
- the *L*(*ām*)-*A*(*lif*), that is, the passing from the second *L*(*ām*) to the second *A*(*lif*), which together form the word *lā* ("no"): these signify the automatic negation of any form of negation (such as ignorance or otherness) within His Essence, which is symbolized by the second *A*(*lif*);
- the *H*(*ā*), the ideogram of *Huwa* ("He"): the Essence that rests in His absolutely non-manifested Selfhood;
- finally, the "*u*"—*W*(*āw*) that appears as the diacritical mark *ḍamma* above the *Hā* (and is pronounced only if the Name *Allāh* is followed in a sentence and in the nominative case by another word): this signifies the world eternally non-manifested in the absolute non-Manifestation of the one Real.[5]

Thus, as Muḥyi 'd-Dīn says, "It is He alone, *Huwa*, that remains, and it is He that is sought" in His Name. He Himself seeks Himself

(6) The sixth letter, *wāw*. The sound is similar to the pure "oo" sound in "room" (without any additional vowel diphthongs). It should be noted that this letter is not actually part of the Name. It is added to the Name when grammatical considerations require it.

When the Name is written, only (1), (2), (3), and (5) are fully visible. When joined together, they are:

الله

When written, the Name usually includes other characters, particularly to indicate the second *alif*, but those above are the essential components. It might be noted, too, that the written Name is sometimes used as a contemplative support in Sufism.

[5] We cannot enter here into all nuances and variants of this symbolism offered by the writing of Ibn 'Arabī.

through the "other," to whom He makes known that this other is not other than He; and the "other," which is dualistic ignorance, evaporates within His Knowledge of Himself, and "it is He only that remains." All this is achieved in the eternal "instant" within the uncreated Name, so that, actually, ignorance is perpetually erased in the one Real that knows Itself. Yet, from the illusory point of view of this "other," there seems to be progressive extinction of "otherness" within "Selfhood" (*al-huwiyya*): the "other" invokes the Name *Allāh* while searching for Him through the meditation of His Aspects and the concentration of the mind on His Unity, until "He alone remains." This reintegration and dissolution of "otherness" into "Selfhood" is traced out in the Name by a secret language spoken by Sufis: in invoking the Name *Allāh*:

- one passes from the *A*(*lif*) to the *L*(*ām*), so that the Name is reduced to *L-L-a-H*, which one will read as *liLlāh* ("to *Allāh*"), which signifies that the illusory appearances of "otherness" form an integrative part of the divine All-Reality;
- in continuing the invocation, the Name is reduced to *L-a-H*, which must be read as *la-Hu*, ("to Him"), which means that man and all things essentially identify with the divine "Self," called "Him";
- the invocation [ultimately] reaches the *H*(*ā*), which indicates *Huwa* ("Him"): "it is He alone that remains."

The Name is Essence and Knowledge of Essence; man is Essence and ignorance of Essence. After having been the representative of God or of His plan for a perfect reflection of Himself, man has become like His broken and inoperative mirror, while God's Name is, to every degree and in all cycles of universal existence, His incorruptible and revealing Form. Earthly man is no longer attended by the real Presence of God except in Its latent and virtual state, while the Name contains this Presence in Its permanent Actualization: the Name communicates this Presence to man to the extent that the latter calls to God with a true "thirst." *Allāh* made His Name known to man so that the latter would recover his lost Unity in the invocation, for He, His Name, and man are of a single Essence. In other words, *Allāh* is the Essence of the Name and of man; He is truly present in man, as in His Name;

but after Adam's fall, He is hidden in man and is only revealed to him by His Name.

When the Koran (29:45) says that "the invocation of *Allāh* is the greatest (thing of all)" it is not only affirming the superiority of the Name *Allāh* over all other Divine Names revealed in Arabic, but also that the most perfect invocation is the one in which God is seen as being the Invoker.* In truth, He who invokes, the Name, and Named are but one. This is, as we have said, the mystery of the invocation, and it is this very thing that man must achieve while invoking God. That which in itself is one, appears first of all through the "prism" of cosmic distinctivity as being separated, but God reveals the "link"—which leads to "unity"—between Himself and the one who invokes Him, in this appeal: "Remember Me [or: 'invoke Me'] and I will remember you . . ." (Koran 2:152). God thus establishes, says Ibn ʿArabī,

> the existence of His remembrance of His subjects in relation to our remembrance of Him. . . . He won't remember you before you have remembered Him. But you will not be able to remember Him until He has granted you adequate assistance and inspired in [or: 'breathed into'] you His invocation. [Ibn ʿArabī also says:] The invocation carried out by the servant is accomplished through the actualizing power (of the real Presence of the Lord), whereas the one performed by the Lord is accomplished by (His) real Presence (*al-ḥuḍūr*).

The "effort of actualization" or the "exercise of the real Presence" (*al-istiḥdār*) comes about first in spiritual "retreat" (*al-khalwa*) ordained and supervised by a spiritual Master. Al-Ghazzālī, in his *Revivification of the Sciences of Religion*, says on this topic:

> When the intense desire to follow this way [i.e. Sufism] seized me, I consulted one of the main Sufis, a very famous man, on the ardent recitation of the Koran. He gave different advice, saying: "The best

* Editors' Note: The Arabic phrase can be interpreted as both "the invocation of God" (i.e. our invoking God) and "God's invocation" (i.e. God's invocation of Himself). This latter invocation would then naturally be interpreted to be greater than any other.

> method consists of completely cutting ties with the world, in such a way that your heart does not occupy itself with family, nor with children, nor with money, nor with homeland, nor with science, nor with government—the existence or the non-existence of these things being for you of equal value. In addition, for you to be alone in a retreat, it is necessary to accomplish among your duties of worship only the prescribed prayers, those that precede them and those that follow them, and being seated, to concentrate your thought on *Allāh*, without other interior occupation. You will first accomplish this by pronouncing the Name of *Allāh* with your tongue, repeating without ceasing: *Allāh, Allāh*, without losing your concentration.[6] The result will be a state in which you will feel this Name in the spontaneous movement of your tongue without any effort on your part."

Al-Ghazzālī specifies that the one who has reached the "state in which one stops the movement of the tongue and sees the word (*Allāh*) as flowing over it . . . moves from there to the point where he erases all traces of the word on the tongue and finds his heart continually engaged in the *dhikr*, he perseveres in this assiduously until it comes about that he erases the image—the letters and the form—of the word from his heart, and the sense (that is, the supra-formal and infinite Reality) of the word alone abides in his heart, present in him, as if conjoined to him, never departing from him."

The spiritual "retreat"—which must be carried out only under the direction of an authentic Master—thus requires in the beginning "completely cutting ties with the world," not only in the way that it surrounds us, but also, and especially, in the way that it lives within us under the form of cosmic illusion, which separates us from the one Real. This requires the continual pronunciation of the Divine Name. "Say *Allāh* and put aside existence and that which surrounds it, if you want to accomplish my perfection. If you accomplish this well, everything, except God, is nothingness, both individually and all together," said Abū Madyan, the great saint of Algeria. The Sufi ʿAbd al-Qādir al-Jīlānī stated: "When you say *Allāh*, He answers you; none other than He enters your heart."

[6] The scriptural foundation of this Sufi method is found in the following verse of the Koran: "And invoke *Allāh* much and often" (33:41).

To the extent that a man joins himself to the world, he distances himself from God. In attaching himself to the multiplicity of created things, he exteriorizes through his thoughts and actions the spirit that resides within him as a direct manifestation of the Divine Immanence. Though lost within the multiplicity that surrounds him and fills his soul, man does enjoy glimmers of the Divine Immanence by which all things maintain their very life and shape. Yet, he forgets that the Divine Immanence gives Itself to him and to the world in order that created beings may affirm the one Real within It, and in order that human beings, who are endowed with intelligence and free will, may contemplate Him within the Divine Immanence until there is full identification with Him. This is why man must strip his thoughts of the multiplicity of created things, detach his bodily and psychic vigor from the world, focus on God, and invoke Him with his whole heart. Then his mind, free of the fetters of illusory existence, itself goes into retreat and his whole being enters with him into his divine Essence.

According to Ibn ʿArabī,

> The messenger of *Allāh* (may *Allāh* bless and give him peace!) said: "The final Hour will only come when there is no longer on the face of the earth anyone who says *Allāh, Allāh*!" He did not stipulate (the invocation of God) by anything other than this word *Allāh*, because this word is the one of the invocation practiced by elite beings, those through whom *Allāh* preserves this lower world, as well as every house in which they are found. When there are no longer any of them in this world, there will no longer be a protective force for the world, and then the world will come to an end and destroy itself.

And the Prophet transmitted these words from God:

> *Allāh* the Most High has said: "O son of Adam, so long as you call upon Me, and hope in Me, I shall forgive you for what you have done, and I shall not concern (Myself with it). O son of Adam, if your sins were to reach to the clouds of the sky and were you then to ask forgiveness of Me, I would forgive you. O son of Adam, if you come to Me with so many sins that they fill the earth, and you meet Me without having ascribed partners to Me, I will forgive you with the same great amount of forgiveness."

JESUS IN THE QUR'AN: SELFHOOD AND COMPASSION—AN AKBARI PERSPECTIVE

Reza Shah-Kazemi

Ibn ʿArabī refers to Jesus as a "symbol of engendering" (*mathalan bi-takwīn*). It is my intention in this paper to show that, in the metaphysical perspective of Ibn ʿArabī's school, one of the most important principles of which the "Qur'anic" Jesus stands forth as a "symbol," sign, and concrete embodiment, is the following: mercy and compassion are the fruits of the realization of the true Self—or the Self of the Real, the *Nafs al-Ḥaqq*, as Ibn ʿArabī calls it. Compassion, in turn, should be understood not only morally *but* also, and *a priori*, metaphysically, in terms of the bestowal of life: God gives life to the cosmos out of compassion for His own hidden qualities that long to be known; and man participates in this process both positively—through being compassionate towards his own self, as well as towards others—and inversely, by enlivening his own soul and that of others through the knowledge of God. The Qur'anic narratives concerning Jesus, together with the esoteric interpretations thereof from the Akbari perspective, illuminate these intertwined realities of selfhood and compassion in a particularly fruitful manner. Jesus is described in the Qur'an "as a sign for mankind and a mercy from Us."[1] Ibn ʿArabī draws out in a most instructive way how these two aspects of Jesus can be spiritually understood: what Jesus is a sign of, and how this relates to mercy or compassion.

I shall begin this paper by referring to the Qur'anic passages in the *Sūra Maryam* that relate the stories of the birth of John and Jesus. One

[1] He is, according to Qāshānī, "a spiritual form of divine compassion" (*ṣūra al-raḥma al-ilāhiyya al-maʿnawiyya*). This comes in his comment on the words in verse 21 of *Sūra Maryam* (chap. 19) ". . . a mercy from Us." See his *Tafsīr*, mistakenly attributed to Ibn ʿArabī, *Tafsīr al-Shaykh al-Akbar* (Cairo, 1283 AH), vol. II, p. 6.

observes a number of remarkable similarities in these two passages.[2] There is in both cases—to Zachariah, the father of John, and Mary, mother of Jesus—the apparition of an angel to announce the news of the imminent birth of a son; the words addressed to them by the angel, and the responses given by them are similar; several of the phrases used to describe John and Jesus are identical; a vow of silence is observed by both Zachariah and Mary after their vision of the angel, etc. But there are also notable differences between the two narratives, in particular the following one: whereas it is the angel who describes John, it is Jesus who describes himself, through the miraculous words uttered by him as a baby still in his cradle. Indeed, it is the degree of miraculousness that, in general, distinguishes the two narratives: the birth of Jesus to the Virgin was a more absolute kind of miracle as compared with the lesser prodigy of John's being begotten by Zachariah, though "my wife is barren and I have reached infirm old age" (19:8). But one should pay particular attention to the words at the end of Jesus' discourse: "Peace be upon me the day I was born, the day I die, and the day I shall be raised up alive." In the case of John, it is the angel who invokes peace upon him: "Peace be on him the day he was born, the day he dies and the day he shall be raised up alive."

The reader is struck by the contrast between the invocation of peace upon oneself, and the invoking of peace on another. Furthermore, it is peace with the definite article, *al-salām*, that Jesus invokes upon himself, whereas it is the indefinite form, *salāmun*, that is invoked by the angel on John. It is as if there is a deliberate juxtaposition here between the divine attribute of peace, in respect of Jesus, and the general quality of peace—ultimately divine, in its essence, but considered here at the level of its formal manifestation—in regard to John. This contrast might be interpreted as an allusion to the fullness of divine life, and the totality of supreme Self-consciousness that infused the human substance of Christ from his very inception, this substance itself being the very Word of God. In this connection, Ibn ʿArabī alerts our attention to an extremely important analogy. The Qurʾan tells us that Jesus was indeed God's Word, "cast unto Mary, and a spirit from

[2] *Sūra Maryam* (chap. 19): verses 1-15 give the story of Zachariah/John; and 16-33, that of Mary/Jesus.

Him" (4:171): Ibn 'Arabī comments upon this, saying that Gabriel transmitted this Word to Mary just as a prophet transmits God's Word to his community.[3] Ibn 'Arabī thus shows that there is something in the very substance of Jesus that is, in and of itself, a revelation, "a sign for mankind," as the Qur'an says (19:21). Such a view of Jesus narrows, in certain respects at least, the gap that separates a Muslim from a Christian conception of the "message" of Christ.[4]

In the *Fuṣūṣ al-Ḥikam* we find Ibn 'Arabī commenting on this contrast between the two greetings of peace. In the chapter on John we read:

> If the speech were that of the spirit: Peace be upon me the day I was born, the day I die, and the day I shall be raised up alive—that is more complete as regards the reality of union and as regards doctrine, and more lofty in interpretation.[5]

'Abd ar-Razzāq Qāshānī provides just such a "lofty interpretation" with his comment on this invocation of peace upon oneself:

[3] *Fuṣūṣ al-Ḥikam* (Cairo, 1321), p. 173; see the English translation of the *Fuṣūṣ* by Ralph Austin, *Bezels of Wisdom* (New York: Paulist Press, 1980), p. 175.

[4] Meister Eckhart may be said to have made the inverse movement, by coming close to an "Islamic" conception of Christ, in some of his pronouncements. For example: "Now you might ask me, since I have everything in this (human) nature that Christ can perform according to his humanity, why then do we praise and magnify Christ as our Lord and our God? That is because he was a messenger from God to us and has brought our blessedness to us. The blessedness he brought us was our own" (*Meister Eckhart: Sermons and Treatises*, translated and edited by M.O'C. Walshe [Longmead: Element, 1979], vol. I, p. 116).

[5] *Fuṣūṣ*, p. 220. In the *Futūḥāt* (Cairo, 1911), Ibn 'Arabī writes: "One who praises himself is more authoritative and more complete than one who is praised, as in the case of John and Jesus. . ." (I:109.4). This sentence was cited by Layla Shamash in "The Cosmology of Compassion or Macrocosm in the Microcosm," in *Journal of the Muhyiddin Ibn 'Arabi Society*, XXVIII, 2000, p. 31. (I have slightly modified the translation.)

> God bestows on Himself the salutation of peace, because of His own Self-determination within the *ʿĪsawī* substance; and this also shows the perfection of Jesus' station in the witnessing of this oneness.[6]

In other words, it is God Himself who greets Himself within and through the very form of Jesus. Now this touches on many key themes of Ibn ʿArabī's metaphysics, but let us note the following point: the greeting offered to God by Himself through another can be taken as a symbol of the principle that God reveals Himself to Himself through the whole of creation. As we saw earlier, Ibn ʿArabī says that Jesus is a symbol of *takwīn*, of engendering, or of creative activity. This comes in the following poem, which opens the chapter of the *Fuṣūṣ* on Jesus:

> From the water of Mary or from the breath of Gabriel,
> In the form of a mortal fashioned of clay
> The Spirit came to be in an essence
> Purified of nature, which you call *Sijjin*.
> . . . A Spirit from God, not from anything else.
> Thus he raised up the dead and made birds from clay.
> . . . God purified him in body and exalted him in spirit,
> And made of him a symbol of engendering.[7]

Let us briefly consider this "symbol of engendering" in four ways. First, the creation of Jesus himself—by means of a breath, a word, a spirit, cast into Mary—is a miraculous sign of God's creativity in general, of the way in which the spirit enlivens matter. Secondly, the creation of Jesus is a recapitulation of the specific miracle of the creation of Adam. Thirdly, at the level of cosmogenesis, the birth of Jesus to the Virgin Mary expresses the principle by which the cosmos itself is brought into being: according to Ibn ʿArabī the universe originates in the epiphany of the "Muhammadan Reality" (*al-ḥaqīqa al-muḥammadiyya*), this reality being the most receptive of all realities—contained within the

[6] *Fuṣūṣ*, p. 220.

[7] *Fuṣūṣ*, pp. 170-172. I benefited from, but did not follow, R. Austin's English rendition of the poem in *Bezels of Wisdom*, pp. 174-175.

primal "Cloud"—to the creative Light of God.[8] It is by virtue of the Prophet's total receptivity to this Light that his passivity (*infiʿāliyya*) is transformed into activity (*fāʿiliyya*):

> Muhammad was created as a slave, in principle; he never raised his head seeking leadership, nay, he ceaselessly prostrated in humility, standing [before his Lord] in his condition of passivity, until God engendered (*kawwana*) from him all that He engendered, bestowing upon him the rank of activity (*fāʿiliyya*) in the world of Breaths. . . .[9]

One is reminded here of the words addressed to Mary in the Qurʾan by the angels:

> O Mary, truly God has chosen you and purified you, and preferred you above all the women of creation. O Mary, be obedient to your Lord, prostrate to Him and bow with those who bow (3:42-43).

It is not Jesus alone who was made a "sign" but he and his mother together:

> And We made the son of Mary and his mother a sign (23:50).

Thus Jesus here can be seen as a symbol of the cosmos itself, the "fruit" of the activity that is rooted in total, virgin receptivity to the Word from above, Mary's role here mirroring that of the Muhammadan Reality.

Finally, continuing this process of *fāʿiliyya*, Jesus' own activity positively reflects this divine creativity: his healing of the blind, the

[8] See Chodkiewicz's illuminating discussion of this theme in the chapter entitled "The Muhammadan Reality," in *Seal of the Saints*, translated by Liadain Sherrard (Cambridge: Islamic Texts Society, 1993); and the fascinating description of the origination of the cosmos in *Islamic Sainthood in the Fullness of Time: Ibn al-ʿArabī's Book of the Fabulous Gryphon*, Gerald Elmore (Leiden: Brill, 1999), the chapter entitled "The Emergence of the World out of the Muḥammadan Reality."

[9] *Fuṣūṣ*, p. 275; see *Bezels*, p. 278.

leper, his creating a bird from clay, and most importantly, his raising up of the dead. As the Qur'an tells us, Jesus says:

> Truly I come unto you with a sign from your Lord. Truly, I create for you out of clay the shape of a bird, and I breathe into it, and it becomes a bird, by God's permission. I heal him who was born blind and the leper, and I give life to the dead, by God's permission (3:49).

It is very instructive to see how Qāshānī draws out the esoteric meaning of these miraculous acts. In his *Tafsīr* he gives the following commentary:

> *Truly I create for you*, through spiritual discipline and purification and realized wisdom, from the clay of souls still deficient but nonetheless receptive, *the shape of a bird*, one that flies to the realm of holiness through the intensity of its longing. *Then I breathe into it* the breath of divine knowledge and true life, through the influence of my presence and my teaching. *And it becomes a bird*, that is, a living soul, flying with the wings of longing and aspiration towards the Real. *I heal the blind*, the one who is veiled from the light of the Real, one whose eye of insight had always been closed, and had never seen the sun of the face of the Real, nor its light . . . *and the leper*, the one whose soul is disfigured by the disease of vices and corrupt beliefs, blemished by the love of this world and besmirched by the stain of concupiscence. *And I give life* to the death of ignorance with the life of knowledge.[10]

In the spirit of this kind of commentary, one might venture to add that the words of the Qur'an, *by God's permission*, which qualify the miraculous acts of Jesus, can be understood, esoterically, as meaning that these acts were performed by Jesus in perfect conformity with his knowledge of who the agent really is; who the true Self is, within him, that is performing these acts. In other words, Jesus was not veiled from the Divine reality by his own performance of these acts: he knew that God was acting through him. The fact that God is the sole

[10] *Tafsīr*, vol. 1, p. 113.

agent emerges in the Akbari perspective as an inescapable subjective corollary of the objective oneness of being, or, to use Ibn ʿArabī's own words, of the reality "that there is nothing in Being but He."[11] Ibn ʿArabī comments in many places on the ontological implications of the verse in the Qurʾan which states: "You did not throw when you threw, but God threw" (8:17). The following few instances will suffice for our purposes:

> *You did not throw*, so He negated, *when you threw*, so He affirmed, *but God threw*, so He negated the engendered existence (*kawn*) of Muḥammad, and affirmed Himself as identical (*ʿayn*) with Muḥammad. . . .[12]

Such ambivalent negations and affirmations give rise to bewilderment:

> You are not you when you are you but God is you.[13]

But they reveal the truth that it is God alone who is the agent of all acts, the agent who acts through all the faculties of man. This truth is affirmed by Ibn ʿArabī by reference to the words of the famous *ḥadīth qudsī*, known as the *ḥadīth al-taqarrub*, "drawing near," in which God says that when He loves His servant, He is "the hearing with which he hears, the sight by which he sees, the hand with which he strikes, and the foot whereon he walks." Ibn ʿArabī draws attention to the important fact that God speaks in the present tense, saying "I am his hearing, his sight, and his hand":

> God's words "I am" show that this was already the situation, but the servant was not aware. Hence the generous gift which this nearness gives to him is the unveiling of the knowledge that God is his hearing and his sight.[14]

[11] *Futūḥāt*, IV 272.22; as cited by W. Chittick in *The Sufi Path of Knowledge* (Albany: SUNY Press, 1989) p. 327.

[12] Ibid., II 216.12; as cited in *Sufi Path*, p. 114.

[13] Ibid., II 444.13; as cited in *Sufi Path*, p. 115.

[14] Ibid., III 67.29; as cited in *Sufi Path*, p. 326.

What this implies is that there is no change of ontological agency: God does not "become" the faculties of the servant after having allowed the servant to enjoy, in his previous condition, the prerogative of autonomous agency. God is and cannot but be the true agent of all the servant's actions and perceptions. The only change is in the awareness of the servant, his assimilation of the truth that God's sole reality includes all other agencies and excludes all ontological alterity, a truth from which the servant had been veiled by his own faculties. But it is important to add that, if one must not be veiled by the creature and its activities from true Selfhood, one must also avoid the opposite veil; that is, one must not allow the Real to veil the creature from the property that accompanies him perpetually, the property of slavehood. The relationship between the receptivity of pure slavehood and the activity of engendering was noted above; but at this point, what should be stressed is that one of the fruits of this paradoxical combination of realized Selfhood and immutable slavehood is compassion, as the following lines from the chapter on Jesus tell us:

> I worship truly, and God is our Master;
> and I am His very identity, so understand.
> When I say "man," do not be veiled by man,
> for He has given you proof.
> So be the Real and be a creature.
> You will be, by God, compassionate.[15]

The last line expresses the essence of the argument of this paper: "being" the Real—while remaining a creature—means "being" compassionate, merciful, kind. The one cannot "be" without the other. When Ibn ʿArabī writes *takun biʾLlāhi raḥmānan*, this sounds rather like an oath: by God, you will be compassionate—in the measure that you realize the true Self, which is veiled by your outer self, your ego. It should be noted that it is not a question here of realizing "*one's* true Self," inasmuch as the Self cannot be the property of any individual; the only thing that the individual can be said to possess is the property of essential poverty. In this perspective, no individual owns anything;

[15] *Fuṣūṣ*, p. 180. See the translation in *Bezels*, p. 179, which I have not followed.

on the contrary, all individuals "belong" to the Self. This point emerges clearly from the following *ta'wīl* by Qāshānī of the verses in the Qur'an in which God addresses Jesus: "O Jesus, son of Mary, did you say unto people: worship me and my mother as two gods beside God? He said: Glory to You, never could I say what I had no right to say. . ." (5:116).

> *Did you* invite people to your own soul and to your mother—or to the station of your heart and your soul; for truly he in whom subsists the reality of egoity (*anā'iyya*) and the residue of the soul and passion, or in whom there takes place the fluctuations of the heart and its manifestation through its quality—such a one invites the creature to the station of his soul or to the station of his heart, not to the Real. *He said: Glory to You, never could I say what I had no right to say*, for indeed I have no being in reality, nor is it appropriate or correct for me to utter speech which I do not really possess; for truly speech and act, quality and being—all of this belongs to You.[16]

If, then, compassion flows from the creature, this is nothing but the compassion of God, not that of the creature; and this compassion flows all the more strongly in the measure that the creature does not

16 *Tafsīr*, p. 194. It is interesting to note a similar principle expressed in the *Tafsīr* attributed by the Sufis to the sixth Shi'ite Imam, Ja'far aṣ-Ṣādiq; the following is his commentary on the words addressed to Moses by God: ". . . when he came to it [the burning bush on Mount Sinai], he was addressed, O Moses, I, I am your Lord" (20:11-12): "It is not proper for anyone but God to speak of himself by using these words *innī anā*, 'I am I.' I [that is Moses, according to aṣ-Ṣādiq's commentary] was seized by a stupor (*dahsh*) and annihilation (*fanā'*) took place. I said then: 'You! You are He who is and who will be eternally, and Moses has no place with You nor the audacity to speak, unless You let him subsist by your subsistence (*baqā'*)'" (Quoted in C.W. Ernst, *Words of Ecstasy in Sufism* [Albany: SUNY Press, 1985]), p. 10). One finds an echo of this formulation in al-Kharrāz: "Only God has the right to say 'I.' For whoever says 'I' will not reach the level of gnosis" (Cited in A. Schimmel, *Mystical Dimensions of Islam* [Chapel Hill: University of North Carolina Press, 1975], p. 55). Also, as-Sarrāj, in the chapter on *tawḥīd* makes the statement that none can say "I" but God, adding that "egoity" (*al-anniyya*) pertains only to God (*Kitāb al-Lumā'*, ed. R.A. Nicholson [London: E.J. Gibb Memorial Series XXII, 1963], p. 32 [Arabic text]).

appropriate it to himself. Ibn ʿArabī tells his readers to be the Real *and* a creature, only then will compassion flow from them; and then, not from them in respect of their own creaturely properties, but from them *biʾLlāh*, by or through God. If the consciousness of being the Real is not balanced by the consciousness that one is a creature, a slave, at the same time and for as long as one persists as an individual, then the result is in fact far from compassion, it is pride, self-delusion, and self-divinization. In other words humility and compassion are two complementary virtues that flow from a proper awareness of reality: a "proper" awareness being one that puts each thing in its right place, knowing that the creature is nothing *but* the Real, in respect of Its Self-manifestation within and through it, and that the creature is nothing *before* the Real. In both cases, the individual as such is reduced to nothing: self-effacement is the *conditio sine qua non* of Self-realization.

If one only has an awareness of being a creature, however, with no sense of the inner reality of divine Selfhood, then one's virtues, compassion included, will lack that all-embracing totality and that infinite depth which comes from realized spiritual knowledge. The more one is aware of the sole reality of God as the true ontological agent, the only true Self, the more naturally and spontaneously will compassion flow forth. In other words, the closer the individual comes to the source of compassion, the more fully will compassion be manifested through him; that is, such a one becomes not only a *marḥūm*, one upon whom compassion or mercy is bestowed, but also a *rāḥim*, one who bestows mercy to others. This is what distinguishes the "veiled ones" (*al-maḥjūbūn*) from the "folk of unveiling" (*ahl al-kashf*). As Ibn ʿArabī says:

> The veiled ones, in accordance with their belief, ask the Real to have compassion upon them, while the folk of unveiling ask that the compassion of God abide through them. They ask for this with the name *Allāh*, saying "O *Allāh*, have compassion upon us," and He only has compassion upon them by causing compassion to abide through them. Compassion has a property which in reality belongs to the essence of "that which abides through a locus" (*al-qāʾim biʾl-maḥall*).

Qāshānī comments:

> The property of compassion rules over them, for that which abides through a locus exercises its ruling property over the receptacle, in accordance with its reality; so He only has compassion upon them by causing compassion to abide through them, thus making them compassionate ones (*rāḥimīn*). . . .[17]

Those who have been rendered compassionate in this way are said to find the property of compassion by way of mystical "taste" (*dhawqan*);[18] their spiritual intuition not only gives them a taste of the essence of compassion, but shows them also that compassion is the very essence of the Real. There are many indications that compassion expresses the fundamental nature of God. The Qur'an tells us that "My compassion encompasses all things" (7:156). The name of God, *ar-Raḥmān*, is practically synonymous with *Allāh*: "Call upon *Allāh* or call upon *ar-Raḥmān*" (17:110). Repeatedly in the Qur'an *ar-Raḥmān* is referred to as the divine creative force from which all things arise.[19] Now according to Ibn 'Arabī, it was precisely because of His compassion that God created the world: the whole of creation is thus itself a *marḥūm*, an object of compassion. Every *mawjūd* is a *marḥūm*: every thing that is made existent is an object of compassion.[20] This perspective on creation might be seen as a commentary on one of the most important "explanations" of the reason behind the creation of the world by God. According to a famous holy utterance, a *ḥadīth qudsī*, which Ibn 'Arabī often cites, God says: "I was a hidden treasure and I loved to be known, so I created." Here the purpose of creation

[17] *Fuṣūṣ*, pp. 225-226. See Austin's translation, p. 225, which I have not followed. See also Izutsu's illuminating discussion of mercy as a key theme of Ibn 'Arabī's metaphysics, in the chapter "Ontological Mercy" in *Sufism and Taoism: A Comparative Study of Key Philosophical Concepts* (Berkeley: University of California Press, 1983).

[18] *Fuṣūṣ*, p. 226.

[19] For example, the chapter of the Qur'an named *ar-Raḥmān* (chap. 55) begins thus: "*Ar-Raḥmān*, taught the Qur'an, created man."

[20] *Fuṣūṣ*, p. 225; *Bezels*, p. 224.

is explicitly tied to God's desire to be known; He wished to manifest His inner perfections; and this is one way of becoming known, that is, knowing Himself outwardly, as distinct from knowing Himself inwardly. As the opening lines of the chapter on Adam in the *Fuṣūṣ* have it:

> The Real willed, by virtue of His Beautiful Names, which are innumerable, to see their identities—if you wish you can say: to see His identity—in a comprehensive engendered being that comprises the entire affair. . . . His mystery is manifest to Himself through it, for the vision a thing has of itself in itself is not like the vision it has of itself in another thing, which will serve as a mirror for it.[21]

One of Ibn ʿArabī's most startling declarations comes, though, when he says that the first object of God's compassion was not in fact the creation, it was God Himself. In other words, God had compassion[22] for His own Names and Qualities that wished to manifest themselves, but were hidden in His own essence. In other words, He had compassion for His own hidden "treasures." As Ibn ʿArabī writes:

> Through the breath of the All-Merciful, God gave relief (*tanfīs*) to the divine names. . . . He relieved the divine names of the lack of displaying effects.[23]

So the supreme archetype or model of all compassion, of all love and feeling for the "other," is this love of God's Essence for Its own

[21] *Fuṣūṣ*, p. 8. I am following Caner Dagli's translation of *ʿayn* as "identity" rather than using the other available translations, "entity," "essence," "archetype," etc. See the convincing reasons he gives for using this term, in the introduction to his translation of the *Fuṣūṣ* (The Great Books of the Islamic World, 2002).

[22] The root of the word "com-passion" expresses well this aspect of the creative function of divine *raḥma*: "to suffer with."

[23] *Futūḥāt*, II 487.34, 123.26; *Sufi Path*, p. 130. See Corbin's inspiring exploration of this theme in "Divine Passion and Compassion," chapter 1 of *Creative Imagination in the Sufism of Ibn ʿArabī*, trans. Ralph Mannheim, (Bollingen Series XCI, Princeton University Press, 1969).

Self-manifestation, for Its own theophany to an "other," and through the "other": everything is ultimately manifested by compassion, is woven of compassion, and returns to compassion: "My compassion encompasses all things," as we saw earlier. Ibn ʿArabī stresses that everything returns to mercy and compassion, but this does not deny the terrible reality of hell nor does it preclude the wrathful side of God. Ibn ʿArabī often cites the *ḥadīth* in which it is stated that God's compassion takes precedence over His wrath, but he does not deny the reality of this wrath: he attributes it, though, not to God's intrinsic nature, but to the creature's willful rejection of the mercy that is being offered to him "ontologically," that is, by virtue of the compassion that inheres in the very nature of being. As Qāshānī says, in his commentary on the opening line of the chapter on Zachariah:

> For compassion is of the Essence, as it is generous by nature, overflowing with generosity from the treasury of compassion and bounty. Being is the first effusion of the all-embracing compassion which encompasses everything. But as for wrath, it does not essentially pertain to the Real, rather, it consists in a property of a non-existential nature (*ḥukm ʿadamī*), arising out of the absence of receptivity (*ʿadam qābiliyya*), on the part of certain things, to the perfect manifestation of the effects of Being and its properties within them. . . . This absence of the effusion of compassion over a given thing, resulting from its lack of receptivity, is called "wrath" in relation to that thing, in the face of the compassionate one (*ar-rāḥim*).[24]

Therefore the compassion of being not only takes precedence ontologically over the non-existential property of wrath, it also prevails, ultimately over the accidental properties of evil and suffering, the concomitants of non-being: "Everyone will end up with mercy."[25] This truth is grasped in the measure of one's awareness—spiritually and not just notionally—of the absolute and infinite reality of goodness and the relative and limited reality of evil.

[24] *Fuṣūṣ*, p. 222.

[25] *Futuḥāt*, III 465.26, as cited in *Sufi Path*, p. 338.

Returning to the theme of selfhood and compassion, the following affirmation by Ibn ʿArabī is of great importance:

> God is qualified by love for us, and love is a property that demands that he who is qualified by it be merciful towards himself.[26]

We have seen how God has mercy upon His own Names and Qualities; on the human plane, this "self-compassion" implies radical objectivity towards one's own self. This idea is expressed in a most incisive manner by Ibn ʿArabī in the following dialogue with his own soul: the very fact of the dialogue itself implies the "otherness within," the objectivity that one must have towards one's own soul. The dialogue involves two of the greatest saints of Islam, Manṣūr al-Ḥallāj and Uways al-Qaranī. Ibn ʿArabī's soul argues that al-Ḥallāj surpassed the degree of Uways because, while Uways satisfied his own needs before giving away his surplus in charity, al-Ḥallāj was prepared even to sacrifice his own needs for the sake of others. To this argument of his own soul, Ibn ʿArabī replies:

> If the gnostic has a spiritual state like al-Ḥallāj, he differentiates between his soul and that of others: he treats his own soul with severity, coercion, and torture, whereas he treats the souls of others with preference and mercy and tenderness. But if the gnostic were a man of high degree . . . his soul would become a stranger to him: he would no longer differentiate between it and other souls in this world. . . . If the gnostic goes out to give alms, he should offer it to the first Muslim whom he meets. . . . The first soul to meet him is his own soul, not that of another.[27]

To digress a little, although the focus in this paper is on the "Qurʾanic" Jesus, the perspectives opened up by Ibn ʿArabī enable one

[26] *Futuḥāt*, III 429, as cited in *Sufi Path*, p. 132.

[27] Quoted on pp. 56-57 of "Excerpts from the Epistle on the Spirit of Holiness (*Risāla Rūḥ al-Quds*)," translated by R. Boase and F. Sahnoun. In *Muhyiddin Ibn ʿArabi: A Commemorative Volume*, ed. S. Hirtenstein and M. Tiernan (Longmead: Element Books, 1993).

to see the Biblical message of Jesus, also, in quite a new light. Through the Akbari perspective on ontological compassion, one comes to appreciate deeper aspects of Christ's biblical injunctions: For instance, in Mark:

> The Lord our God is one Lord. And thou shalt love the Lord thy God with all thy heart, and with all thy soul, and with all thy mind, and with all thy strength: this is the first commandment. And the second is like, namely this, thou shalt love thy neighbor as thyself (12:29-31).

The meaning of "loving oneself" is altogether transfigured in Ibn ʿArabī's metaphysics of Self-compassion. It is also significant that the second commandment is described as "like" the first. In Ibn ʿArabī's perspective, it is likely that the word *ʿayn* would be used: it is identical to the first. For he would stress that there is but one God, one reality; thus love of God must be directed to the divine nature in itself, above and beyond all creatures, but also to the divine nature immanent *within* all creatures, the divinity that constitutes the true being of the creatures. Both modes of love relate to the one and only Beloved. One recalls here another of Christ's sayings:

> Inasmuch as ye have done it unto one of the least of these my brethren, ye have done it unto me (Matthew, 25:40).

And this saying in Luke, after taking a child's hand:

> Whosoever shall receive this child in my name receiveth me: and whosoever shall receive me, receiveth Him that sent me (9:48).

The idea that every *mawjūd* is by definition already a *marḥūm* raises the pitch of Christ's message of charity and compassion, a message which is so often limited to a purely moral application. For example:

> Love your enemies, do good to them which hate you, bless them that curse you. . . . Ye shall be the children of the Highest: for He is kind unto the unthankful and to the evil. Be ye therefore merciful as your Father is merciful (Luke, 6:27-28; 35-36).

This verse from Matthew evokes with particular clarity the universal compassion which embraces all things by virtue of giving them life:

> Your Father . . . maketh His sun to rise on the evil and the good, and sendeth rain on the just and the unjust (5:45).

It was stated above that it is not just compassion but also humility that flows from an understanding of true Selfhood. Returning to the verses in the *Sūra Maryam* with which this discussion began, it is important to note that the first words of Jesus in the cradle were "Truly I am the slave of God" (19:30). Now it might seem at first sight that creaturely slavehood and divine Selfhood are diametrically opposed, yet in Ibn ʿArabī's perspective, as we have observed above, only he who knows that he is a slave of God will come to know that God is the only true Self of all. In his description of the climax of his own spiritual ascension, Ibn ʿArabī makes clear the relationship between slavehood and Selfhood:

> God removed from me my contingent dimension (*imkānī*). Thus I attained in this nocturnal journey the inner realities of all the Names, and I saw them all returning to One Subject (*musammā wāḥid*) and One Entity (*ʿayn wāḥida*): that Subject was what I witnessed and that Entity was my being. For my voyage was only in myself and pointed to myself, and through this I came to know that I was a pure "slave" without a trace of lordship in me at all.[28]

Again, let us note that the first thing that he says after this remarkable experience of *tawḥīd* in subjective mode, that is, the realization of the oneness of true Selfhood, is that he came to know his own slavehood. What this shows clearly is that self-effacement is the consequence of true Self-realization. When the subjective core of individuality is effaced, there can be nothing to which pride can attach

[28] *Futūḥāt*, III 350.30; what we cite here is the translation given by James Morris, "Ibn ʿArabī's Spiritual Ascension," p. 380 in *Les Illuminations de La Mecque—The Meccan Illuminations, selected texts* (under the direction of M. Chodkiewicz) (Paris: Sindbad, 1988).

itself: with the effacement of individuality, there is the uprooting of pride, and the consummation of a humility that is as ineradicable as the knowledge upon which it is based is indubitable.

To complete our reflections on the relationship between Selfhood, slavehood, and compassion, let us consider the following remarkable commentary by Qāshānī on verses in the *Sūrat al-Insān.* Here, self-extinction is seen as inextricably tied to self-giving. In the verses in question we are presented with a distinction between the righteous (*al-abrār*) and the slaves of God (*'ibād Allāh*):

> Truly the righteous shall drink from a filled cup [containing a drink] flavored with Kāfūr—a fountain from which the slaves of God drink, making it flow with greater abundance (74:5-6).

Qāshānī interprets this fountain as a symbol of the divine Essence, beyond the divine Qualities. The righteous, he writes,

> are the joyous ones who have gone beyond the veils of traces and actions, and are now veiled by the veils of the divine Qualities. But they do not completely stop at this level, rather, their orientation is towards the Fountain of the Essence . . . they are midway along the Path.

The slaves, on the other hand, who drink directly from the fountain itself, without diluting the drink at all, are distinguished by their exclusive devotion to the unity of the Essence.

> Their love is for the Fountain of the Essence beyond the Qualities, not differentiating between compulsion and kindness, gentleness and harshness. . . . Their love abides in the midst of contraries, their joy remains in the face of graces and trials, compassion and distress.

The important point comes now. It shows the clear relationship between slavehood, selfhood, and self-giving: for these slaves not only love the Fountain of the Essence, they are submerged in it, totally and indistinguishably one with it. The words of the Qur'an powerfully evoke this identity, *yufajjirūnahā tafjīran*, they make the fountain flow all the more abundantly, the more they drink from it. Why is this? Because, according to Qāshānī, the slaves

> are [themselves] the sources of this Fountain; there is no duality or otherness. . . . Were it otherwise, it would not be the Fountain of Kāfūr, because of the darkness of the veil of egoity (*anā'iyya*) and duality.[29]

There is no ego-consciousness in the Essence, for there are no distinct egos, although all are nonetheless mysteriously contained by the Essence, in absolute non-differentiation; there is but the one Self, the *Nafs al-Ḥaqq*, the Self of the Real, and there are no distinctions, no *tafāḍul*, therein. It is only in the Paradises that one finds such ranking in degrees between the prophets, saints, martyrs, and righteous ones. In the *Futūḥāt* one finds Ibn ʿArabī making this point by means of distinguishing between "essential (*dhātī*) perfection" and "accidental (*ʿaraḍī*) perfection," the first pertaining to pure "slavehood" (*ʿubūdiyya*), the second to "manliness" (*rajuliyya*):

> The degree of the essential perfection is in the Self of the Real (*Nafs al-Ḥaqq*), while the degrees of accidental perfection are in the Gardens. . . . Ranking according to excellence (*tafāḍul*) takes place in accidental perfection, but not in essential perfection.[30]

In other words, "accidental perfection" pertains to the individual, whether in the world or in the heavens—this mode of unavoidable self-affirmation is thus "manly," in contrast to the ontological effacement of the individual in the highest realization, such effacement being evoked by the term "slave." Thus, to return to Qāshānī's *ta'wīl*, the drinking of the "slaves of God" at the fountain of the Essence—together with the fact that such drinking only increases the flow of the fountain—symbolizes their inner identity with the Essence, but as persons they remain distinct in the various levels of Paradise. And, one might venture to add, in the spirit of this perspective, this is not just the case in the

[29] *Tafsīr*, vol. II, pp. 360-361.

[30] *Futūḥāt*, II 588.10, 13; as cited in *Sufi Path*, p. 366.

Hereafter, it is also the situation herebelow: the prophets and the saints are inwardly at one with the Essence, while outwardly, as slaves, they imbibe from this fountain, the source of essential identity, the one and only Self of the Real; and this is why they are not just slaves, but veritable streams of grace by which the infinite compassion of *ar-Raḥmān* flows through the veins of the entire cosmos:

> And We sent you not save as a mercy to all the worlds (21:107).

ASPECTS OF ISLAMIC ESOTERISM*

William Stoddart

Esoterism is the correlative of exoterism. The latter is the outward and general religion of dogmas and observances, to which, in a traditional society, the whole community adheres, and which promises, and provides the means for achieving, salvation. The former is the "total truth" (spiritually and metaphysically speaking) behind—and only symbolically expressed by—the dogmas of the general religion and at the same time it is the key to, and the *raison d'être* of, the religious observances. What, in exoterism, are dogmas and observances, become, in esoterism, unconditioned truth and ways of realization. In both exoterism and esoterism the same two poles are present: theory and practice, or doctrine and method; they are simply envisaged at different levels. The first of these two poles, incidentally, clearly has a primary role or function: one must understand before one can do. Any practice without theory lacks both motivation and goal.

Exoterism is interested: it aims at transforming the collectivity, and saving as many souls as possible. Esoterism is disinterested and impersonal. As "total truth," it "saves" *a fortiori*,[1] but whereas exoterism, to be itself, inevitably has a moralizing and to some extent a subjectivistic character, esoterism is dispassionate and totally objective.

What is meant by a universalist point of view can perhaps best be summed up in the following saying: "All religions come from God, and all religions lead back to God." The first clause refers to doctrine, and the second to method (or "way," or "path"). This saying presupposes that we are talking about "revealed" religions (or religious

* First published in German in *Initiative 42*, a special volume devoted to Esoterism Today, with contributions by several authors (Herder, Freiburg-im-Breisgau, 1981).

[1] "Ye shall know the truth, and the truth shall make you free" (John 8:32).

revelations), and also that the religions in question have retained their "orthodoxy" (i.e. fidelity to truth) and have remained "traditional" (i.e. have not undergone any essential innovation).

From the universalist point of view, the various revealed religions are sometimes represented as sectors of a circle, the sectors, by definition, coming together at the central point. The larger and wider area of the sector, bordering on the circumference, represents a given exoterism; the smaller and narrower area of the sector that is close to the center is the corresponding esoterism; and the dimensionless center itself is esoterism in the pure state: the total truth.

The same symbolism can also be represented in three dimensions, in the form of a cone or a mountain. Here it will be said that "all paths lead to the same summit." Once again, the dimensionless central point (this time the summit of the mountain) represents the total truth. The cone or the mountain is made up of sectors, each one representing a religion. The lower slopes of each sector represent a given exoterism, while the upper slopes of the same sector represent the corresponding esoterism. The summit represents esoterism in the pure state.

Perhaps the most direct of all the symbolisms referring to the genesis, mutual relationship, and saving role of the various revelations, is that which likens esoterism (in the pure state) to the uncolored light, and the various religions to red, green, yellow, and the other colors of the spectrum. Depending on their distance from the source of light, the colored rays will be more intense or more weak (i.e. more esoteric or more exoteric). Each color is a form or a vehicle of the truth. Each color "represents" the total truth. But the supra-formal total truth, the plenitude of uncolored light, is not exhausted by or limited to one single color. Incidentally, this symbolism has the merit of showing, amongst many other things, just how precious exoterism is. A weak, colored, light shining in unfavorable circumstances is in itself sufficient (if we genuinely try to see by it) to save us from outer darkness. Despite "refraction" (and let us remember that it is precisely its "color" which makes it accessible to the majority of men), and despite its weakness, it is the same light as the uncolored light of God, and its merciful role is precisely to lead us back to its own absolute and infinite source.

Terminologically one may regard esoterism and mysticism as synonymous. Mysticism is known to be the inward or spiritual dimension within every religion, and this is precisely what esoterism is. This may prompt the question: does the mystic who has reached the end of the path (who has achieved "salvation," "liberation," or "enlightenment") leave religion behind? To this the answer must be yes and no. Returning to our symbolism of the uncolored light which is refracted into many colors, one may say that he has left "color" behind, but not light. And yet, when one recalls that each color is fully present in the uncolored light (in harmonious union with all the other colors in what amounts to a principial plenitude of light), one cannot truly say that he has left color behind either. What he has done is to trace his own color back to its essence or source, where, although infinitely clarified, it is essentially and abundantly present. The uncolored light, source of all the colors, has also been called the *philosophia perennis* or *religio perennis*. This is one with what was earlier called esoterism in the pure state.

And this has an important practical consequence for the beginner. One cannot take the view that, since mysticism or esoterism is the inner truth common to all the religions, one can dispense with religion (exoterism) and seek only mysticism (esoterism). Man's situation is such that with God's grace, he may be made worthy of turning towards the uncolored light only if he approaches it by way of "red" or "green" or some other color. (And his "red" or his "green" must be as pure and intense as possible.) To believe that we can lay hold on the uncolored light without arduously proceeding along a "colored ray" is not only arrogance, it is illusion.

One should perhaps add at this point that any "syncretism" (or pseudo-theosophy) is likewise vain. To pick and choose bits and pieces from each religion (allegedly those relating to an imagined "highest common factor") is to try to mix the immiscible. It leads not to clarity, but to a sterile and opaque "muddy brown."

* * *

In the foregoing symbolisms, the relationships between Islamic exoterism, Islamic esoterism, and the *religio perennis* will be clearly apparent. Islamic exoterism, the *sharīʿa*, is incumbent upon the whole collectivity. It is the corpus of religious beliefs and practices which shapes the community and leads individuals to salvation. Islamic esoterism or Sufism (in Arabic *taṣawwuf*) is the inward or spiritual dimension of the religion, and is the concern only of those possessed of the appropriate vocation. From the "operative" point of view, the main difference between exoterism and esoterism (i.e. between the outward Islamic religion and Sufism) is as follows: whereas the goal of the *sharīʿa* is salvation, conceived as something attainable only after death—a rejoining of the saints in Paradise—Sufism envisages as its main end the attaining of salvation or liberation (or the embarking on the path that leads to salvation or liberation) even in this life, here and now. This is nothing other than the path of sanctification, the goal of which is union with God, whatever be the degree or mode of this union. The Koran declares: "Verily we are God's and unto Him we shall return." The function of Sufism (and indeed that of the general religion also, although in a less direct, less active, and more outward fashion) is to teach that, for salvation or liberation, this "return" must necessarily engage the will of the individual. Let it be added that all religions likewise teach that "perdition" or "damnation" is the result, precisely, of the individual's refusing his co-operation with the divine will as expressed, for example, in the relevant religious revelation. Revelation, incidentally, represents the "objective" pole of religion, in that it comes to the individual from outside. The "subjective" pole is that which comes to the individual from within. It includes both the voice of conscience and also that intuitive assent to the truths of religion which constitutes faith. For religion and spirituality, revelation and faith are the twin sources, objective and subjective respectively, of knowledge.

One of the most easily graspable keys to the origin, and so to the meaning, of the concepts "objective" and "subjective" is furnished by the Hindu doctrine of *Sat-Cit-Ānanda*. In Hinduism, this term is one of the names of God. Its constituent elements are usually translated as (infinite) Being, (infinite) Consciousness, and (infinite) Bliss. This enables us to see that Being is the Divine Object, Consciousness the Divine Subject, while Bliss—the joyous coming together of the two—is Divine Union. The most "essential" translation, therefore, of *Sat-Cit-Ānanda* is "Object-Subject-Union." This is the model and origin of all possible objects and subjects, and of the longing of the latter for the former.[2]

This trinitarian aspect of the Divinity is universal and is to be found in all religions. In Christianity it is the central dogma: God viewed as Father, Son, and Holy Spirit. The analogy between the Christian Trinity and "Being-Consciousness-Bliss" is best seen in the doctrinal expositions of the Greek Fathers and also in St. Augustine's designation of the Christian Trinity as "Being-Wisdom-Life," which carries the same connotation of "Object-Subject-Union." In Islam, although it is the religion of strict monotheism, certain Sufi formulations evoke the selfsame trinitarian aspect of the Divinity. Reference will be made later to the question of "spiritual realization" in Sufism, the essential means of which is the invocation (*dhikr*) of the Name of God. In this connection it is said that God is not only That which is invoked (*Madhkūr*), but also, in the last analysis, That within us which invokes (*Dhākir*), and furthermore that *Dhikr* itself, being one with the internal Activity of God,[3] is also Divine. We thus have the ternary *Madhkūr-Dhākir-Dhikr*, meaning "Invoked-Invoker-Invocation," the relationship of these elements to one another being precisely that of "Object-Subject-Union." This is the very essence of the theory and practice of esoterism—Islamic or other—for this "Union" *in divinis* is the prefiguration of and pattern for the union of man with God. Hindu, Christian, and Sufi doctrines coincide in elucidating just why this is so.

* * *

The mystery of union, from whichever doctrinal point of view it may be approached, carries an inescapable "operative" implication and is the basis of the mystical path and the motivation for all spiritual striv-

[2] *Sat-Cit-Ānanda* may also be interpreted as "Known-Knower-Knowledge" or "Beloved-Lover-Love."

[3] That this Divine Act should pass through man is the mystery of salvation.

ing. One of the most esoteric of all doctrines expressing the mystery of union is that concerning the Logos. This doctrine has its origin in the distinction, within God Himself, between God and the Godhead, or between "Being" and "Essence." This distinction is to be found in the esoterisms of several religions, and is made explicit in the treatises of such great "gnostics" as Śaṅkara, Eckhart, and Ibn ʿArabī.[4] Ordinary theology distinguishes simply between God and man, between the Uncreated and the created. But in each of these categories, esoterism makes a distinction. For example, within God Himself, there is already a prefiguration of creation, and this is God as "Being." God as "Being" is the immediate Creator of the world. This is the source of the metaphysical distinction between "Beyond-Being" ("Essence") and "Being," or between the Godhead and the Personal God. Likewise, within the created, there is a distinction to be made. There is something within the created itself that reflects the Uncreated (something, within the relative, that reflects the Absolute). For Christianity, this is the Savior; for Islam, the Prophet. In more general terms, it is truth and virtue, or symbol and sacrament.

These different strands are brought together by the concept of the Logos: the prefiguration of the created in the Uncreated (the Personal God) is the *uncreated* Logos. The reflection of the Uncreated in the created or the Absolute in the relative—(Savior; Prophet; truth and virtue; symbol and sacrament) is the *created* Logos. Hence the indispensability of the Logos (with its *two* faces) as "bridge" between created and Uncreated, or between man and God.

Without the Logos, no contact between man and God would be possible. This seems to be the position of the Deists. Without the Logos, there would be a fundamental dualism, not "Non-Dualism" (*Advaita*), as the Vedantists call it. This indeed is the blind alley that Descartes (with his unbridgeable dichotomy of "spirit and matter") has led us into.

This doctrine can be summarized in diagrammatic form as follows:

[4] The same distinction is also made by St. Gregory Palamas in his doctrine of the Divine Essence and the Divine Energies.

	"Beyond-Being"	
God (the Uncreated)	"Being" (the Personal God or Creator) —uncreated Logos	
	man as Prophet or Savior (man in so far as he personifies truth and virtue) —created Logos	"bridge"
man (the created)	fallen, individual, man	

Esoterism thus renders explicit the reality of mystical union, for it is by uniting himself with the "created" Logos (for example, in the Eucharist, or in the Invocation of the Divine Name, or in the practice of the virtues), that the spiritual aspirant (the *faqīr*, as he is called in Sufism) realizes his union with, or reintegration into, the uncreated Divinity.

The Logos is everywhere and always the same, but its personification is "unique" within each different religion, in the shape of the Founder. Jesus and Muhammad are personifications of the Logos, and this is what enables them to speak in such absolute terms. Muhammad said: "He that has seen me has seen God." That is, whoever has seen the created (and visible) Logos has, sacramentally, also "seen" the uncreated (and invisible) Logos, namely God as "Being" or Creator. Similarly, Jesus said: "No man cometh to the Father but by me." This has the same meaning. It is for this precise reason that Muhammad for Muslims (like Jesus for Christians) is "absolutely" indispensable. In Islam, this is the ultimate, or esoteric, reason for conformity to the *Sunna*, the "Wont" or "Practice" of the Prophet. Outwardly the *Sunna* constitutes a norm for the whole Islamic community, but for the *faqīr*, conformity to the "inward" or essential *Sunna* is as it were a "sacrament," and a central mode of realizing union.

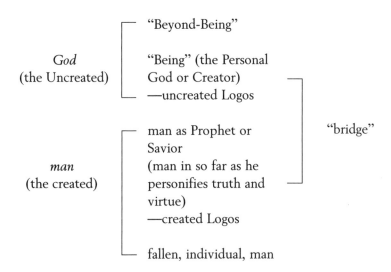

Mutatis mutandis the Virgin Mary plays the same role. She is the feminine personification of the Logos—or the personification of the feminine aspects of the Logos, namely Purity, Beauty, and Goodness. This is why, in Christianity, she is called "Co-Redemptrix."

The above doctrinal considerations let it be seen that mystical union, whatever be its degree or mode, is realizable only through the Logos.[5]

* * *

It has been mentioned more than once that Sufism is the spiritual and metaphysical interpretation and application of the religion of Islam. The central doctrine of Islam is the "testimony of faith" (*Shahāda*): "There is no god but God; Muhammad is the Messenger of God" (*lā ilāha illā 'Llāh; Muḥammadur Rasūlu 'Llāh*). The esoteric interpretation of the *Shahāda* generally takes the form of the doctrine known as *waḥdat al-wujūd*, or the "oneness of being." According to this, the *Shahāda* means not merely "there is no god but God," but also, and even more, "there is no reality except Reality." One of the names of God, indeed, is *al-Ḥaqq*, which means "Reality" or "Truth."

This doctrine also means that the relative has no reality other than in the Absolute, and the finite has no reality other than in the Infinite. The Muslim or the Sufi has access to the Absolute and the Infinite in the Koran (God's revealed words), in the *Shahāda*, and, most intensely of all, in the Divine Name, *Allāh*. He also has access through the Prophet who, within the world itself, is God's very reflection. The Prophet's name is communicated in the second clause of the *Shahāda*. Thus through these two revealed and sacred clauses, man has access, on the one hand, to the Divine Immutability and, on the other, to the Muhammadian or Prophetic Norm. In and through the two *Shahādas*, the imperfect is overwhelmed by the Perfect (the Muhammadian Norm) and the impermanent is extinguished by the Permanent (God

[5] This exposition is taken from the writings of Frithjof Schuon. See especially *Esoterism as Principle and as Way* (London: Perennial Books, 1981).

Himself). As the Koran says: "Truth hath come, and falsehood hath vanished away. Verily falsehood is ever bound to vanish."[6]

* * *

The above considerations enable us to see how the spiritual method, or means of realization, in Sufism is above all the "remembrance of God" (*dhikru 'Llāh*). The verbal root concerned also means "to mention" or "to invoke," and the practice is sometimes called "invocation" (i.e. the invocation of the Divine Name). Reference was made to this above. This spiritual practice is derived from numerous Koranic injunctions, amongst which are: "Remember God with much remembrance" (*idhkurū 'Llāha dhikran kathīran*); "Verily in the remembrance of God do hearts find rest" (*a lā bidhikri 'Llāhi tatma'innu 'l-qulūb*); and "Remember Me and I shall remember you" (*idhkurū-nī adhkur-kum*). *Dhikr* may be performed only with the permission and guidance of a spiritual master or Shaykh. It can be performed either in solitude or in a gathering (*majlis*) of *fuqarā'* (plural of *faqīr*) convened for that purpose, and led by a Shaykh or his representative (*muqaddam*). From another point of view, *dhikr* should, in principle, be constant. This is analogous to the "prayer without ceasing" of St. Paul (the Jesus-Prayer of the Eastern Church) and to the *japa-yoga* of the Hindus.

The immediate, practical motivation for *dhikr* is that man finds himself entrapped in manifestation. Manifestation is doomed to impermanence, and this impermanence inevitably entails separation, suffering, and death. Islamic esoterism teaches that the Principle alone is permanent—and blissful. Once again we are brought back to the message of the *Shahāda*: "There is no permanent except in the Permanent," "there is no reality other than the Real." The doctrine of the *dhikr* is that the Divine Name (*Allāh*) directly vehicles the Principle, and when the believer unites himself with the Divine Name in fervent invocation, he inwardly frees himself from manifestation

[6] For a detailed esoteric interpretation of the *Shahāda*, see *Mirror of the Intellect* (Albany: State University of New York Press, 1987), chapter entitled "Concerning the *Barzakh*," by Titus Burckhardt, edited by William Stoddart.

and its concomitant suffering. The essential condition for *dhikr* is *faqr*, i.e. "spiritual poverty" or self-effacement. Without *faqr*, *dhikr* is self-delusion and pride, and a dangerous poison for the soul. Only the *faqīr* (the one who is "poor in spirit") may be a *dhākir* (one who invokes God).

Dhikr, in the wider sense, includes any devotion that serves as a support for the remembrance of God, in particular the *wird*, or rosary, which most *fuqarā'* recite morning and evening. The *wird* comprises three Koranic formulas, each of which is recited one hundred times. The first formula pertains to individual man and its aim is to establish contrition and resolution. The second formula contains the name of the Prophet, and seeks to confer on the *faqīr* the perfection pertaining to the human state as it was created. The third formula contains the Name of God, and enshrines and vehicles the mystery of Union. The three formulas thus correspond to the three "stages" known in the mysticisms of various religions, namely: purification, perfection, union. And in their essence, they correspond to the three fundamental aspects of all spirituality: humility, charity, truth.

* * *

The last-mentioned words lead us directly to a well-known Islamic ternary, namely, *makhāfa*, *maḥabba*, and *ma'rifa*. These may be translated as "Fear of God," "Love of God," "Knowledge of God." "Fear," "Love," and "Knowledge" (or "Gnosis"[7]) may be regarded either as simultaneous aspects or successive stages. They correspond to the perhaps better known Hindu ternary: *karma-mārga* (the Way of Action), *bhakti-mārga* (the Way of Love), and *jñāna-mārga* (the Way of Knowledge). Strictly speaking, it is only *bhakti* and *jñāna* (i.e. *maḥabba* and *ma'rifa*) that constitute esoterism: esoterism is either a Way of Love, or a Way of Knowledge, or a combination of both.

[7] This word is used purely etymologically, and does not hark back to the current, in the early history of Christianity, known as "gnosticism." "Gnosis," from the Greek, is the only adequate English rendering for the Sanskrit *jñāna* (with which in fact it is cognate) and the Arabic *ma'rifa*.

Since comparisons with Christianity may be useful, let us recall the incident in the life of Christ when he was received in the house of the sisters Martha and Mary. What has come to be known in Christianity as the "Way of Martha" corresponds to *karma-mārga*, the way of religious observance and good works. The esoteric or mystical way, on the other hand, is the "Way of Mary," which comprises two modes, namely *bhakti-mārga* (the Way of Love) and *jñāna-mārga* (the Way of Knowledge). *Karma* as such is purely exoteric, but it is important to stress that there is always a karmic component within both *bhakti* and *jñāna*. Sufism teaches quite explicitly that the Way of Love (*maḥabba*) and the Way of Knowledge (*maʿrifa*) both necessarily contain an element of Fear or conformity (*makhāfa*). Likewise the Way of Knowledge invariably contains within it the reality of Love. As for the Way of Love, which is composed of faith and devotion, it contains an indirect element of *jñāna* or *maʿrifa* in the form of dogmatic and speculative theology. This element is in the intellectual speculation as such, and not in its object which, for the Way of Love, is restricted to God as "Being," "Creator," or "Lord." When the object is God as "Beyond-Being" or "Essence," it is no longer a case of *bhakti* (or *maḥabba*), but of *jñāna* (or *maʿrifa*).

In spite of the presence in each "Way" of elements of the two others, the three Ways, *karma*, *bhakti*, and *jñāna* (or *makhāfa*, *maḥabba*, and *maʿrifa*), represent three specific and easily distinguishable modes of religious aspiration.

As for the question as to which of these paths a given aspirant adheres to, it is overwhelmingly a matter of temperament and vocation. It is a case where the Way chooses the individual and not the individual the Way.

Historically speaking, Christian mysticism has been characterized in the main by the "Way of Love," whereas Islamic mysticism (like Hindu mysticism) comprises both the "Way of Love" and the "Way of Knowledge." The language of the "Way of Love" has a remarkably similar ring in whichever mysticism it crops up, but the more "gnostic" formulations of Islamic esoterism (as of Vedanta) tend to strike a foreign note in the ears of those who are familiar only with Christian, or at any rate bhaktic, forms of spirituality.[8]

[8] Those who, by way of exception, have manifested the "Way of Knowledge" in Christianity include such great figures as Dionysius the Areopagite, Meister

The fact that the spiritual method *par excellence* consists in "sacramental" concentration on the revealed Name of God (*dhikru 'Llāh*) indicates clearly that the practical side of Islamic esoterism is the very opposite of giving free play to man's unregenerate subjectivity. Indeed, it amounts to the exposing of his unregenerate subjectivity to the normative and transforming influence of the Divine "Object," God transcendent. At the same time, and even more esoterically, it is the exposing of man's paltry egoism, seen in turn as an "object" (illusorily other than God), to the withering and yet quickening influence of the Divine "Subject," God immanent; the Name of God (*Allāh*) being both transcendent Object and immanent Subject (*Madhkūr* and *Dhākir*). These two contrasting attitudes or "stations" (*maqām*)—spiritual extinction before the Divine Object and spiritual rebirth in the Divine Subject—are the two aspects, objective and subjective, of unitive Knowledge (*ma'rifa*).[9] In Sufi treatises, they have been called, respectively, *fanā'* (extinction) and *baqā'* (permanence).[10]

* * *

The organization or framework within which Sufism historically exists is that of the *ṭurūq* (plural of *ṭarīqa*, which on the one hand, means "path" or "way" and, on the other, "spiritual order or brotherhood"). The first great Sufi order to appear in the form in which *ṭurūq* are now known was the Qādirī *ṭarīqa* which took its name from its illustrious founder 'Abd al-Qādir al-Jilānī (1078-1166). This was an offshoot of the older Junaydī *ṭarīqa* which stemmed from the great Abū 'l-Qāsim al-Junayd of Baghdad (d. 910). Amongst the next to appear were the Suhrawardī *ṭarīqa*, whose founder was Shihāb ad-Dīn as-Suhrawardī

Eckhart, and Angelus Silesius. It is significant that it is the works of "gnostics" such as these that have tended to cause ripples in the generally "bhaktic" climate of Christianity.

9 This synthesis of the dual aspects of spiritual realization or method is taken from the writings of Frithjof Schuon. See especially *The Eye of the Heart* (Bloomington: World Wisdom, 1997), chapter "Microcosm and Symbol."

10 The Sufi expression *fanā' al-fanā'i* ("the extinction of extinction") is a synonym for *baqā'*.

(1144-1234), and the Shādhilī *ṭarīqa*, founded by one of the greatest luminaries of Western Islam, Abū 'l-Ḥasan ash-Shādhilī (1196-1258). Another order to be created about the same period was the Maulawī *ṭarīqa* (more famous under its Turkish name Mevlevi), so called after the title *Maulā-nā* ("our Lord"), given by his disciples to the founder of the order, Jalāl ad-Dīn Rūmī (1207-1273), author of the *Mathnawī*, and perhaps the greatest mystical poet of Islam. The most renowned Sufi order to originate in India is the Chishtī *ṭarīqa*, founded by Muʿin ad-Dīn Chishtī (1142-1236), whose tomb at Ajmer is one of the greatest shrines of the sub-continent, and is much visited and revered by Hindus and Moslems alike. Another order important throughout the East is the Naqshbandī order, founded in the fourteenth century by Pīr Muḥammad Naqshbandī. A widely disseminated order in Western Islam is the Darqāwī, a relatively recent sub-group of the Shādhilī *ṭarīqa*, having been founded by the Moroccan Shaykh Mulay al-ʿArabī ad-Darqāwī (c.1743-1823). An illustrious spiritual descendant of Mulay al-Arabī ad-Darqāwī was the Algerian Shaykh Aḥmad al-ʿAlawī (1869-1934), "whose erudition and saintliness" as A. J. Arberry has written, "recall the golden age of the medieval mystics."[11]

It should be stressed that these orders are not sects, but mystical brotherhoods whose purpose is to vehicle and enshrine the traditions and inheritance of Islamic spirituality, and above all to guarantee the transmission of the initiatic rite (passed on from shaykh to shaykh, and originating in Muhammad himself who, through God's grace, received it from the Archangel Gabriel) that is the *sine qua non* of entering and following the Sufi path. Without this initiation, followed by a long and arduous discipleship under a spiritual master, there is no Sufism, and no possible spiritual rebirth or sanctification.

[11] *Luzac's Oriental List* (London), October-December 1961.

THE QUINTESSENTIAL ESOTERISM OF ISLAM

Frithjof Schuon

The Islamic religion is divided into three constituent parts: *Īmān*, Faith, which contains everything one must believe; *Islām*, the Law, which contains everything one must do; *Iḥsān*,[1] operative Virtue, which confers upon believing and doing the qualities that make them perfect—in other words, that intensify or deepen both faith and works. *Iḥsān* in short is the sincerity of the intelligence and the will: it is our complete adherence to the Truth and our total conformity to the Law, which means that we must on the one hand know the Truth entirely, not only in part, and on the other hand conform to it with our deepest being and not only with a partial and superficial will. Thus *Iḥsān* opens onto esoterism—which is the science of the essential and total—and is even identified with it; for to be sincere is to draw from the Truth the maximal consequences from the point of view of both intelligence and will; in other words, it is to think and will with the heart, hence with our entire being, with all we are.

Iḥsān is right believing and right doing, and it is at the same time their quintessence: the quintessence of right believing is metaphysical truth, *Ḥaqīqa*, and that of right doing is the practice of invocation, *Dhikr*. *Iḥsān* comprises as it were two modes, depending on its application: the speculative and the operative, namely, intellectual discernment and unitive concentration; in Sufi language this is expressed precisely by the terms *Ḥaqīqa*[2] and *Dhikr* or by *Tawḥīd*, "Unification", and *Ittiḥād*, "Union". For Sufis the "hypocrite" (*munāfiq*) is not mere-

[1] Literally *Iḥsān* means "embellishment", "beautiful activity", "right doing", "charitable activity"; and let us recall the relationship that exists in Arabic between the notions of beauty and virtue.

[2] It is to be noted that in the word *ḥaqīqa*, as in its quasi-synonym *ḥaqq*, the meanings "truth" and "reality" coincide.

ly someone who gives himself airs of piety in order to impress people, but it is the profane man in general, someone who fails to draw all the consequences implied in the Dogma and Law, hence the man who is not sincere since he is neither consequential nor whole; now Sufism (*taṣawwuf*) is nothing other than sincerity (*ṣidq*), and the "sincere" (*ṣiddīqūn*) are none other than Sufis.

Iḥsān, since it is necessarily an exoteric notion as well, may be interpreted at different levels and in different ways. Exoterically it is the faith of the fideists and the zeal of the ritualists; in this case it is intensity and not profundity and thus has something quantitative or horizontal in it when compared with wisdom. Esoterically one can distinguish in *Iḥsān* two accentuations: that of gnosis, which implies doctrinal intellectuality, and that of love, which requires the totality of the volitive and emotive soul, the first mode operating with intellectual means—without however neglecting the supports that may be necessitated by human weakness—and the second with moral and sentimental means. It is in the nature of things that this love can exclude every element of intellection and that it can readily if not always do so—precisely to the extent it constitutes a way—whereas gnosis, on the contrary, always contains an element of love, doubtless not violent love but one akin to Beauty and Peace.

* * *

Iḥsān includes many ramifications, but it is obviously constituted most directly by quintessential esoterism. At first sight the expression "quintessential esoterism" looks like a pleonasm; is esoterism not quintessential by definition? It is indeed so "by right" but not necessarily "in fact", as is amply proven by the unequal and often disconcerting phenomenon of average Sufism. The principal pitfall of this spirituality—let it be said once again—is the fact that in it metaphysics is treated according to the categories of an anthropomorphist and voluntaristic theology and of an individualistic piety above all obediential in character. Another pitfall, which goes hand in hand with the first, is the insistence on a certain hagiographic "mythology" and other preoccupations that enclose the intelligence and sensibility within the phenomenal order; finally there is the abuse of scriptural interpretations and metaphysico-mystical speculations, which are derived from an ill-defined and poorly disciplined inspirationism or from an esoterism that is in fact insufficiently conscious of its true nature.

An example of "moralizing metaphysics" is the confusion between a divine decree addressed to creatures endowed with free will and the ontological possibility that determines the nature of a thing; as a result of this confusion one asserts that Satan, by disobeying God—or Pharaoh, by resisting Moses—obeyed God in that by disobeying they obeyed their archetype, hence the existentiating divine "will", and that they have been—or will be—pardoned for this reason. Now the ideas of "divine will" and "obedience" are being used here in an abusive manner, because in order for an ontological possibility to be a "will" or an "order" it must emanate from the legislating *Logos* as such, and in this case it is expressly concerned with free and therefore responsible creatures; and in order for the submission of a thing or a being to constitute an "obedience", it is clearly necessary for there to be a discerning consciousness and freedom, hence the possibility of not obeying. In the absence of this fundamental *distinguo* there is merely doctrinal confusion and misuse of language as well as heresy from the legitimate point of view of theologians.

The general impression given by Sufi literature must not cause us to forget that there were many Sufis who left no writings and were strangers to the pitfalls we have just described; their influence has remained practically anonymous or blends with that of well-known individuals. Indeed it may be that certain minds instructed in the "vertical" way—and this refers to the mysterious filiation of al-Khiḍr—and outside the requirements of a "horizontal" tradition shaped by an underlying theology and dialectical habits, may have voluntarily abstained from formulating their thought in such an environment, without this having prevented the radiance proper to every spiritual presence.

To describe known or what one may call literary Sufism in all its *de facto* complexity and all its paradoxes would require a whole book, whereas to give an account of the necessary and therefore concise character of Sufism, a few pages can suffice. "The Doctrine—and the Way—of Unity is unique" (*at-Tawḥīdu wāḥid*): this classic formula succinctly expresses the essentiality, primordiality, and universality of Islamic esoterism as well as of esoterism as such; and we might even say that all wisdom—all *Advaita Vedānta* if one prefers—is contained for Islam within the *Shahāda* alone, the twofold Testimony of faith.

Before going further and in order to situate Islam within the totality of Monotheism, we wish to draw attention to the following: from the point of view of Islam, which is the religion of the primordial and universal—analogically and principially speaking—Mosaism appears as a kind of "petrifaction" and Christianity by contrast as a kind of "disequilibrium". Leaving aside any question of exaggeration or stylization, we can say that Mosaism has the vocation of being the preserving ark of both the Abrahamic and the Sinaitic heritage, the "ghetto"* of the One and Invisible God, who speaks and acts, but who does so only for an Israel which is impenetrable and turned in on itself and which puts all the emphasis on the Covenant and obedience; whereas the sufficient reason for Christianity, at least with regard to its specific mode, is to be the incredible and explosive exception that breaks the continuity of the horizontal and exteriorizing stream of the human by a vertical and interiorizing irruption of the Divine, the entire emphasis being placed on the sacramental life and penance. Islam, which professes to be Abrahamic, hence primordial, seeks to reconcile all oppositions within itself, just as the substance absorbs accidents but without abolishing their qualities; by referring to Abraham and thereby to Noah and Adam, Islam seeks to bring out again the value of the immense treasure of pure Monotheism, whence its accentuation on Unity and faith; it frees and reanimates this Monotheism, the Israelization and Christification of which had actualized specific potentialities while dimming its substantial light. All the unshakable certitude and propulsive power of Islam are explained by this and cannot be explained otherwise.

* * *

The first Testimony of faith (*Shahāda*) consists of two parts, each of which is composed of two words: *lā ilāha* and *illā 'Llāh*, "no divin-

* Editors' Note: The author uses the term "ghetto" to designate an insular ethnic community that is formed by shared traditions, unlike the term's more limited and pejorative usages in current English.

ity—except the (sole) Divinity". The first part, the "negation" (*nafy*), corresponds to universal Manifestation, which is illusory in relation to the Principle, whereas the second part, the "confirmation" (*ithbāt*), corresponds to the Principle, which is Reality and which in relation to Manifestation is alone real.

Nevertheless Manifestation possesses a relative reality without which it would be pure nothingness; in a complementary way there must be within the principial order an element of relativity without which this order could not be the cause of Manifestation, hence of what is relative by definition; this is visually expressed by the Taoist symbol of the *Yin-Yang*, which is an image of compensatory reciprocity. This means that at a level below its Essence the Principle contains a prefiguration of Manifestation, which makes Manifestation possible; and Manifestation for its part contains in its center a reflection of the Principle, without which it would be independent of the Principle, which is inconceivable, relativity having no substantiality of its own.

The prefiguration of Manifestation in the Principle—the principial *Logos*—is represented in the *Shahāda* by the word *illā* ("except" or "if not"), whereas the name *Allāh* expresses the Principle in itself; and the reflection of the Principle—the manifested *Logos*—is represented in turn by the word *ilāha* ("divinity"), whereas the word *lā* ("there is no" or "no") refers to Manifestation as such, which is illusory in relation to the Principle and therefore cannot be envisaged outside of it or separately from it.

This is the metaphysical and cosmological doctrine of the first Testimony, that of God (*lā ilāha illā 'Llāh*). The doctrine of the second Testimony, that of the Prophet (*Muḥammadun Rasūlu 'Llāh*), refers to a Unity not exclusive this time but inclusive; it expresses not distinction but identity, not discernment but union, not transcendence but immanence, not the objective and macrocosmic discontinuity of the degrees of Reality but the subjective and microcosmic continuity of the one Consciousness. The second Testimony is not static and separative like the first, but dynamic and unitive.

Strictly speaking, the second Testimony—according to its quintessential interpretation—considers the Principle only in relation to three hypostatic aspects, namely: the manifested Principle (*Muḥammad*), the manifesting Principle (*Rasūl*), and the Principle in itself (*Allāh*).

The entire accent is placed on the intermediate element, *Rasūl*, "Messenger"; it is this element, the *Logos*, which links the manifested Principle to the Principle in itself. The *Logos* is the "Spirit" (*Rūḥ*) of which it has been said that it is neither created nor uncreated or again that it is manifested in relation to the Principle and non-manifested or principial in relation to Manifestation.

The word *Rasūl*, "Messenger", indicates a "descent" of God toward the world; it also implies an "ascent" of man toward God. In the case of the Muhammadan phenomenon, the descent is that of the Koranic Revelation (*laylat al-qadr*), and the ascent is that of the Prophet during the "Night Journey" (*laylat al-miʿrāj*); in the human microcosm, the descent is inspiration, and the ascent is aspiration; the descent is divine grace whereas the ascent is human effort, the content of which is the "remembrance of God" (*dhikru ʾLlāh*), whence the name *Dhikru ʾLlāh* given to the Prophet.[3]

The three words *dhākir, dhikr, madhkūr*—a classic ternary in Sufism—correspond exactly to the ternary *Muḥammad, Rasūl, Allāh*: *Muḥammad* is the invoker, *Rasūl* the invocation, *Allāh* the invoked. In the invocation, the invoker and invoked meet, just as *Muḥammad* and *Allāh* meet in *Rasūl* or in the *Risāla*, the Message.[4]

The microcosmic aspect of *Rasūl* explains the esoteric meaning of the "Blessing upon the Prophet" (*ṣalāt ʿalā ʾn-Nabī*), which contains on the one hand the "Blessing" properly so called (*Ṣalāt*) and on the other hand "Peace" (*Salām*), the latter referring to the stabilizing, appeasing, and "horizontal" graces and the former to the transforming, vivifying, and "vertical" graces. Now the "Prophet" is the immanent universal Intellect, and the purpose of the formula is to awaken within us the Heart-Intellect in the twofold relationship of receptivity and enlightenment—of the Peace that extinguishes and of the Life that regenerates, by God and in God.

[3] Jacob's Ladder is an image of the *Logos*, with the angels descending and ascending, God appearing at the top of the ladder and Jacob remaining below.

[4] Another ascending ternary is that of *makhāfa, maḥabba, maʿrifa*: fear, love, knowledge—modes at once simultaneous and successive; we shall return to this later.

* * *

The first Testimony of faith, which refers *a priori* to transcendence, includes secondarily and necessarily a meaning according to immanence: in this case the word *illā*, "except" or "if not", means that every positive quality, every perfection, every beauty belongs to God or even "is" God in a certain sense, whence the divine Name "the Outward" (*aẓ-Ẓāhir*), which is the complementary opposite of "the Inward" (*al-Bāṭin*).[5]

In a similar but inverse manner, the second Testimony, which refers *a priori* to immanence, includes secondarily and necessarily a meaning according to transcendence: in this case the word *Rasūl*, "Messenger", means that Manifestation—*Muḥammad*—is but the trace of the Principle, *Allāh*, hence that Manifestation is not the Principle.

These underlying meanings must accompany the primary meanings because of the principle of compensatory reciprocity to which we referred when speaking of the first Testimony and with regard to which we mentioned the well-known symbol of *Yin-Yang*. For, Manifestation is not the Principle, while nonetheless being the Principle through participation in "non-inexistence"; and Manifestation—the word says as much—is the Principle manifested, but without being able to be the Principle in itself. The unitive truth of the second Testimony cannot be absent from the first Testimony any more than the separative truth of the first can be absent from the second.

And just as the first Testimony, which has above all a macrocosmic and objective meaning, necessarily includes a microcosmic and subjective meaning as well,[6] so the second Testimony, which has

[5] This interpretation has given rise to the accusation of pantheism, wrongly of course since God cannot be reduced to outwardness, that is, since outwardness does not exclude inwardness any more than immanence excludes transcendence.

[6] An initiatic, or if one prefers "advaitic", meaning: "There is no subject ('me') except the sole Subject (the 'Self')." It should be noted that Rāmaṇa Maharṣi and Rāmākrishna seem to have failed to recognize in their teachings the vital importance of the ritual and liturgical framework of the way, whereas neither the great Vedantists nor the Sufis ever lost sight of this.

above all a microcosmic and subjective meaning, necessarily includes a macrocosmic and objective meaning as well.

The two Testimonies culminate in the word *Allāh*, which being their essence contains them and thereby transcends them. In the name *Allāh* the first syllable is short, contracted, absolute, whereas the second is long, dilated, infinite; it is thus that the Supreme Name contains these two mysteries, Absoluteness and Infinitude, and thereby also the extrinsic effect of their complementarity, Manifestation, as is indicated by this *ḥadīth qudsī*: "I was a hidden treasure, and I wanted to be known; hence I created the world." Since absolute Reality includes intrinsically Goodness, Beauty, Beatitude (*Raḥma*) and since it is the Sovereign Good, it includes *ipso facto* the tendency to communicate itself, hence to radiate; this is the Absolute's aspect of Infinity, and it is this aspect that projects Possibility, Being, from which the world, things, and creatures spring forth.

The Name *Muḥammad* is that of the *Logos*, which is situated between the Principle and Manifestation or between God and the world. Now the *Logos* is on the one hand prefigured in the Principle, which is expressed by the word *illā* in the first *Shahāda*, and on the other hand projects itself into Manifestation, which is expressed by the word *ilāha* in the same formula. In the Name *Muḥammad* the whole accent and all the fulgurating power are situated at the center between two short syllables, one initial and one final, without which this accentuation would not be possible; it is the sonorous image of the victorious Manifestation of the One.

* * *

According to the school of *Wujūdiyya*,[7] to say that "there is no divinity (*ilāha*) if not the (sole) Divinity (*Allāh*)" means that there is only God, that as a consequence everything is God, and that it is we creatures who see a multiple world where there is only one Reality; the question that remains is why creatures see the One in multiple mode

[7] The ontological monism of Ibn ʿArabī. It should be noted that even in Islam this school does not have a monopoly on unitive metaphysics despite the prestige of its founder.

and why God Himself, insofar as He creates, legislates, and judges, sees the multiple and not the One. The correct answer is that multiplicity is objective as well as subjective—the cause of diversifying contingency being in each of the two poles of perception—and that multiplicity or diversity is in reality a subdivision, not of the divine Principle of course, but of its manifesting projection, which is existential and universal Substance. Diversity or plurality is therefore not opposed to Unity; it is within it and not alongside it. Multiplicity as such is the outward aspect of the world; but it is necessary to look at phenomena according to their inward reality, hence as a diversified and diversifying projection of the One. The metacosmic cause of the phenomenon of multiplicity is All-Possibility, which coincides by definition with the Infinite, the latter being an intrinsic characteristic of the Absolute. The divine Principle, being the Sovereign Good, tends by this very fact to radiate, hence to communicate itself—to project or make explicit all the "possibilities of the Possible".

To say radiation is to say increasing distance, hence progressive weakening or darkening, which explains the privative—and finally subversive—phenomenon of what we call evil; we speak of it thus for good reason and in conformity with its nature and not because of a particular, even arbitrary, point of view. But evil must have a positive function in the economy of the universe or else it would not be possible, and this function is twofold: first of all there is manifestation which contrasts, that is, which highlights the good by means of its opposite, for to distinguish a good from an evil is a way of better understanding the nature of the good;[8] then there is transitory collaboration, which means that it is also the role of evil to contribute to the realization of the good.[9] It is in any case absurd to assert that evil is a good because it is "willed by God" and because God can will only the good; evil

[8] At first sight one might think that this highlighting is a merely circumstantial and therefore secondary factor, but this is not the case, for it is a question here of the quasi-principial opposition of phenomena—or categories of phenomena—and not of accidental confrontations. Qualitative "contrasting" is indeed a cosmic principle and not a question of encounters or comparisons.

[9] Evil in its aspect of suffering contributes to the unfolding of Mercy, which in order to be plenary must be able to save in the fullest meaning of this word;

always remains evil in relation to the privative or subversive character that defines it, but it is indirectly a good by virtue of the following factors: by existence, which detaches it so to speak from nothingness and causes it to participate, with everything that exists, in the divine Reality, the only one there is; by superimposed qualities or faculties, which as such always retain their positive character; and finally, as we have said, by its contrasting function with regard to the good and its indirect collaboration in the realization of the good.

To consider evil in relation to cosmogonic Causality is at the same stroke and *a priori* to consider it in relation to universal Possibility: if manifesting Radiation is necessarily prefigured in the divine Being, the privative consequences of this Radiation must be so in a certain manner as well, not as such of course but as "punitive" functions—morally speaking—pertaining essentially to Power and Rigor and thus making manifest the "negation" (*nafy*) of the *Shahāda*, namely, the exclusiveness of the Absolute. These functions are expressed by the divine Names of Wrath, such as "He who contracts, tightens, tears away (*al-Qabiḍ*)", "He who avenges (*al-Muntaqim*)", "He who injures (*aḍ-Ḍarr*)", and several others;[10] these are altogether extrinsic functions, for "Verily, my Mercy (*Raḥma*) precedeth my Wrath (*Ghaḍab*)", as the inscription on the throne of *Allāh* declares; "precedeth", hence "takes precedence over" and in the final analysis "annuls". Moreover the wrathful functions are reflected in creatures in just the same way as the generous ones, whether positively by analogy or negatively by opposition; for holy anger is something other than hatred, just as noble love is something other than blind passion.

We shall add that the function of evil is to permit or introduce the manifestation of divine Anger, which means that this Anger in a

in other words divine Love in its dimension of unlimited compassion implies evil in its dimension of unfathomable misery; to this the Psalms and the Book of Job bear witness, and to this the final and quasi-absolute solution is the *Apocatastasis*, which reintegrates everything in the Sovereign Good.

10 Vedantic doctrine discerns in the substantial or feminine pole (*Prakṛti*) of Being three tendencies: one ascending and luminous (*Sattva*), one expansive and fiery (*Rajas*), and one descending and obscure (*Tamas*); the last does not in itself constitute evil but prefigures it indirectly and gives rise to it on certain levels or under certain conditions.

certain way creates evil for the sake of its own ontologically necessary manifestation: if there is universal Radiation, there is by virtue of the same necessity both the phenomenon of evil and the manifestation of Rigor, and then the victory of the Good, hence the eminently compensatory manifestation of Mercy. We could also say very elliptically that evil is the "existence of the inexistent" or the "possibility of the impossible", this paradoxical possibility being required as it were by the limitlessness of All-Possibility, which cannot exclude even nothingness, for however null in itself, this nothingness is nonetheless "conceivable" existentially as well as intellectually.

Whoever discerns and contemplates God, first in a conceptual way and then in the Heart, will finally see Him in creatures as well, in the manner permitted by their nature and not otherwise. From this comes on the one hand charity toward one's neighbor and on the other hand respect toward even inanimate objects, always to the extent required or permitted by their qualities and defects, for it is not a question of deluding oneself but of understanding the real nature of creatures and things;[11] this means that one must be just and—depending on the case—more charitable than just, and also that one must treat things in conformity with their nature and not with a profaning inadvertence. This is the most elementary manner of seeing God everywhere, and it is also a way of feeling that we are everywhere seen by God; and since there are no strict lines of demarcation in charity, we may say that it is better to be a little too charitable than not charitable enough.[12]

* * *

Each verse of the Koran, even if it is not metaphysical or mystical in itself, includes a meaning in addition to its immediate sense that pertains to one or the other of these two domains; this certainly does not

[11] Love of beauty and the sense of the sacred are also situated in this context.

[12] According to the Koran God rewards merits much more than He punishes faults, and He more readily forgives a fault on account of a small merit than reduces a reward on account of a small fault—always according to the measures of God, not according to ours.

authorize setting aside an underlying meaning in favor of an arbitrary and forced interpretation, for neither zeal nor ingenuity can replace the real intentions of the Text, whether these are direct or indirect, essential or secondary. "Lead us on the straight path": this verse refers first of all to dogmatic, ritual, and moral rectitude, but it cannot but refer also and more especially to the way of gnosis; on the other hand, when the Koran institutes some rule or other or when it relates some incident, no higher meaning imposes itself in a necessary way, which is not to say that this is excluded *a priori*, provided that the symbolism is plausible. It goes without saying that the exegetical science (*'ilm al-uṣūl*) of theologians, with its classification of explanatory categories, does not take account—and this is its right—of the liberties of an esoterist reading.

A point we must take into account here, even if only to mention it, is the discontinuous, allusive, and elliptical character of the Koran: it is discontinuous like its mode of revelation or "descent" (*tanzīl*) and allusive and therefore elliptical through its parabolism, which insinuates itself into secondary details that are all the more paradoxical in that their intention remains independent of context. Moreover it is a fact that the Arabs, and with them the Arabized, are fond of a separating and accentuating discontinuity, of allusion, ellipsis, tautology, and hyperbolism; all this seems to have its roots in certain characteristics of nomadic life, with its alternations, mysteries, and nostalgias.[13]

[13] With regard to allusive ellipticism, here are some examples: Solomon arrives with all his army in the "Valley of the Ants", and one of these says to the others: "O ants! Enter your dwellings so that Solomon and his armies will not crush you without knowing it." The meaning is first that even the best of monarchs, to the very extent he is powerful, cannot prevent injustices committed in his name and second that the small, when confronted with the great, must look to their own safety by remaining in a modest and discrete anonymity, not because of a voluntary ill will on the part of the great, but because of an inevitable situation; the subsequent prayer of Solomon expresses gratitude toward God, who gives all power, as well as the intention of being just, of "doing good". Then Solomon, having inspected his troops, notices that the hoopoe is absent, whose important function is to discover water holes, and he says: "Verily I will punish it with a severe chastisement or I will slay it unless it bring me a worthy excuse"; the teaching which slips here into the

Let us now consider the Koranic "signs" in themselves. The following verses—and many others as well—have an esoteric significance that is at least certain and therefore legitimate even if it is not always direct; or more precisely, each verse has several meanings of this kind, if only because of the difference between the perspectives of love and gnosis or between doctrine and method.*

> "*God is the Light of the heavens and the earth* (the Intellect that is both "celestial" and "terrestrial" = principial or manifested, macrocosmic or microcosmic, the transcendent or immanent Self)" (*Sūra* "Light" [24]:35).

> "*Unto God belong the East and the West, and whithersoever ye turn, there is the Face of God*" (*Sūra* "The Cow" [2]:115).

general narrative is that it is a grave matter to fail without a serious reason in fulfilling the obligations of an office, the degrees of seriousness being expressed by the degrees of punishment. Finally, the hoopoe having recounted that it had seen the Queen of Sheba, a worshipper of the sun, Solomon says to it: "We shall see whether thou speakest truth or whether thou art of the liars." Why this distrust? It is to emphasize that a leader must verify the reports of his subordinates, not because they are liars, but because they may be so; but the distrust of the king is also explained by the extraordinary nature of the account, and it thereby includes an indirect homage to the splendor of the kingdom of Sheba. These are so many psychological, social, and political teachings inserted into the story of the meeting between Solomon and Queen Bilqis (*Sūra* "The Ant" [27]:18, 21, 27). That these incidents can also have profound meanings we have no reason to doubt, but we nonetheless do not wish to abolish the distinction between interpretations that are necessary and those that are merely possible. Let us add, regarding the quotations we have presented here, that it is completely in the style of Islam to mention, explicitly or implicitly, practical details that at first sight seem obvious and thus to provide points of reference for the most diverse situations of individual and collective life; the *Sunna* is an abundant proof of this.

* Editors' Note: The list of quotes from the Koran that follow have been formatted with the actual translations in italics and the author's comments in parentheses. In other citations from the Koran or Ḥadīth in this essay, the parenthetical comments are once again the author's explanations.

"*He is the First and the Last, and the Outward* (the Apparent) *and the Inward* (the Hidden); *and He knows infinitely all things*" (*Sūra* "Iron" [57]:3).

"*He it is who hath sent down the profound Peace* (*Sakīna* = Tranquility through the divine Presence) *into the hearts of the believers* (the heart being either the deep soul or the Intellect) *that they might add faith unto their faith* (a reference to the illumination that superimposes itself on ordinary faith)" (*Sūra* "Victory" [48]:4).

"*Verily we belong to God and verily unto Him we shall return*" (*Sūra* "The Cow" [2]:156).

"*And God summoneth to the abode of peace, and leadeth whom He will* (whoever is qualified) *to a straight* (ascending) *path*" (*Sūra* "Jonah" [10]:25).

"*Those who believe and whose hearts find peace in the remembrance* (mention = invocation) *of God; is it not through the remembrance of God that hearts find peace?*" (*Sūra* "The Thunder" [13]:28).

"*Say: 'Allāh!' Then leave them to their vain discourse*" (*Sūra* "The Cattle" [6]:91).

"O *mankind, ye are the poor* (*fuqarā* from *faqīr*) *in relation to God, and God is the Rich* (*al-Ghanī* = the Independent), *the universally Praised* (every cosmic quality referring to Him and bearing witness to Him)" (*Sūra* "The Angels" [35]:15).

"*And the Hereafter* (the principial night) *is better for thee than the here-below* (the phenomenal world)" (*Sūra* "The Morning Hours" [93]:4).

"*And worship thy Lord till Certitude* (metaphysical certitude, gnosis) *cometh unto thee*" (*Sūra* "The Rock" [15]:99).

We have quoted these verses as examples without undertaking to make explicit the specifically esoteric undercurrents hidden in their respective symbolisms. But it is not only the verses of the Koran that are important in Islam; there are also the sayings (*aḥādīth*) of the

Prophet, which obey the same laws and in which God sometimes speaks in the first person; a saying in this category, to which we referred above on account of its doctrinal importance, is the following: "I was a hidden treasure, and I wanted to be known; hence I created the world." Or a saying in which the Prophet speaks for himself: "Spiritual virtue (*iḥsān* = right doing) is that thou shouldst worship God as if thou sawest Him, for, if thou seest Him not, He nonetheless seeth thee."

A key formula for Sufism is the famous *ḥadīth* in which God speaks through the mouth of the Messenger: "My servant ceaseth not to draw nigh unto Me by devotions freely accomplished[14] until I love him; and when I love him, I am the Hearing whereby he heareth and the Sight whereby he seeth and the Hand wherewith he smiteth and the Foot whereon he walketh." It is thus that the absolute Subject, the Self, penetrates the contingent subject, the ego, and thus the ego is reintegrated into the Self; this is the principal theme of esoterism. The "devotions freely accomplished" culminate in the "Remembrance of God" or are directly identified with it, all the more so since the profound reason for every religious act is this remembrance, which in the final analysis is the very reason for the existence of man.

But let us return to the Koran: the quasi-"eucharistic" element in Islam—that is, the element of "heavenly nourishment"—is the chanting of the Book; the canonical Prayer is the obligatory minimum of this, but it contains as if by compensation a text that is considered to be the equivalent of the entire Koran, namely the *Fātiḥa*, the "*Sūra* that opens". What is important in the rite of reading or reciting the Revealed Book is not only a literal understanding of the text, but also—and almost independently of this understanding—an assimilation of the "magic" of the Book, whether by elocution or audition,

[14] Exoterizing Sufism, which prolongs and intensifies the *Sharīʿa*, deduces from this passage the multiplication of pious practices, whereas the Sufism that is centered on gnosis deduces the frequency of the quintessential rite, *Dhikr*, emphasizing its contemplative quality and not its character of meritorious act. Let us remember, however, that there is no strict line of demarcation between the two conceptions, although this line does exist by right and can always assert itself.

with the intention of being penetrated by the divine Word (*Kalām Allāh*) as such and, consequently, forgetting both the world and the ego.[15] Ejaculatory prayer—*Dhikr*—has in principle the value and virtue of a synthesis of Koranic recitation, both from the point of view of doctrinal content and "real Presence".

* * *

The sayings of Muhammad sometimes contain judgments that appear excessive, which prompts us to give the following explanation. Ibn ʿArabī has been reproached for placing the Sages above the Prophets—wrongly so, for he regarded all the Prophets as Sages too, though their quality of wisdom took precedence over that of prophecy. Indeed the Sage transmits truths as he perceives them whereas the Prophet as such transmits a divine Will, which he does not spontaneously perceive and which determines him in a moral and quasi-existential manner; the Prophet is thus passive in his receptive function whereas the Sage is active by his discernment, although in another respect the Truth is received passively, just as inversely and by way of compensation the divine Will confers upon the Prophet an active attitude. And here is the point we wish to make: when a Prophet proclaims a point of view whose limitations one can perceive without difficulty, whether from the standpoint of another religious system or from a perception of the nature of things, he does so because he incarnates in this case a particular divine Will: for example, there is a divine Will which, for a given mentality, inspires the production of sacred images just as there is another divine Will which, for another mentality, proscribes images; when the Arab Prophet, determined by this second Will, proscribes the plastic arts and anathematizes artists, he does not do so on the basis of prevailing opinion or as the result of a personal intellection, but under the effect of a divine Will that seizes him and makes of him its instrument or spokesman.

[15] It does happen that non-Arab Muslims, who to a large extent do not know the language of the Koran, recite or read parts of the Book in order to benefit from its *baraka*, a practice considered perfectly valid.

All this is said to explain the "narrowness" of certain positions taken by the founders of religion. The Prophet as Sage has access to every truth, but there are some truths which do not actualize themselves concretely in his mind or which he places in parentheses unless an occasional cause makes him change his attitude, and this depends on Providence, not chance. By his nature, the Prophet does not belie as Sage what he must personify as Prophet, except in some exceptional cases, which believers may understand or not and of which they are not meant to be judges.

* * *

The twofold Testimony is the first and most important of the five "Pillars of the Religion" (*arkān ad-Dīn*). The others have a meaning only in reference to it, and they are canonical Prayer (*Ṣalāt*), the Fast of Ramadan (*Ṣiyām*), Almsgiving (*Zakāt*), Pilgrimage (*Ḥajj*). The esoterism of these practices is not only in their obvious initiatic symbolism but in the fact that our practices are esoteric to the extent we ourselves are, first by our understanding of the Doctrine and then by our assimilation of the Method,[16] these two elements being contained, precisely, in the twofold Testimony. Prayer marks the submission of Manifestation to the Principle; the Fast is detachment with regard to desires, hence with regard to the ego; Almsgiving is detachment with regard to things, hence with regard to the world; finally, the Pilgrimage is the return to the Center, the Heart, the Self. A sixth Pillar is sometimes added, Holy War: this is combat against the profane soul by means of the spiritual weapon; it is therefore not the Holy War that is outward and "lesser" (*aṣghar*), but the Holy War that is inward and "greater" (*akbar*), according to a *ḥadīth*. Islamic initiation is in fact a pact with God for the sake of this "greater" Holy War; the battle is fought by means of the *Dhikr* and on the basis of *Faqr*, inward "Poverty", whence the name of *faqīr*, given the initiate.

What is distinctive about Prayer among the "Pillars of the Religion" is that it has a precise form and includes bodily positions,

[16] Which essentially includes the virtues, for there is no path that is limited to an abstract and in a sense inhuman *yoga*; Sufism is, precisely, one of the most patent proofs of this.

which as symbols necessarily have meanings specific to esoterism; but these meanings are simply explanatory and do not enter consciously and operatively into the accomplishment of the rite, which requires only a sincere awareness of the formulas and the pious intention of the movements. The reason for the existence of the canonical Prayer lies in the fact that man always remains an individual interlocutor before God and that he need not be anything else; when God wants us to speak to Him, He does not accept from us a metaphysical meditation. As for the meaning of the movements of the Prayer, all we need to say here is that the vertical positions express our dignity as free and theomorphic "vicar" (*khalīfa*) and that the prostrations on the contrary manifest our smallness as "servant" (*ʿabd*) and as dependant and limited creature;[17] man must be aware of the two sides of his being, made as he is of clay and spirit.

* * *

For obvious reasons the Name *Allāh* is the quintessence of Prayer just as it is the quintessence of the Koran; containing in a certain manner the whole Koran, it thereby also contains the canonical Prayer, which is the first *Sūra* of the Koran, "that which opens" (*al-Fātiḥa*). In principle the supreme Name (*al-Ism al-Aʿẓam*) even contains the whole religion and all the practices it requires, and it could therefore replace them;[18] but in fact these practices contribute to the equilibrium of the soul and society, or rather they condition them.

[17] The gestures of the ritual ablution (*wuḍūʾ*), without which man is not in a state of prayer, constitute various psychosomatic purifications, so to speak. Man sins with the members of his body, but the root of sin is in the soul.

[18] "Remembrance (*dhikr*) is the most important rule of the religion. The law was not imposed upon us nor the rites of worship ordained except for the sake of establishing the remembrance of God (*dhikru ʾLlāh*). The Prophet said: 'The circumambulation (*ṭawāf*) around the Holy House, the passage to and fro between (the hills of) Safa and Marwa, and the throwing of the pebbles (on three pillars symbolizing the devil) were ordained only for the sake of the Remembrance of God.' And God Himself has said (in the Koran): 'Remember God at the Holy Monument.' Thus we know that the rite that consists in stopping there was ordained for remembrance and not specifically

In several passages the Koran enjoins the faithful to remember God, hence to invoke Him and frequently repeat His Name. Likewise the Prophet said: "It behooves you to remember your Lord (to invoke Him)." He also said: "There is a means of polishing everything and removing rust; and that which polishes the heart is the invocation of *Allāh*; and there is no act that removes God's punishment as much as does this invocation." The Companions of the Prophet said: "Is the fight against infidels equal to this?" He replied: "No, not even if one fights until one's sword is broken." And he said further on another occasion: "Should I not teach you an action that is better for you than fighting against infidels?" His Companions said: "Yes, teach it to us." The Prophet said: "This action is the invocation of *Allāh*."

Dhikr, which implies spiritual combat since the soul tends naturally toward the world and the passions, coincides with *Jihād*, Holy War; Islamic initiation—as we said above—is a pact in view of this War, a pact with the Prophet and with God. After the return from a battle, the Prophet declared: "We have returned from the lesser Holy War (performed with the sword) to the greater Holy War (performed with invocation)."

Dhikr contains the whole Law (*Sharīʿa*), and it is the reason for the existence of the whole Law;[19] this is declared by the Koranic verse:

for the sake of the monument itself, just as the halt at Muna was ordained for remembrance and not because of the valley. Furthermore He (God) has said on the subject of the ritual prayer: 'Perform the prayer in remembrance of Me.' In a word, our performance of the rites is considered ardent or lukewarm according to the degree of our remembrance of God while performing them. Thus when the Prophet was asked which spiritual strivers would receive the greatest reward, he replied: 'Those who have remembered God most.' And when asked which fasters would receive the greatest reward, he replied: 'Those who have remembered God most.' And when the prayer and the almsgiving and the pilgrimage and the charitable donations were mentioned, he said each time: 'The richest in remembrance of God is the richest in reward'" (Shaykh Aḥmad al-ʿAlawī in his treatise *Al-Qawl al-Maʿrūf*).

[19] This is the point of view of all invocatory disciplines, such as Hindu *japa-yoga* or the Amidist *nembutsu* (*buddhānusmṛti*). This *yoga* is found in *jñāna* as well as in *bhakti*: "Repeat the Sacred Name of the Divinity," said Śaṅkarāchārya in one of his hymns.

"Verily, prayer (the exoteric practice) prevents [man from committing] what is shameful (degrading) and blameworthy; certainly, the remembrance (invocation) of God (the esoteric practice) is greater" (*Sūra* "The Spider" [29]:45).[20] The expression "the remembrance of God is greater" or "the greatest thing" (*wa la-dhikru 'Llāhi akbar*) evokes and paraphrases this formula from the canonical Prayer: "God is greater" or "the greatest" (*Allāhu akbar*), and this indicates a mysterious connection between God and His Name; it also indicates a certain relativity—from the point of view of gnosis—of the outward rites, however indispensable in principle and in the majority of cases. In this connection we could also cite the following *ḥadīth*: one of the Companions said to the Prophet: "O Messenger of God, the prescriptions of Islam are too numerous for me; tell me something I can hold fast to." The Prophet replied: "Let thy tongue always be supple (in motion) with the mention (the remembrance) of God." This *ḥadīth*, like the verse we just quoted, expresses by allusion (*ishāra*) the principle of the inherence of the whole *Sharīʿa* in *Dhikr* alone.

"Ye have indeed in the Messenger of God a beautiful example for him whose hope is in God and the Last Day, and who remembereth God much" (*Sūra* "The Clans" [33]:21). "Him whose hope is in God": this is he who accepts the Testimony, the *Shahāda*, not merely with his mind but also with his heart; this is expressed by the word "hope". Now faith in God implies by way of consequence faith in our final ends; and to act in consequence is quintessentially to "remember God"; it is to fix the mind upon the Real instead of squandering it in the illusory, and it is to find peace in this fixation, according to the verse we have quoted above: "Is it not through the remembrance of God that hearts find peace?"

"Through the firm Word, God maketh steadfast, in the life of this world and in the Hereafter, those who believe" (*Sūra* "Abraham" [14]:27). The "firm Word" (*al-qawl ath-thābit*) is either the *Shahāda*, the Testimony, or the *Ism*, the Name, the nature of the *Shahāda* being *a priori* intellectual or doctrinal and that of the *Ism* being existential or alchemical; but this is not in an exclusive manner, for each of the two

[20] "God and His Name are identical," as Rāmākrishna said; and he was certainly not the only one or the first to say so.

divine Words participates in the other, the Testimony being in its way a divine Name and the Name being implicitly a doctrinal Testimony. By these two Words man becomes rooted in the Immutable, in this world as in the next. The "firmness" of the divine Word refers quintessentially to the Absolute, which in Islamic language is the One; thus the affirmative part of the *Shahāda*—the words *illā 'Llāh*—is called a "firming"* (*ithbāt*), which indicates reintegration into immutable Unity.

The whole doctrine of *Dhikr* is brought out by these words: "Therefore remember Me (*Allāh*), I will remember you (*Fadhkurunī adhkurkum*)" (*Sūra* "The Cow" [2]:152). This is the doctrine of mystical reciprocity, such as appears in the following formulation of the early Church: "God became man that man might become God"; the Essence became form that form might become Essence. This presupposes a formal potentiality within the Essence and a mysterious immanence of the essential Reality within form; the Essence unites because it is one.

* * *

Every way includes successive stages, which can at the same time be simultaneous modes; these are the "stations" (*maqāmāt*, singular: *maqām*) of Sufism. The fundamental stations are three: "Fear" (*Makhāfa*), "Love" (*Maḥabba*), and "Knowledge" (*Ma'rifa*); the number of the other stations, which in principle is indeterminate, is obtained by the subdivision of the three fundamental stations, whether the ternary is reflected in each of them or each is polarized into two complementary stations, each of which may in its turn contain various aspects, and so on. Moreover the "stations" are also manifested as passing "states" (*aḥwāl*, singular: *ḥāl*), which are anticipations of the stations or which cause a given station already acquired to participate in another station still unexplored.

* Editors' Note: In other words, "making firm" or "making immovable." The French term used by the author also has the meanings of "steadying," "strengthening," and "consolidating." The Arabic term *ithbāt* is a verbal noun that has a wealth of meanings including "confirming," "affirming," "testifying," "proving," "asserting," and "substantiating."

That each of the three fundamental modes of perfection or of the way is repeated or reflected in the other two appears to us obvious and easy to imagine; we shall therefore not seek to describe these reciprocal reverberations here. However, we must give an account of a subdivision which is not self-explanatory and which results from the bipolarization of each mode because of the universal law of complementarity; this complementarity is expressed fundamentally, for example, by the divine Names "the Immutable" (*Al-Qayyūm*) and "the Living" (*Al-Ḥayy*). We may thus distinguish within *Makhāfa* a static pole, Abstention or Renunciation (*Zuhd*), and a dynamic pole, Accomplishment or Effort (*Jahd*), the first pole realizing "Poverty" (*Faqr*), without which there is no valid work, and the second giving rise to "Remembrance" (*Dhikr*), which is work in the highest sense of the word and which eminently contains all works, not from the point of view of worldly necessities or opportunities, but from that of the fundamental divine requirement.

In *Maḥabba* there are likewise grounds for distinguishing between a static or passive pole and a dynamic or active pole: the first is Contentment (*Riḍā*ʾ) or Gratitude (*Shukr*), and the second is Hope (*Rajā*ʾ) or Trust (*Tawakkul*). Moreover the second pole implies Generosity (*Karam*), just as Contentment for its part implies or requires Patience (*Ṣabr*); these virtues are necessarily relative, hence conditional, except toward God.[21]

As for *Maʿrifa*, it includes an objective pole, which refers to transcendence, and a subjective pole, which refers to immanence: on the one hand there is the "Truth" (*Ḥaqq*) or Discernment of the One (*Tawḥīd*), and on the other hand there is the "Heart" (*Qalb*) or Union with the One (*Ittiḥād*).

The three formulas of the Sufi rosary retrace the three fundamental degrees or planes: the "Asking of forgiveness" (*Istighfār*) corresponds to "Fear", the "Blessing on the Prophet" (*Ṣalāt ʿalā ʾn-Nabī*)

[21] We give here only the "archetypes" or "keys" of the virtues—or "stations"—which sum up their multiple derivations. The *Risāla* of Qushayrī or the *Maḥāsin al-Majālis* of Ibn al-ʿArif, and other treatises of this kind, contain enumerations and analyses of these subdivisions, which have been studied by various Arabists.

to "Love", the "Testimony of faith" (*Shahāda*) to "Knowledge". The higher planes always include the lower whereas the lower planes prefigure or anticipate the higher if only by opening onto them; for Reality is one, in the soul as in the Universe. Moreover, Action reunites with Love to the extent that it is disinterested; and it reunites with Knowledge to the extent that it is accompanied by an awareness that God is the true Agent; and the same applies to Abstention, the *Vacare Deo*, which likewise can have its source only in God in the sense that mystical emptiness prolongs the principial Void.

In fact, classical Sufism has a tendency to seek to obtain cognitive results by volitive means rather than seeking to obtain volitive results by cognitive means, that is, by what is intellectually self-evident;[22] the two attitudes must in reality be combined, especially since in Islam the supreme and decisive merit is acceptance of a truth and not a moral attitude. There is no question that profound virtues predispose to Knowledge and can even bring about its blossoming in cases of heroism, but it is no less true, to say the least, that when Truth is well assimilated it produces the virtues in the very measure of this assimilation or—what amounts to the same—this qualification.

* * *

The Koran repeatedly cites the names of earlier Prophets and relates their stories; this must have a meaning for the spiritual life, as the Koran itself attests. It can happen indeed that a Sufi is attached—within the very framework of the Muhammadan Way, which is his by definition—to some pre-Islamic Prophet; in other words the Sufi places himself under the symbol, influence, and affective direction of a Prophet who personifies a congenial vocation. Islam sees in Christ—Sayyidnā ʿIsā—the personification of renunciation, interiorization, contemplative and solitary sanctity, Union; and more than one Sufi has claimed this spiritual filiation.

The series of the great Semitic Prophets includes only one woman, Sayyidatnā Maryam; her prophetic—but not law-giving—dignity is

[22] As was understood by the best of the Greeks, the word "philosophy" implied for them virtue through wisdom.

made clear by the way the Koran presents her and also by the fact that she is mentioned in the *Sūra* "The Prophets" together with other Messengers. Maryam incarnates inviolable purity to which is joined divine fecundation;[23] she also personifies spiritual retreat and abundance of graces[24] and, in an altogether general manner and *a priori*, celestial Femininity, Purity, Beauty, Mercy. The Message of the Blessed Virgin was Jesus, not Jesus as the founder of a religion but the Child Jesus[25]—not such and such a *Rasūl* but the *Rasūl* as such, who contains all possible prophetic forms in their universal and primordial indifferentiation. Thus the Virgin is considered by certain Sufis as well as Christian authors to be Wisdom-Mother or Mother of Prophecy and all the Prophets; thus Islam calls her *Ṣiddīqa*, the "Sincere"—sincerity being none other than total conformity to the Truth—which is indicated by the identification of Mary with Wisdom or with Sanctity in itself.

* * *

The Sufi readily calls himself "son of the Moment" (*ibn al-Waqt*), which means that he is situated in God's Present without concern for yesterday or tomorrow, and this Present is none other than a reflection of Unity; the One projected into time becomes the "Now" of

23 "And Maryam, daughter of 'Imrān, who kept her virginity intact; and We (*Allāh*) breathed into her of Our Spirit (*Ruḥ*)" (*Sūra* "The Banning" [66]:12).

24 According to the Koran, Mary spent her early youth in the "prayer-niche" (*miḥrāb*) of the Temple and was nourished there by angels. When Zachariah asked her whence came this food, the Virgin replied: "It is from God; verily, God provideth sustenance to whom He will without measure" (*Sūra* "The Family of 'Imrān" [3]:37). The image of the "prayer-niche"—or spiritual retreat (*khalwa*)—is found in the following verse: "And mention (O Prophet), in the Book, Maryam: when she withdrew from her family (from the world) to a place facing the East (facing the Light); and she placed a veil between her and her people" (*Sūra* "Mary" [19]:16, 17).

25 "And We (*Allāh*) have made the Son of Mary and his mother a sign (*āya*)" (*Sūra* "The Believers" [23]:50). It will be noted that the "sign" is not Jesus alone, but he and his Mother.

God, which coincides with Eternity. The Sufi cannot call himself "son of the One", for this expression would evoke Christian terminology, which Islam must exclude because of its perspective; but he could call himself "son of the Center"—according to a spatial symbolism in this case—and he does so indirectly by his insistence on the mysteries of the Heart.

The whole of Sufism, it seems to us, is summed up in these four words: *Ḥaqq*, *Qalb*, *Dhikr*, *Faqr*, "Truth", "Heart", "Remembrance", "Poverty". *Ḥaqq* coincides with the *Shahāda*, the twofold Testimony: the metaphysical, cosmological, mystical, and eschatological Truth. *Qalb* means that this Truth must not be accepted with the mind alone but with the Heart, hence with all we are. *Dhikr*, as we know, is the permanent actualization of this Faith or Gnosis by means of the sacramental word; while *Faqr* is simplicity and purity of soul, which make this actualization possible by conferring on it the sincerity without which no act is valid.[26]

The four most important formulas in Islam, which correspond in a sense to the four rivers of Paradise gushing forth from beneath the Throne of *Allāh*—the earthly reflection of this Throne being the Kaʿba—are the first and second *Shahāda*, then the Consecration and the Praise: the *Basmala* and the *Ḥamdala*. The first *Shahāda*: "There is no divinity except the (sole) Divinity"; the second *Shahāda*: "Muhammad is the Messenger of God (of the sole Divinity)"; the *Basmala*: "In the Name of God, the Clement, the Merciful";[27] the *Ḥamdala*: "Praise be to God, the Lord of the worlds."

[26] "Blessed are the pure in heart: for they shall see God" (Matt. 5:8).

[27] God is clement or benevolent in Himself in the sense that Goodness, Beauty, and Love are contained in His very Essence (*Dhāt*), and that He therefore manifests them necessarily in and through the world; this is expressed by the Name *Raḥmān*, which is almost synonymous with the Name *Allāh*. And God is also good toward the world in the sense that He manifests His goodness toward creatures by according them subsistence and all possible gifts, including, above all, salvation; it is this that is expressed by the Name *Raḥīm*.

GLOSSARY

a priori: literally, "from the former." This refers to what one can know "before experience," that is, innate knowledge that does not require observation.

ʿabd: slave, servant; this designates the worshiper and the creature dependent on his Lord.

abṣār (sing. *baṣar*): looks, glances. However, the term also has extended meanings of sight, seeing, vision, insight, discernment, penetration, mental perception, and even intelligence.

adab (pl. *ādāb*): outward attitude; pious courtesy, standards of pious decorum.

Advaita-Vedānta: the school of Hindu philosophy which is founded upon non-dualism and which asserts that the Self (*Ātman*) is not other than the Absolute (*Brahman*).

afrād: in Sufism, those very rare individuals who are chosen by Heaven to be "given" certain spiritual experiences, even though they are not systematically practicing a regular spiritual way.

aḥwāl: plural form of *ḥāl*.

Allāhu akbar: "God is the most-Great"; both a war-cry and spiritual invocation asserting the preeminence of God above all contingent creation.

amr: the order, the commandment; in theology, it is the divine Command symbolized by the creative word *kun* ("be").

anāʾiyya: the contingent reality of the separative ego that "veils" spiritual aspirants from the divine Reality.

ʿaqīda (pl. *ʿaqāʾd*): literally, "creed." These dogmas or doctrinal statements summarize the basic tenets of faith in exoteric Islam.

ʿaql: the intellect; the faculty of discursive reasoning. When used in the expression *al-ʿAql al-awwal* (the "first or primordial Intellect"), it corresponds to the transcendent *Nous* as explained by Plotinus.

avatāra (Sanskrit): literally, "a descent." The descent of the Divine to earth, especially in the sense of an incarnation, for the purpose of restoring the link of humankind with Absolute Reality.

awliyāʾ: plural form of *walī*.

ʿayn: the essence, the first determination, the eye, the spring, the source.

ʿayn ath-thābita: the "immutable essence" or principial possibility; the Archetype. Can also be expressed simply as *al-ʿayn*.

baqāʾ: subsistence, duration. In Sufism, it signifies the spiritual state of pure "subsistence" beyond all form; in other words, reintegration into the Spirit or even in pure Being. It also means the Divine Eternity. This eternal subsistence is the opposite of *fanāʾ*, spiritual extinction.

baraka: spiritual influence, blessedness, grace.

barzakh: the isthmus; symbol of an intermediate state or of a mediating principle.

bāṭin: inner, hidden. In Sufism this refers to the esoteric dimension of Islam. It is the opposite of *ẓāhir*, the outer. *Al-Bāṭin*, the Inner, the Hidden, is one of the Names of God in the Koran.

bayʿa: a pact, a giving of allegiance. In the spiritual order, this means the rite of initiation.

bhakti (Sanskrit): in Hinduism, the way of love and devotion. Cf. *jñāna*.

conditio sine qua non (Latin): an indispensable condition.

dār al-islām: literally, "realm of submission"; generally meaning the geographical areas of Muslim influence or the Muslim world.

aḍ-Ḍarr: a divine Name taken to mean "He who injures" but more subtly "He who creates that which harms." This name is not found in the Koran but was said by the Prophet to be an attribute of God. The name is usually paired with *an-Nafiʿ*, "He who creates Good," indicating that creation can be attributed solely to God.

dhākir: the invoker, that which invokes.

dhāt: personality; essence.

adh-Dhāt: the Divine Essence, the Subject of the Qualities or Attributes (*ṣifāt*), the God Beyond-Being.

dhawq: tasting, a taste. It has been said that Sufism itself can be defined as a *dhawq*, a taste here and now of the divine Presence to be found in the hereafter.

dhikr: the recollection or remembrance of the Divine. The term can also be used for the recitation, silent or aloud, of sacred litanies and invocations by Sufis.

distinguo (Latin): literally, "I mark or set off, differentiate"; a philosophical distinction.

duʿāʾ: a prayer of personal supplication.

Empedocles (c. 492-432 B.C.E.): a pre-Socratic philosopher and poet of Acagras in Sicily who postulated the four-element theory of matter (earth, air, fire, and water).

fanāʾ: extinction (in God), evanescence of transitory things. In Sufism, it designates extinction of individual limitation in the state of union with God. The opposite is *baqāʾ*, subsistence.

faqīr: he who is imbued with *faqr*, one who has attained true spiritual "poverty." This term is often used as a synonym of *ṣūfī*, dervish, etc.

faqr: indigence, spiritual poverty; the state of detachment from worldly forms and temptations, or the state of inner "emptiness."

fatḥ (pl. *futūḥ*): in Sufism, illumination, or the anticipation of illumination. It also means "opening," unfolding, triumph, and victory.

fiat lux (Latin): "Let there be light" (cf. Gen. 1:3).

fiṭra: the natural predisposition of man, as created by God, to act in accordance with the will of Heaven; the original uprightness of humanity. In Sufism, it often refers to the theomorphic nature of human beings.

fuʾād: the inmost self, the heart.

fuqahāʾ (sing. *faqīh*): experts in Islamic law or jurisprudence.

fuqarāʾ: plural of *faqīr*.

Fuṣūṣ al-Ḥikam: *Bezels of Divine Wisdom*, a short and influential masterpiece of Islamic metaphysics by Ibn ʿArabī. It addresses the human and spiritual natures of various prophets.

al-Futūḥāt al-Makkīyya: *The Meccan Revelations*, an extensive and influential work by Ibn ʿArabī that incorporates his mystical philosophy.

ghafla: negligence, forgetfulness, heedlessness. Said to be a characteristic of fallen mankind unaware of God's Presence.

Ghazzālī: Abu Ḥāmid Muḥammad ibn Muḥammad al-Ghazzālī (1058-1111 C.E.). Author of *Iḥyāʾ ʿUlūm ad-Dīn* and other renowned Sufi texts; an authority on Islamic jurisprudence as well as Sufism.

ḥadīth (pl. *aḥādith*): a "report" of the Prophet Muhammad's spoken utterances or actions. *Aḥādith* are transmitted through a chain of known and trusted intermediaries. There are two kinds of *aḥādith*: *ḥadīth qudsī* (sacred sentence or utterance), a type of direct revelation in which God speaks in the first person through the mouth of the Prophet, and *ḥadīth nabawī* (prophetic utterance), an indirect revelation in which the Prophet speaks as himself.

ḥaḍra: "presence," being present. The term is also used to designate the ecstatic dance of some Sufi orders. In the plural, *al-Ḥaḍarāt*, it refers to the divine Presences, the modes of divine Presence in contemplation.

ḥāl (pl. *aḥwāl*): state, a spiritual state. Sometimes *ḥāl* is seen in distinction to *maqām* (spiritual station), with the former considered as something that passes away while the latter refers to something stable or that cannot be lost.

al-Ḥaqīqa (pl. *ḥaqā'iq*): the truth, reality, pure knowledge; in Sufism, the divine Truth or Reality, the quintessence of a thing.

al-Ḥaqq: Truth or Reality (name of God). In Sufism, the term designates the Divinity as distinguished from that which is created (*al-khalq*).

Hermes Trismegistos: founder of Hermeticism, a philosophy well-known to the medieval Christian schools of Western Europe.

ḥijāb: veil, curtain, illusion. That which obscures God's Reality from human perception.

himmah: the force of decision; spiritual aspiration or will.

ḥuḍūr: the Real Presence of God; also the sense of the Presence of God by a spiritual seeker.

al-Huwiyya: a term derived from the pronoun *Huwa* (He): the divine Aseity or Ipseity, the Supreme "Self."

Ibn ʿArabī: Muḥyi ʾd-Dīn ibn al-ʿArabī (1165-1240 C.E.). A Sufi theorist and poet, known as "the great master." The prolific author of the *Fuṣūṣ al-Ḥikam* and *al-Futūḥāt al-Makkīyya* and many other works of mystical philosophy, he was the first to formulate explicitly many of the metaphysical and cosmological doctrines of Sufism.

iḥsān: spiritual virtue. See *islām*.

imago Dei (Latin): image of God.

imām: in Muslim rituals, the person who presides when a number pray together. The term can also be used to designate the head of a religious community.

īmān: faith. See *islām*.

in divinis (Latin): "in or among divine things"; within the divine Principle.

insān al-kāmil: "the perfect man" (i.e., human being) or "the universal man"; this is the Sufi term for one who has realized all levels of Being;

also designates the permanent prototype of humankind. It is also the title of a masterpiece of Islamic metaphysics by al-Jīlī.

ipso facto (Latin): "by the fact itself," meaning "by that very fact," or "as an unavoidable result."

ishāra: allusion, symbolism.

islām: literally, "submission" (to God's will). In Sufism, a fundamental phase of spiritual development (along with *īmān*, faith, and *iḥsān*, sanctifying virtue, spiritual beauty).

jabarūt: the world (or sphere) of the divine Omnipotence or Immensity.

jadhb: the divine attraction, which enters to some extent into every spiritual process. It is an aspect of grace.

japa (Sanskrit): invocation (a form of yoga in the Hindu tradition). *Japa-yoga* is based on the repetition of a sacred syllable, phrase, or Name of God, much like the *dhikr* of the Sufis.

jihād al-akbar: the greater holy war, i.e., the inward holy war against one's own passions and ignorance.

jihād al-aṣghar: the lesser holy war, i.e., the external holy war against enemies.

jñāna (Sanskrit): in Hinduism, the spiritual path of knowledge (i.e., gnosis) and intellection. Cf. *bhakti*.

kashf: intuition; literally, "the raising of a curtain or veil."

khalīfa: representative. Often applied in Sufism to the concept that man, by his primordial nature, is the vicegerent or representative of God on earth. Also used in some Sufi orders to designate those who have an advanced function.

khalwa: seclusion; a retreat in which a Sufi separates himself from the world to concentrate on spiritual practices.

khayāl: the faculty of imagination. This is conceived to be a purely passive faculty that depends on other faculties (e.g., a lower one of conjecture or a higher one of the Intellect) to derive objects of either illusion or Truth.

khayāl muṭlaq: the absolute Imagination.

lauḥ al-maḥfūẓ: the Guarded Tablet, symbol of universal receptive Substance or of the universal Soul.

laylat al-miʿrāj: the Prophet's "Night Journey," his ascension through the various levels of Heaven.

laylat al-qadr: the "Night of Power"; the night upon which the Koran was first revealed to the Prophet.

lubb: the kernel. Figuratively, the hidden meaning, the essence of a thing, the heart. The contrary is *al-qishr*, the shell or husk.

Madhkūr: That which is invoked, namely God, by the invoker.

majdhūb: one who undergoes the Divine attraction (*jadhb*); the spiritual person whose mental faculties are as it were paralyzed or confused by the effect of the Divine attraction.

makhāfa: fear or reverent awe of God; one of the Sufi triad of motives or qualities which lead to God. The others are *maḥabba* (spiritual love) and *maʿrifa* (gnosis, knowledge of God).

maqām (pl. *maqāmāt*): in Sufi terminology, the spiritual "station" of a seeker, which is permanent as compared to the state of *ḥāl*.

Meister Eckhart (c. 1260-1327/8 C.E.): a great Christian mystic.

mokṣa (Sanskrit): in Hinduism, deliverance from ignorance, liberation from earthly bondage.

muʾadhdhin: the person who calls the faithful to the five daily Islamic prayers. This call to prayer (*adhān*) is often chanted from the minarets of mosques.

murād: willed, desired by Him whom he claims to reach by his own powers.

mutatis mutandis (Latin): "upon changing what needs to be changed" (i.e., "after having taken respective differences into consideration").

nafs: ego, psyche, soul, passionate self, the subtle reality of an individual.

nirvāṇa (Sanskrit): in Hinduism and Buddhism, literally, "extinction" (of desire or ignorance); the state of bliss.

Nous: intelligence, immediate awareness, intuition, intuitive intellect. Plato distinguished *nous* from *dianoia* (the discursive mind). It is the divine Intellect, independent of body and thus immune to destruction.

Plotinus (c. 204-270 C.E.): the philosopher who is considered to have founded Neoplatonism.

pūjā (Sanskrit): in Hinduism, a ritual of honor, worship, reverence, or homage to superiors or the Divine.

qishr: casing, shell, husk. The opposite is *lubb*, kernel.

ar-Raḥmān: the divine Mercy. The same root RḤM is to be found in both the divine Names *ar-Raḥmān* (the Compassionate, He whose Mercy envelops all things) and *ar-Raḥīm* (the Merciful, He who saves by His grace). It is sometimes said that the former pertains to the endless outpouring of the Divine which wishes to communicate Itself and the latter to the reintegrating attraction of the Divine.

rasūl (pl. *rusūl*): envoy, messenger; in theology, the one who is the receptacle for a divine Message. It is in his function of *rasūl* that a prophet (*nabī*) promulgates a new sacred law; not every prophet is necessarily a *rasūl*, although he enjoys divine inspiration, but every *rasūl* is necessarily a *nabī*.

ar-Rūḥ: the spirit. In Sufism, this word has a variety of meanings, including: (1) the Divine, and therefore uncreated Spirit (*ar-Rūḥ al-ilāhī*), also called *ar-Rūḥ al-Qudūs*, the Holy Spirit; (2) the Universal, created, Spirit (*ar-Rūḥ al-kullī*); (3) the individual Spirit, or rather the Spirit polarized in relation to an individual; (4) the vital spirit, intermediate between soul and body. The precise meaning may be understood through qualifying terms (e.g., *ar-Rūḥ al-ilāhī*) or through context.

Rūmī: Jalāl ad-Dīn Rūmī (1207-1273 C.E.) was the founder of the Mevlevī dervish order, and a great mystical poet of Islam.

Sakīna: the divine Peace which dwells in a sanctuary or in the heart.
ṣalāt: ritual prayer or prayer service; also used in the sense of a recited blessing, as in a prayer said as a blessing upon the Prophet, etc.

sālik: a spiritual "traveler," one who follows a Sufi path.

sayyidnā: an honorific title meaning "our lord." It is used in Islam when referring to prophets and various other important spiritual personages.

shahāda: testimony, and in particular the Muslim profession of faith that "There is no divinity but the Divinity," (i.e., the One God). The *shahāda* is also used in Sufi invocations and rituals.

sharīʿa: the revealed, exoteric religious Law which is addressed to all and which is made to be followed by all. The goal of the *sharīʿa* is individual salvation for the multitude of believers.

shaykh: in Sufi terminology, a spiritual master. Other terms used more or less synonymously are *murshid*, and *pīr*.

Shaykh al-akbar: "the greatest of spiritual masters," an honorific title typically used for the great Sufi master, philosopher, and poet, Muḥyi ʾd-Dīn ibn al-ʿArabī (1165-1240 C.E.).

ṣifa (pl. *ṣifāt*): quality, attribute. This can apply to created things or to God. God's *ṣifāt* exist at a different level than His Pure Essence (*Dhāt*).

silsila: chain. In Sufism, the initiatic chain of spiritual influence that joins present Sufi practitioners to the Prophet.

Sirr: secret, mystery, hidden nature. In Sufism, this designates the intimate and ineffable center of consciousness, the "point of contact" between the individual and his Divine principle.

stricto sensu (Latin): "in its strictest sense."

sulūk: in Sufism, spiritual wayfaring or journeying.

tafsīr: the term used for the exegesis, or explanation of the Koran. Commentators have undertaken Koranic exegesis from a wide variety of perspectives (e.g., historical, linguistic, theological, etc.).

tajallī (pl. *tajallīyat*): unveiling, revelation, irradiation, shining forth, theophany; a manifestation of God within creation.

ṭarīqa (pl. *ṭurūq*): in Sufism, the spiritual Way or Path; also, a Sufi brotherhood. There is a Sufi saying: "The ways (*ṭurūq*) toward God are as numerous as the souls of men."

Taṣawwuf: Sufism; Islamic esoterism. The whole of the contemplative ways founded on the sacred forms of Islam.

tawḥīd: the affirmation of Unity, which is the doctrinal basis of Islam. In common usage this means the recognition of the Divine Unity. In Sufism it sums up all levels of the knowledge of Unity.

Vacare Deo (Latin): "to be empty for God."

walī: literally, "one who is near" or under special protection (of God), thus, a saint. There is no formal process in Islam for canonizing a "saint" and the concept is problematic for exoteric Islam, though not for Sufism. The plural form is *awliyā'*.

wird: litany; a term that would later come to designate the set of daily recitations characteristic of every initiatic path.

yaqīn: certainty.

ẓāhir: the exterior, the outer, apparent. Its opposite is *bāṭin*. *Aẓ-Ẓāhir*, the External, the Apparent, is one of the Names of God in the Koran.

For a glossary of all key foreign words used in books published by World Wisdom, including metaphysical terms in English, consult: www.DictionaryofSpiritualTerms.org.
This on-line Dictionary of Spiritual Terms provides extensive definitions, examples and related terms in other languages.

ACKNOWLEDGMENTS

The editors wish to thank the following authors, editors, and publishers for their consent to publish the articles in this anthology:

Titus Burckhardt, "Sufi Doctrine and Method" (the chapter in the present volume includes the chapters "*At-Taṣawwuf*," "Sufism and Mysticism," and "Rites" from):
An Introduction to Sufi Doctrine, Thorsons Publishers Limited, 1976, pp. 15-27, 99-105. Translated from French by D. M. Matheson.

William C. Chittick, "Sufism and Islam":
The Sufi Doctrine of Rumi, World Wisdom, 2005, pp. 9-21.

Michel Chodkiewicz, "The Vision of God According to Ibn ʿArabī":
Journal of the Muhyiddin Ibn ʿArabi Society, Volume 14, 1993, pp. 53-67. Translated from French by Cecilia Twinch.

Éric Geoffroy, "Approaching Sufism" (this chapter is taken from a longer chapter entitled "Approches" in):
Initiation au Soufisme, Librairie Arthème Fayard, 2003, pp. 15-30. Translated from French by Roger Gaetani.

Denis Gril, "The Prophetic Model of the Spiritual Master in Islam" ("Le Modèle Prophétique du Maître Spirituel en Islam"):
Maestro e discepolo, ed. Giovanni Filoramo, Morcelliana, 2002, pp. 345-360. Translated from French by Roger Gaetani.

René Guénon, "*Ḥaqīqa* and *Sharīʿa* in Islam" (the chapter in the present volume includes the chapters "Islamic Esoterism" and "The Shell and the Kernel [*Al-Qishr wa al-Lubb*]" from):
Insights into Islamic Esoterism and Taoism, Sophia Perennis, 2004, pp. 1-13. Translated from French by Henry D. Fohr.

Martin Lings, "Sufi Answers to Questions on Ultimate Reality": *Studies in Comparative Religion*, 13:.3 & 4, 1979, pp. 137-148.

Angus Macnab, "Sufism in Muslim Spain" (the chapter in the present volume includes the chapters "Spanish Sufism" and "Sultans and Sufis" from):
Spain Under the Crescent Moon, Fons Vitae, 1999, pp. 129-140.

Maria Massi Dakake, "'Walking upon the Path of God like Men'?: Women and the Feminine in the Islamic Mystical Tradition":
Sophia 8:2, Winter 2002, pp. 117-138.

Jean-Louis Michon, "Sacred Music and Dance in Islam":
Islamic Spirituality: Manifestations, ed. Seyyed Hossein Nasr, The Crossroad Publishing Company, 1997, pp. 469-483 & 486-489. Translated from French by Katherine O'Brien.

Seyyed Hossein Nasr, "The Spiritual Needs of Western Man and the Message of Sufism":
Islam and the Plight of Modern Man, ABC International Group, Inc., 2001, pp. 71-100.

Leo Schaya, "On the Name *Allāh*" ("Du Nom d'*Allâh*"):
La Doctrine Soufique de l'Unité, Adrien-Maisonneuve, 1962, pp. 79-86. Translated from French by Roger Gaetani.

Reza Shah-Kazemi, "Jesus in the Qur'an: Selfhood and Compassion—An Akbari Perspective":
Journal of the Muhyiddin Ibn ʿArabi Society, Volume 29, 2001, pp. 57-75.

William Stoddart, "Aspects of Islamic Esoterism":
Studies in Comparative Religion, 13:.3 & 4, 1979, pp. 215-224.

Frithjof Schuon, "The Quintessential Esoterism of Islam":
Sufism: Veil and Quintessence, World Wisdom, forthcoming in 2007. Translated from French by Mark Perry.

CONTRIBUTORS

ROGER GAETANI is an editor and educator who lives in Bloomington, Indiana. He lived and traveled in Muslim countries for a number of years and has had a deep interest in Sufism, Islam, and other world religions for many years. He has contributed articles and poetry to several journals and books.

JEAN-LOUIS MICHON is a traditionalist French scholar, translator, and writer who specializes in Islam in North Africa, Islamic art, and Sufism. He was associated with both René Guénon and Frithjof Schuon, and lived and worked in several Muslim countries both as a teacher and as a consultant on the reestablishment of traditional arts and crafts, including architecture. He has written many articles that have appeared in journals and collections on Islam and Sufism, including a number of articles in the *Encyclopaedia of Islam* (by Brill Academic Publishers). His books include the much-respected area study, *Autobiography of a Moroccan Sufi: Ahmad Ibn 'Ajiba.*

SEYYED HOSSEIN NASR is University Professor of Islamic Studies at George Washington University. The author of over thirty books and three hundred articles, he is one of the world's most respected writers and speakers on Islam, its arts and sciences, and its traditional mystical path, Sufism. His publications include *Sufi Essays*, *Knowledge and the Sacred*, *Religion and the Order of Nature*, *A Young Muslim's Guide to the Modern World*, *The Heart of Islam: Enduring Values for Humanity*, and *Islam: Religion, History, and Civilization.* A volume in the prestigious *Library of Living Philosophers* series has been dedicated to his thought. World Wisdom will be publishing *The Essential Seyyed Hossein Nasr* in 2007.

TITUS BURCKHARDT was one of the primary authors of the Traditionalist school of thought. He wrote on metaphysics, cosmology, art, architecture, alchemy, symbolism, and traditional civilization and devoted all his life to the study and exposition of the different aspects of Wisdom and Tradition. His book *An Introduction to Sufi Doctrine* (1976) is widely considered a classic in the area of Sufi studies. Burckhardt's translations of and commentaries on books by Ibn ʿArabī and Jīlī are also substantial contributions to the field. A collection of his writings, *The Essential Titus Burckhardt: Reflections on Sacred Art, Faiths, and Civilizations*, was published by World Wisdom in 2003.

WILLIAM C. CHITTICK is one of the most important contemporary translators and interpreters of Islamic mystical texts and poetry. He is also a professor in the Department of Comparative Studies at the State University of New York, Stony Brook. Among his publications are *The Sufi Path of Love: The Spiritual Teachings of Rumi, The Psalms of Islam, The Self-Disclosure of God: Principles of Ibn al-ʿArabī's Cosmology, Sufism: A Short Introduction, The Heart of Islamic Philosophy: The Quest for Self-Knowledge in the Teachings of Afdal al-Dīn Kāshānī*, and *The Sufi Doctrine of Rumi: Illustrated Edition* (World Wisdom, 2005).

MICHEL CHODKIEWICZ is the Director of Studies at the École des Hautes Études en Sciences Sociales in Paris. His teaching, research, translations, and writing focus on Sufism, particularly on the important figures of Ibn ʿArabī and his direct and indirect disciples. He is the author of *The Seal of the Saints: Prophethood and Sainthood in the Doctrine of Ibn ʿArabī, An Ocean Without Shore: Ibn ʿArabī, the Book, and the Law*, and *The Spiritual Writings of Amīr ʿAbd al-Kader.* He is also the editor of *The Meccan Revelations, vols. 1 and 2.*

ÉRIC GEOFFROY is an Islamicist and Arabist at the Université Marc Bloch in Strasbourg. He specializes in Sufism and sainthood within Islam, as well as in issues of spirituality in the modern world (e.g., globalization, ecology, etc.). Geoffroy has contributed numerous articles to the *Encyclopaedia of Islam* (by Brill Academic Publishers) and translations and books under his own name such as *Initiation au Soufisme* and *Ibn ʿAtāʾ Allāh—La sagesse des maîtres soufis.*

DENIS GRIL is a scholar, translator, and writer who teaches Arabic and Islamic studies at the Université de Provence in France, where he has been since 1981. He has devoted himself to the study of the work of Ibn 'Arabī, but also to the study of sainthood within Islam. His other research interests include Islamic spirituality and its scriptural foundations. His published works include translations (along with commentaries) of works by Ibn 'Arabī: *Le Livre de l'Arbre et des quatre oiseaux* and *Le dévoilement des effets du voyage.* Gril has also translated and published *La Risāla de Safī al-Dīn Ibn Abī l-Mansūr Ibn Zāfir: Biographies des maîtres spirituels connus par un cheikh égyptien du viie/xiiie siècle.*

RENÉ GUÉNON was a writer of extraordinary power and insight—in the early decades of the 20th century, it was Guénon who reintroduced the importance and necessity of integral metaphysics to thinkers in the West, and who delivered scathing indictments of the pomp and hollowness of much of modernism. Traditionalists and Perennialists everywhere tend to view Guénon's writings as having had a profound and critical influence on their thinking. Among his most influential books are *The Crisis of the Modern World* (2004) and *The Reign of Quantity & the Signs of the Times* (2004). He died in Egypt in 1951.

MARTIN LINGS was an author, editor, translator, and specialist in Islamic art and esoterism. From 1970-74 he was Keeper of Oriental Manuscripts and Printed Books at the British Museum (in 1973 his Department became part of the British Library) where he had been in special charge of the Koran manuscripts, amongst other treasures, since 1955. His authoritative biography, *Muhammad: His Life Based on the Earliest Sources*, has become a classic and is widely read in both East and West as an unbiased, clear, and profound source on the Prophet of Islam.

ANGUS MACNAB was a gifted translator of Latin and Greek poetry, but as a profession he chose teaching. His interest in Spain began in 1936, and after World War II he learned Spanish and decided to make Spain his home. In 1938, under the influence of G.K Chesterton and Hilaire Belloc, Angus Macnab embraced neo-scholasticism and traditional Catholicism.

MARIA MASSI DAKAKE is Assistant Professor of Religious Studies at George Mason University in Fairfax, Virginia, where she teaches courses on various areas of Islam and on women in world religions. Her research encompasses areas of Islamic theology, philosophy, and mysticism, and she has a particular interest in Shiite and Sufi traditions. Dakake has completed a book entitled, *The Charismatic Community: Shi'ite Identity in Early Islam* and is an active contributor to current traditionalist thought and writing.

LEO SCHAYA was born in Switzerland where he received a traditional Jewish upbringing. From his early youth he devoted himself to the study of the great metaphysical doctrines of the East and West, particularly the works of Neoplatonism, Sufism, and Advaita Vedanta. He published several articles on the metaphysical and esoteric wisdom of the Jewish Kabbalah, as well as his well-known book *The Universal Meaning of the Kabbalah*, and a book on Sufism, *La doctrine soufique de l'unité.*

REZA SHAH-KAZEMI is a Research Associate at the Institute of Ismaili Studies in London. He has also contributed articles to *Paths to the Heart: Sufism and the Christian East* (World Wisdom, 2003) and *Islam, Fundamentalism, and the Betrayal of Tradition: Essays by Western Muslim Scholars* (World Wisdom, 2004). He has regularly contributed to *Sophia*, *Sacred Web*, and *The Journal of Islamic Studies* (Oxford Center for Islamic Studies). He also translated *Doctrines of Shi'i Islam* (*Manshur-i Aqa'id-i Imamiyya*), and edited *Algeria: Revolution Revisited.* His book *Paths to Transcendence: According to Shankara, Ibn Arabi, and Meister Eckhart* has recently been published by World Wisdom (2006).

WILLIAM STODDART is a translator, editor, and writer. He studied modern languages, and later medicine, at the universities of Glasgow, Edinburgh, and Dublin. For many years he was assistant editor of the British journal *Studies in Comparative Religion.* He spent most of his working life in London and retired to Windsor, Ontario, in 1982. His books include: *Sufism: The Mystical Doctrines and Methods of Islam* (editions in seven languages), *Outline of Hinduism*, and *Outline of*

Buddhism. Stoddart is also known for translating and editing the works of the important perennialist author, Titus Burckhardt, including *The Essential Titus Burckhardt: Reflections on Sacred Art, Faiths, and Civilizations* (World Wisdom, 2003), as well as for many translations of the essays and poems of Frithjof Schuon.

FRITHJOF SCHUON was the foremost expositor of the Perennialist perspective in the twentieth century. He is best known as a philosopher in the metaphysical current of Shankara and Plato, writing more than 25 books on metaphysical and religious themes, and publishing other books of his selected paintings and mystical poetry. His analyses of spiritual problems facing modern people and societies were unique in content and style and continue to influence a new generation of Traditionalist/Perennialist thinkers. Among his many books on a vast range of spiritual subjects, Schuon's book *Understanding Islam* (1998) remains essential reading on the inner meaning of the doctrines and practices of Islam, while *Sufism: Veil and Quintessence* (forthcoming new edition, 2007) sheds similar light on many aspects of Sufism, the esoterism of Islam.

INDEX

Abraham, 4, 65, 78, 78n, 254, 270
Absolute: 21, 22, 31, 58, 101-105, 108-109, 112, 114, 242, 244, 258-260; Being, 167; Essence, 208; Self, 211
Abū Bakr, 43, 82-83, 112, 158, 175
Abū Hurayra, 34, 81-84
actualization, actualizing, 14, 22, 102, 181, 191n, 192n, 201, 210, 213-214, 267, 275
adab, 56, 63, 67-68, 114
al-ʿAlawī, Shaykh Aḥmad, 192n, 249, 269
al-Baṣrī, Ḥasan, 64, 145-146, 150
alchemy, 32, 32n, 95, 111, 163, 270
al-Futūḥāt al-Makkīya, 26, 38-41, 43-47, 55, 126, 128, 219, 223, 228, 232, 234
al-ism al-aʿẓam (the Supreme Name), 208, 258, 268
alms, 71-72, 82, 230, 267, 269
Andalusia, 117, 122, 125-126, 168
angels, 17, 40n, 85, 85n, 111, 154, 174, 188, 218, 221, 256n, 264
ʿaql, 50, 133
Archangel Gabriel, 71, 74-77, 163, 249
archetype, 115, 228, 228n, 253, 272n
asceticism, ascetics, 1n, 12, 55, 57-58, 83, 103, 143, 148, 150-151
aspiration (*spiritual*), 55, 66, 79, 104, 117, 163, 210, 222, 247
Attributes (*of God*), 23, 41, 43, 59, 80, 90, 218. *See also* Qualities
authorization: spiritual masters' authority, 6, 66-67, 74-75, 105; authorization for practitioners, 20, 64, 68, 177, 245
ʿayn (*identity, eye, source*), 34, 183, 194, 223, 228, 231-232
aẓ-Ẓāhir, 40, 97, 100, 257
baqāʾ, 1, 46, 48, 59-60, 90, 171, 225n, 248, 248n
Baqlī, Rūzbihān, 37, 37n, 41
baraka, 5, 28, 93, 202, 266n
barzakh(ī), 41-42, 84, 245
beauty, 9, 17, 19n, 27, 41, 111, 134, 162, 166, 179, 244, 251-252, 257, 258, 261n, 274, 275n
Bektāshiyya (*Sufi order*), 168
Bhagavad-Gītā, 180, 197, 203
bhakti, (bhakta), 7-8, 118n, 119-120, 126, 187, 198, 198n, 246-247, 248n, 269n
al-Bisṭāmī, Abū Yazīd , 35, 54, 109n, 144, 148-149
body (human), 12n, 18, 40, 48, 97, 138, 149, 160, 172, 175, 177, 188, 220, 268n
bravery, 140, 142, 160, 168
breath: Divine Breath, 132, 214, 220-222, 228, 274; human breath, 18, 167, 172, 176
brotherhoods (*Sufi Orders*), 19, 28-29, 31, 102, 104, 106, 141, 163, 165, 168, 172, 174-176, 199- 201, 248-249
Buddhism, 11n, 15n, 101, 110, 114, 128n, 182, 195, 269n
Burckhardt, Titus, 1n, 21n, 24n, 32n, 94n, 115n, 187n, 192n, 195n, 208n, 209n, 245n
celibacy, 143, 144n, 148
certainty, 51, 183, 183n, 194, 194n
charity, 129, 205, 230-231, 246, 251n, 261, 269
Chittick, William, 135n, 138n, 195n, 223n
Chodkiewicz, Michel, 63n, 221n, 232n
Christianity: 3-5, 7-8, 15n, 19n, 58, 93, 101, 104, 117-119, 121, 126, 128, 143-144, 182, 196-197, 199, 219, 241-242, 247, 247n, 248n, 254;

114, 181, 202, 234, 263
hell, 66, 78, 85, 147, 150-151, 229
Hereafter, 66, 79, 87, 154, 235, 264, 270
heresy, 104, 120, 155, 253
Hermeticism, 95, 121
hermits, 121, 199n
hierarchy: of the arts, 158; of Being, 52, 154, 183; initiatic, 95-96; between intellect and passionate soul, 139; of men and women, 139; in Paradise, 112; of spiritual figures, 107, 111; of theophanies, 41, 48
ḥikmat al-ilāhiyya, 1, 91-92, 181, 195
Hinduism, 2-3, 7, 15n, 19n, 99n, 105, 120, 128, 176, 187, 195, 198n, 240-241, 246-247, 269n
holiness, 63n, 80, 126, 222
holy war, 16, 56, 126, 138, 267, 269
hope, 17, 54, 73, 150, 216, 270, 272
Hujwīrī, 35-36, 49, 153, 155, 163
humanity: as "humankind," 1, 15, 56, 65, 72, 132, 210; as communities, 25, 56, 181
humility, humbleness, 16-17, 67, 74, 146, 221, 226, 232-233, 246
Huwa, 33, 100, 211-213
hypocrisy, 57, 118, 163-164, 176, 251-252
Ibn 'Abbās, 34-35, 81
ibn 'Ajība, Aḥmad, 165, 165n, 166n
Ibn 'Arabī, 7, 8n, 12n, 13, 26, 26n, 34-40, 40n, 41-42, 42n, 43, 43n, 44, 44n, 45-47, 47n, 49, 51, 55, 57, 59, 109, 112, 120, 122, 126-127, 127n, 128, 131, 135-136, 139, 141n, 142, 148, 180, 181n, 195, 195n, 198, 207, 210-211, 211n-212n, 214, 216-217, 217n, 218-219, 219n, 220, 223-224, 226-227, 227n, 228, 228n, 229-232, 232n, 234, 242, 258n, 266
Ibn al-Jawzī, 144, 149, 157
ibn al-Waqt, 274
Ibn 'Aṭa'illāh al-Iskandarī, 194, 198
identifying, spiritually: with aspects of the Divine, 8, 90, 208, 213, 216; with the divine Name, 15, 209; with the ego, 9, 22, 137; with prophetic model, 63n; with the "void", 11; with the spirit, 138
ignorance, ignorant, 77, 90, 92, 95, 128, 135, 155, 212-213, 222
Iḥyā' 'Ulūm ad-Dīn, 20n, 156n, 162, 162n, 164
illusion, 12, 38, 54, 182, 189, 191, 197, 210, 215, 239
'ilm, 50-51, 183, 194, 262
imagining, imaginal, imagination, 41-43, 168, 172
īmān, 16, 192, 251
incarnation 56, 59, 75, 106, 266, 274
individual, individuality, individualism, 2, 7-9, 9n, 11-12, 14-15, 20-21, 25, 59, 66, 90, 98, 127, 224-226, 232-234, 252
Infinite, divine Infinity, 15, 35, 44, 108, 112, 189, 240, 244, 258-259
initiates, 6n, 50, 54, 58-60, 120, 137, 141, 267
initiation, 5-6, 28, 52, 55, 70, 73, 77, 90, 94, 96, 105-106, 119-120, 187n, 200n, 201, 201n, 249, 267
al-Insān al-Kāmil (book and concept), 4, 139, 141, 172, 195, 195n, 208n
inspiration (*spiritual*), 5, 50-51, 57, 70-71, 75n, 79, 150, 214, 256, 266
Intellect, intellection, 5-6, 6n, 8-10, 10n, 11n, 23n, 29n, 100, 133-134, 135, 137-139, 143, 160, 191, 194, 194n, 195, 204, 252, 256, 263-264
intention, 14, 55, 174, 262, 266, 268
intercession, 66, 78, 79n, 129, 174
intoxication (*spiritual*), 36, 58-60, 165
intuition, 3, 5, 19n, 29, 31, 52, 181n, 191, 194n, 227, 240
Invocation, 9, 15-18, 18n, 20, 22, 39, 73-74, 80, 107n, 111, 144, 164, 203, 209-210, 211n, 213-214, 214n, 215n, 216, 241, 243, 245-246, 251, 256, 264n, 269-270. See also *dhikr*
'Īsā, Sayyidnā, 4, 95, 126, 273. *See also* Jesus, Christianity
Islam, *passim*

Jesus, 4-5, 39, 65, 75, 78, 78n, 86-87, 87n, 110, 113, 118, 126, 187, 201-202, 217-219, 219n, 220-222, 224-225, 230-232, 243, 247, 273-274, 274n. *See also* Christianity
Jibrīl, *See* Archangel Gabriel
jihād, 16, 56, 269
al-Jīlī, ʿAbd al-Karīm, 4, 41n, 42n, 43, 43n, 195n, 207, 208n
Judaism: 101, 104, 109, 118; and ascetics, 1n; and esoterism, 19n
Junayd, 35, 58-60, 166, 248
Kaʿba, 98n, 127, 275
karma, 118n, 197-198, 246-247
Khaḍir (*or* Khiḍr), 50-51, 71, 108, 200, 253
khalwa, 20, 39, 76, 214-215, 274n
khātam, *See* Seal
Ibn al-Khaṭṭāb, ʿUmar, 43, 82-85,
khayāl, 41-43
knowledge, knowing: 8, 35; and contemplation, 44, 46-47; direct, 1, 25, 51, 71, 208; and doctrine, 3, 5, 10, 57, 95; esoteric, "realized," or related to gnosis, 7, 9, 10, 15, 22, 24, 27, 30, 32, 36, 38, 42, 44, 50-53, 77, 79, 89, 93, 108, 118, 118n, 126, 133, 136, 181, 191n, 197-198, 217, 240, 246, 246n, 247-248, 256n, 271; exoteric, rational, or theoretical, 15, 22, 38, 50, 77, 89, 93, 96, 188, 191n, 194, 240; and Islam, 21, 30n, 119, 198; relationship to love, 23-24, 24n, 119, 199, 246-247, 273; sacred or divine nature of, God's Knowledge of Himself, 11, 51-52, 57, 59, 71, 79, 86, 89, 91, 110, 194, 194n, 210, 212-213, 222, 226-228, 241n; self-knowledge, 136, 162; source is revelation and faith, 240; and Sufism, 30-31, 50-53, 57, 68, 77, 194, 194n, 197-199, 247-248, 271, 273; transmission of by masters and prophets, 79, 80n, 81, 84, 84n, 86; and virtue, 273
Koran (Qurʾan): on creation, 227-228; elliptical character of, 262, 262n-263n; and invocation, recitation, litanies, *dhikr*, 80, 86, 214, 26-266, 266n, 268n, 269; and God's Supreme Name or Names, 210, 214, 245, 268-269; and initiation, 52; on Jesus or Mary, 110, 217-219, 221-222, 225, 274n; and Paradise, 112-113; and the Prophet, prophets, and spiritual masters, 56, 63, 65-67, 69-70, 73-74, 79-80, 80n, 81, 87n, 104, 108-111, 122-123, 256, 273-274, 274n; and signs for contemplation, 47, 58, 263; and spiritual "combat," 73; and spiritual states and stations, 54; and Sufism or esoterism, 33-34, 39, 49, 51, 56, 60, 93, 102, 104, 108-109, 215n, 223, 244-246, 261-265; Western understanding of, 103
liberation (*spiritual*), 13, 13n, 100, 185, 239-240
Lings, Martin, 28n, 30n, 165n, 192n
litanies, 15, 107n, 110-111, 172
Logos, 242-244, 253, 255-256, 256n, 258
Love: aids to, 163, 198; all-encompassing, 147-149, 231, 233, 252; archetype of all, 228-229; and asceticism, 150-151; and gnosis, knowledge, 22-24, 24n, 119, 161, 197-199, 246-247, 252, 263, 273; of God for seekers, servants, 47, 230, 265; and merciful Attributes of God, 23, 147, 230, 275; object of seeker's, 231, 247; and passion, evil, 260, 260n; spiritual state of, 54, 271; spiritual way of, 7-8, 118, 118n, 119-120, 126, 127n, 199, 246-247, 256, 271; in Sufism, esoterism, 24, 119, 199, 231, 247, 265; as symbol of beatitude, 22; transformative, motivating power of, 23, 23n, 24, 53, 55, 172, 231
macrocosm, macrocosmic, 95, 168, 171, 188, 219, 255, 257-258, 263
madhkūr, 241, 248, 256
makhāfa, 118n, 196-197, 246-247, 256n, 271-272
manifestation(s): cause of, 255; and the

Titles in the Perennial Philosophy Series by World Wisdom

The Betrayal of Tradition: Essays on the Spiritual Crisis of Modernity,
edited by Harry Oldmeadow, 2005
Borderlands of the Spirit: Reflections on a Sacred Science of Mind,
by John Herlihy, 2005
A Buddhist Spectrum: Contributions to Buddhist-Christian Dialogue,
by Marco Pallis, 2003
The Essential Ananda K. Coomaraswamy,
edited by Rama P. Coomaraswamy, 2004
The Essential Sophia, edited by Seyyed Hossein Nasr
and Katherine O'Brien, 2006
The Essential Titus Burckhardt: Reflections on Sacred Art,
Faiths, and Civilizations,
edited by William Stoddart, 2003
Every Branch in Me: Essays on the Meaning of Man,
edited by Barry McDonald, 2002
Islam, Fundamentalism, and the Betrayal of Tradition:
Essays by Western Muslim Scholars,
edited by Joseph E. B. Lumbard, 2004
Journeys East: 20th Century Western Encounters with
Eastern Religious Traditions,
by Harry Oldmeadow, 2004
Living in Amida's Universal Vow: Essays in Shin Buddhism,
edited by Alfred Bloom, 2004
Paths to the Heart: Sufism and the Christian East,
edited by James S. Cutsinger, 2002
Returning to the Essential: Selected Writings of Jean Biès,
translated by Deborah Weiss-Dutilh, 2004
Science and the Myth of Progress,
edited by Mehrdad M. Zarandi, 2003
Seeing God Everywhere: Essays on Nature and the Sacred,
edited by Barry McDonald, 2003
Singing the Way: Insights in Poetry and Spiritual Transformation,
by Patrick Laude, 2005
Sufism: Love & Wisdom, edited by Jean-Louis Michon
and Roger Gaetani, 2006
Ye Shall Know the Truth: Christianity and the Perennial Philosophy,
edited by Mateus Soares de Azevedo, 2005